Copyright © 1976 by Little, Brown and Company (Inc.)
First Edition
All rights reserved. No part of this book may be reproduced in any form or by any
electronic or mechanical means, including information storage and retrieval systems,
without permission in writing from the publisher, except by a reviewer who may quote
brief passages in a review.
Library of Congress catalog card No. 75-30296
ISBN 0-316-71483-6
Printed in the United States of America

Mental Health Counseling
with Children

PATRICIA C. POTHIER, R.N., M.S.
Associate Professor and Chairperson, Department of Mental Health and Community Nursing, University of California School of Nursing, San Francisco

Foreword by Marion E. Kalkman, R.N., M.A.
Professor Emerita, Psychiatric Nursing, University of California School of Nursing, San Francisco

Little, Brown and Company, Boston

Mental Health Counseling
with Children

Foreword

Children are the most precious resource of a nation and its legacy to the
future. Yet it is estimated that in this country over 10 million children are
suffering from some form of emotional distress, of whom only 7 percent are
receiving any kind of help. The report of the U.S. Congress, Joint Commission
on Mental Health of Children, *Crisis in Child Mental Health* (1970) has
alerted the nation to the urgent needs of these children, and the writers of
that report have recommended the immediate planning and establishment of
innovative, preventive, and treatment programs for these socially and psychologically handicapped children.[*]

Members of the several health professions are, and increasingly in the future
will be, called upon to do their share in providing needed treatment for these
children. One effective method of treatment is that of counseling. However,
the literature on counseling with children is very meager. Fortunately for
child psychiatric nurses and other child health workers, Patricia Pothier has
given us this much-needed book, *Mental Health Counseling with Children,*
developed from her own rich experience of nearly a decade of practicing
and teaching child psychiatric nursing.

This is a very personal book and a very practical one — personal because
the author shares with the reader those theories of others which she has found
most helpful to her in developing her own concepts and principles of child
counseling; and practical because she has provided copious examples of her
method of working with children. For the would-be counselor who is tenta-
tively taking his first steps in this mode of treatment, these clinical illustrations

[*]U.S. Congress, Joint Commission on the Mental Health of Children. *Crisis in Child
Mental Health: Challenge for the 1970s.* New York: Harper & Row, 1970.

can be both enlightening and supportive. Each stage of the counseling process is thoroughly discussed — the relationship-forming phase, the working phase, and the terminating phase. The chapters on the use of play, the various art media, and dance and movement in child counseling are unusually rich and encourage the neophyte counselor to use his creative abilities. An armamentarium of key strategies, useful when the young counselor finds himself in a situation in which he does not know what to do, is also very valuable.

Mrs. Pothier's discussion of the counseling of the adults most involved in the daily life of the child — parents, other family members, and teachers — sheds light on an important aspect of child counseling intervention.

I feel sure that this book will be warmly welcomed by nurses and others concerned with the welfare of children, and that it will make a useful and significant contribution to the literature on child psychiatric nursing and to the improvement of the care of sociopsychologically neglected children.

Marion E. Kalkman

Preface

Improving the mental health status of our children is one of the most important tasks facing professional personnel in this decade. Medical science has
decreased death and physical handicaps in children, but at the same time, the
number of children suffering some degree of emotional disability has increased
tremendously.

Professional practitioners who are interested in decreasing the incidence of
emotional problems in children and improving the mental health of young-
sters are using a variety of approaches for treatment and prevention. This
book presents one approach — mental health counseling with children. Its
purpose is to provide a guide to the process of direct counseling, a theoretical
background on which this process is based, and an overview of some of the
issues involved in the field of child mental health. The book can be appropriately used by professional personnel with diverse backgrounds.

Many of the techniques and skills described in the text are also used in
psychotherapy with children, for indeed there is a great deal of overlap in the
two processes. The term *counseling,* however, implies that the emotional
problems being dealt with by counseling are not severe or long-standing. The
aim of mental health counseling with children is prevention of further emotional handicapping and the promotion of normal developmental processes.
The setting in which counseling with children occurs is in the community:
mental health centers, homes, day care centers, schools.

In developing this book, I have brought to it my own personal philosophy
regarding the theory and practice of mental health counseling with children.
This philosophy is a reflection of my own struggles for mental health, my
experience as a mother of four children, my educational background, and
my numerous professional relationships with students and clients. I have

included a number of clinical examples so that the concepts, ideas, and skills will become alive and authentic for you, the reader. I hope to encourage you to engage in child counseling — a most demanding, sometimes frustrating, but often rewarding field of practice.

P. C. P.

Acknowledgments

I would like to express my appreciation to each person who played his or her part in my ongoing growth and without whom the statements on these pages would not be possible — most especially to my husband, William, who encouraged me through the long process of writing and rewriting; to all my children and grandchildren; to my students; to my clients, especially Patty; to all my teachers, especially Ki and Agnes; and to my therapists, Gene and Juanita.

I would also like to acknowledge those who contributed to the development of the manuscript — Georgiann M. Gielow, R.N., M.S.N., for her chapter on movement and dance; Marion E. Kalkman, R.N., M.A., for writing the Foreword; Mary Lambert, R.N., M.S., Marcia McLain-Douville, R.N., M.S., Page Kelly Brenner, R.N., M.S., Elizabeth Jordan, R.N., M.S., for their clinical data; Sarah Boardman for her editorial direction; and those who worked on typing and editing: Maria Sandoval, Catherine Murtaugh, Fran Church, Ann McNeill, Page Kelly Brenner, and Joan Rankin.

P. C. P.

Contents

Mental Health Counseling with Children

(1) Introduction: The Challenge

THE SCOPE AND NATURE OF THE PROBLEM

Statistics related to the scope and nature of mental health of children in the
United States indicate that we are in danger of wasting one of the prime
resources necessary for vital, ongoing growth of the nation.

There are more children and youths in the United States today than there
have been at any other time in our history. Over half of the total population
is under 25 years of age. Of the age group 18 years and under, approximately
one-fourth live at or below the poverty level and are considered potentially
at high risk both physically and psychologically. In this age group there are
estimated to be 10 million children who are experiencing some degree of
mental illness for which treatment intervention is needed. Of this number,
only 7 percent are receiving this care. Treatment for the mentally ill child
in our society is uncertain, variable, and inadequate. In addition, there is no
organized or integrated program aimed at the prevention of mental illness or
the promotion of mental health of children and youths. This situation has
quite appropriately been labeled a crisis by the U.S. Congress Joint Commission on Mental Health of Children in its report *Crisis in Child Mental Health:
Challenge for the 1970s* [1]. These data clearly indicate a need for broad
planning that supports innovative programs both remedial and preventive in
nature. The report also indicates the need for more, and perhaps different,
pools of manpower trained for new roles in relation to both treatment and
prevention. It is also essential for professional personnel to continually
evaluate mental health programs and interventions, through basic research,
to determine their effectiveness.

(1)

This report draws attention not only to the number of children needing mental health services but also to the types of mental health problems. The Joint Commission survey found that those children needing mental health services fall into three categories. The first category, which represents approximately 80 percent of those needing these services, are children who have developed surface conflicts arising from normal developmental tasks or from the effects of faulty life experiences happening either to them or to other people in their environment, such as divorce, death, racism, and poverty. The second group has deeper, internalized conflicts and may be labeled neurotic or is physiologically handicapped. This group constitutes about 10 percent of the total. The third group, also 10 percent of the total, is composed of those children who are considered to be most seriously handicapped because of emotional or intellectual factors. Psychotic and severely retarded children fall into this group.

STRATEGIES AIMED AT MEETING THE CHALLENGE

Although there is certainly a need for continuing to develop and refine effective treatment programs for the children who fall into the Joint Commission's third category, there is an even greater opportunity to promote mental health by means of preventive programs within its first two categories, based on a developmental model rather than on the traditional medical or clinical model. Treatment approaches are needed that stress the developmental aspects of cognitive, social, and vocational, as well as emotional, areas.

The Joint Commission's report also calls for a change in delivery of services to include new professional and nonprofessional roles and types of services that differ from the traditional (illness) model. It recommends that mental health services for children be community-based, adapted to community needs, and incorporated in community mental health centers; that mental health principles and services be integrated in school programs; that "disadvantaged" children receive enriched mental health services; and that all services to children focus more on promotion of adaptive and coping skills, particularly those children in high risk groups.

Prevention of Emotional Disorders

Primary prevention of emotional disorders in children relates to reducing the rate of emotional disorders in a population of children rather than to focusing intervention on individual children. The goal is to provide some assurance that the developmental needs of infants and children will be met in order to reduce the rate of emotional disorders in the total population. Preventive programs include prenatal care; perinatal care; day care centers; preschool facilities; provision of home helpers; planned parenthood; assistance to families in crisis, deprivation, or disorganization; mental health planning; community organization; educational changes; and income and health maintenance.

Secondary prevention of emotional disorders is the early intervention in the development of emotional disorders in individual children, the goal being to prevent more severe or complex emotional disability.

Early Identification of Mild Emotional Disorder

The emotionally handicapped child can be identified as a child with any, or a combination, of the following characteristics which are apparent to a marked degree over a period of time and which cannot be accounted for by low intelligence or other defects.

1. Inability to learn, or to master skills
2. Inability to build or maintain satisfactory interpersonal relations with peers or teachers
3. Inappropriate types of behavior or feelings under normal conditions
4. General mood of depression or unhappiness
5. Tendency to develop psychosomatic symptoms, e.g., headaches, stomachaches

Community-initiated programs have been developed that are aimed at early identification of, and intervention in, high risk young children as they enter school settings. In addition, these programs provide special comprehensive services to children, parents, and teachers in an attempt to prevent further disability.

Treatment for Mild Emotional Disorders

As well as the identification of beginning problems, effective intervention strategies should be planned to prevent further damage. Pediatricians, pediatric social workers, community health nurses, child mental-health nurses, and preschool or day care personnel, who are in a position to regularly observe parent-infant and parent-child interaction, can provide the following services.

1. Anticipatory guidance for infant-parent and child-parent interaction before the child moves into a crucial developmental stage

2. Demonstration of appropriate handling of infant and child behavior through role modeling, and supervision and reinforcement to the parents as they interact with the infant or child in subsequent demonstrations
3. Mental health counseling for children and parents whose developmental problems have resulted from inappropriate parent-infant and parent-child interaction
4. Referral of families to other mental health facilities for counseling when the health professional is not able to assume the counseling role
5. Functioning as an advocate for the infant and child when parents are not able to use available resources to reduce abnormal deviation of their infants and children

The school-age child with emotional problems is often identified by a teacher, who may need mental health consultation on how to deal with the child's behavior in the classroom. Both child and family may also benefit from individual or group mental health counseling in the school setting. If school counseling is not available, referral is made to appropriate community resources.

Identification of Severe Emotional Disorders

The severely emotionally disturbed child is one whose progressive personality development shows marked impairment for the appropriate age and endowment in the following areas.

1. Reasonable, accurate perception of the world
2. Impulse control
3. Satisfying relations with others
4. Learning
5. Any combination of these categories

Although these signs and symptoms may appear at a very early age, the children often are not identified as being severely disturbed until their parents attempt to enter them in kindergarten. Before school age, parents and some professional people tend to assume that the children will outgrow their "different" behavior. However, compared to other children in kindergarten, the severely disturbed child becomes obvious. It is at this point that these children are often referred for treatment. It is preferable to initiate family treatment at an earlier age if possible, in order to minimize the amount of emotional damage to the young child in these crucial years of personality formation.

Treatment for Severe Emotional Disorders

When the child is impaired in a severe, complex way, treatment and rehabilitation programs are initiated for both child and family. Such programs are
built on a model of health with a focus on encouraging developmentally appropriate behavior, and with a minimum amount of medically diagnostic classifi-
cation. Services are provided in community-based facilities that allow the
child to remain in as normal a setting as possible. When institutionalization is
necessary, the programs are highly individualized and should also have a treatment and rehabilitation focus.

In the case of infants and young children who are seriously disturbed, the
major focus of treatment is with the parents, who are involved in an intensive
therapeutic program. However, because personality change leading to the
ability to assume a healthier parental role may take a considerable period of
time, it is also important to plan for alternative parental experiences for
infants and young children, such as full-time or part-time day care and foster
home care. The autistic infant or child may also fall into this category. In
the mental health field there is a great deal of controversy regarding the etiology and treatment of autism; however, the fact remains that, regardless of
professional controversy, the parents of these children often cannot cope with
the behavior of the infant or child in a way that fosters development. There
is a need in such cases to provide the parents and children with respite, day,
or foster home care, in addition to whatever treatment program is prescribed.

For the older preschool and school-age child, in addition to parent or family
therapy, direct treatment is often indicated. The preferred approach is to keep
the child in as near a normal setting as possible. There are a growing number
of psychoeducational programs for disturbed children in both public school
settings and separate community-based facilities. Their goal is to provide
additional corrective environmental experiences for disturbed children in
addition to those to which they are exposed in child and family therapy.

SUMMARY

This chapter introduces the nature and scope of the child mental-health challenge in the United States today and includes an overview of activities and
strategies aimed at promotion of mental health and prevention and treatment
of mental illness in children. The balance of this book focuses on one aspect
of treatment: mental health counseling with children.

This book is based on the assumption that mental health counseling with
children can be carried out by a variety of professional practitioners and in a

variety of settings. It is also assumed that the underlying focus of all these activities is to promote optimum development in children who are identified as having early signs of emotional disability, and to prevent the development of further disability.

REFERENCE

1. U.S. Congress, Joint Commission on the Mental Health of Children. *Crisis in Child Mental Health: Challenge for the 1970s.* New York: Harper & Row, 1970.

(2) On Becoming a Counselor

Learning to become an effective counselor usually occurs in stages, the first of which is acquisition of basic knowledge and skills that are essential for counseling. The student integrates and utilizes the principles of therapeutic counseling with children by demonstrating an increased understanding of self and of the influence that he has on his clients; of the clients themselves and their personal dynamics; and of therapeutic communication and skills of observation, assessment, intervention, and evaluation. With this expertise, the counselor can intervene therapeutically in the occurrence of mild emotional disorders in individual children and can assist in creating optimum conditions for each child's continuing growth.

The next stage is group counseling, in which the student counselor applies to a group setting all the previously learned knowledge and skills with children. With young children, group work is still individual relationships with the counselor, but with preadolescents group dynamics and group processes become a more important focus.

After the student counselor has mastered the skills for direct counseling with children, he should expand his therapeutic repertoire by learning parent and family counseling. At this stage the counselor can also engage in consultation with teachers.

BACKGROUND FOR COUNSELING

The counselor needs the following educational preparation: a broad exposure to the social and behavioral sciences, and the study of normal and abnormal child personality development soundly based in theory and research and with ample opportunity to observe normal children. With this background the counselor is able to assess the developmental level of a client as well as the child's strengths and weaknesses, and to plan age-appropriate interventions. The counselor can then appreciate those factors in that child's life that have been deterrents to development. The study of abnormal personality development should include descriptions of the types of disorders, hypotheses regarding etiology, and recommended treatment. Disorders can include the neuroses, learning disabilities, psychosomatic dysfunction, mental retardation, and the psychoses.

The student counselor should also study and discuss the theories of child counseling and therapy, if at all possible observing the counseling process live, on film, or in taped sessions (audio or video). With these experiences the student can select a style and theoretical base that most suits his own personality.

Finally, the counselor should have an understanding of group dynamics and be familiar with the basic premises and modes of group counseling with children.

PSYCHOLOGICAL CHARACTERISTICS OF THE COUNSELOR

A universal requirement for any person who intends to become a counselor with children is a genuine liking for children and an empathy for the vicissitudes of growing up. Liking children also means liking child activities, a willingness to play, and pleasure in playing. Although the adult maintains himself as an adult in play, he must also gear his play and speech to the level of the child's ability to participate and understand. This might mean sitting on the floor, building or watching a house being built out of blocks, engaging in a game of checkers, or perhaps smearing finger paints over paper to demonstrate the use of paints for a young or inhibited child.

SUPERVISED COUNSELING

The most important experience in learning to be a counselor is actually working therapeutically with children. Through practice the theories come alive and are integrated into the therapeutic style of the counselor. Supervision of the student's counseling is an essential part of his education, for it provides opportunities for the student to examine his work closely under the guidance and direction of an experienced counselor. More experienced counselors also seek the assistance of their colleagues when they sense that there is a problem related to their work that they need help in resolving.

In the supervisory session — usually one a week — the student presents clinical data for examination. The supervisor listens to the student's concerns, listens to tape recordings, and reads whatever additional written material the student may bring. From his own knowledge and counseling experience he then directs and guides the student in examination of the material. The supervisor does not provide solutions, but guides the student in discovering and judging alternatives. The student may also ask the supervisor for validation of what was done or said.

In order to gain the maximum amount of learning from supervision, the student can tape-record these weekly supervisory sessions. If there are parts of the supervision that he did not understand, listening to the tapes sometimes helps to clarify them. If, however, he still has questions about material raised in supervision, he can bring the tape to a subsequent supervisory session for review and direction from the supervisor.

Issues Related to Supervision

Because supervision is an interpersonal process that often explores affective material, a number of issues may arise that are similar to the counseling process. Although the two processes are similar, supervision focuses on separating personal problems from counseling; but it also relates these personal issues to how the student functions as a counselor. One role of the supervisor is to continually help the student clarify and define these two interrelated issues.

Parallel Process and Behaviors

Stages that arise in supervision may at times parallel those found in counseling. For example, there is a beginning, a working, and a terminating stage in both counseling and supervision. Similar behaviors may be found in each: initial anxiety, the need to establish trust, working on resolving problems, and separation anxiety.

The student can help reduce initial anxiety by clarifying with the supervisor what to expect of the supervisory process and how best to present clinical material for examination. Through experiencing a helpful relationship with the supervisor, the student learns to trust and develop openness to a more in-depth exploration of clinical material. When the supervisory relationship is terminating, the student may feel some separation anxiety and also some feelings that he has not learned enough. These are feelings that the student can discuss with the supervisor. It is sometimes helpful at this stage for the student to review clinical notes and supervisory tapes in order to assess his learning more appropriately, and to help him take credit for the progress he has made. His supervisor can also help him in evaluating his or her growth as a counselor.

Resistance

Conflicts may arise in the supervisory relationship when a student wants to change, but at the same time resists changing. Some of this resistance may be due to wanting to be independent but finding himself in a dependent relationship. Another factor may be the discovery of how his own unconscious past experience affects his ability to counsel effectively.

However, the student should keep in mind that this period of dependency is temporary and a necessary part of learning, and that the end goal is for him to be able to function independently.

When repressed unconscious experiences are revealed through supervision, the student may feel some anxiety. Normal under the circumstances, this anxiety may be reduced through further exploration with a supportive supervisor. It may inhibit or impede deeper exploration, but the student can come back to the material at another time. When resistance and anxiety remain high regarding specific issues, the student may want to seek professional therapy to work through these issues.

Credit Taking

One of the problems that often arise in supervision is the student's feeling that nothing is happening in the counseling process, and he consequently feels inadequate. It is at this point that the student needs to remember that the therapeutic process is a slow one, and that it often takes considerable time to see significant improvement in the children. It helps if the student can look at small changes in a child and recognize that he did have a part in this growth or change toward health. The supervisor may draw attention to the fact that a student has not been taking credit for his part in the counseling process. By becoming aware of his behavior, the student takes a first step toward accepting and appreciating his growing counseling skills.

AWARENESS OF EMOTIONS

Children in counseling are usually very sensitive to changes in the emotional state of the counselor. The counselor's body and voice are constantly displaying nonverbal cues to internal emotional states. One of the major goals of the counseling student is to grow in awareness and understanding of his own emotions and how these emotions affect the child, how they influence his effectiveness as a counselor, and how to use counseling strategies to counteract undesirable effects.

Types and Sources of Student Emotions

Emotions that the student might feel during counseling are anger, anxiety, fear, or embarrassment. The student may enter the counseling session with remnants of these emotions from previous personal experience. These emotions can also be triggered by the child's behavior during the counseling session. They usually arise as a result of unresolved conflicts in the student's past life. Child behavior that is most likely to instigate anxiety reactions in the counselor are expressions of aggression and affection; physical touching of his own genitals and attempts to touch those of the counselor; and regression, such as sucking a bottle.

Transference and Countertransference Feelings

The phenomena of transference and countertransference are also sources of arousal of emotions in the student. Transference means that the child transfers or extends some of the feelings of love and affection and of hate and anger that he has toward his parents onto the counselor. Countertransference responses can be readily identified when the counselor reacts to the child with a direct return of love for love, anger for anger, or fear for fear. The counselor becomes overinvolved with the child at a subjective level instead of maintaining therapeutic objectivity. Countertransference is an expression of the counselor's identification with the internal conflicts of the child, and thus may provide a great deal of information about the child in addition to his own awareness.

Child counselors may find countertransference reactions more difficult to deal with than do adult counselors. The kind of material that the child brings is often more openly related to conflicts surrounding very basic needs that awaken childhood experiences in the counselor. Also, the child counselor must deal with his countertransference feelings about the child's parents. The child counselor may become very protective of the child and see the parents as "villains" rather than potential allies in helping the child. The counselor needs to explore and work through these issues in supervision and, if they are quite deep seated and well defended, seek professional therapy.

SUMMARY

In learning to become a child mental-health counselor, the student progresses through stages. The first stage, individual counseling, is seen as the base on which more complex forms of counseling may develop, such as group and parent counseling. The student has a theoretical background on which to begin his supervised counseling experience, and through supervised counseling the student learns how to become an effective counselor.

(3) Cultural Values and Counseling

It is possible to engage in mental health counseling without taking into account the cultural values of the child; however, the counselor may be more effective if he has an understanding of the child's cultural background, particularly if it is different from his own. Cultural variables should be considered as a part of the total assessment of the child.

RECOGNITION OF THE INFLUENCE OF VALUES

Every counselor brings to the counseling process his own values and convictions of what is right and wrong, what is mental health and mental illness, and how people should conduct their lives. In fact, in order to be therapeutic the counselor must select certain behaviors to reinforce and encourage, and others to ignore and discourage.

In many subtle ways the counselor communicates his own bias by selective intervention and by his goals for the client. This issue becomes of even greater importance when the client is of a socioeconomic or ethnic group different from that of the counselor, who has a responsibility to understand and respect the values and life styles that are different from his own, to plan intervention based on these differences, and to focus on changing certain aspects of life style and behaviors when they clearly are causing the client pain or retarding the client's development.

Mental health and mental illness both depend on the balance between the individual's own strengths and weaknesses and the strengths and weaknesses of the environment. Therefore it is crucial to understand social and cultural differences among ethnic groups. Each culture provides its own strengths and supports and also problems unique to the environment. The whole concept of what is deviant behavior or healthy, appropriate behavior is also culturally and socially defined. The counselor must be aware of how a specific culture views health and illness, so that a white middle-class counselor will not super-impose white middle-class norms on all clients.

This chapter discusses some of the value differences and behaviors that develop because of poverty and ethnic differences, and some of the strategies that counselors can use to narrow the gap that exists when counselor and client have wide variations in value orientation and life style.

CULTURAL DIFFERENCES

In order to look more closely at differing values, it is helpful to have a systematic method to use in analysis. Kluckhohn and Strodtbeck [4], in their studies of different cultures, have identified definitely patterned principles universally found in all cultures. How cultures relate to these universal principles is a result of reinforcement patterns within the culture itself. They identified the following five value orientations and the range of variations for each.

1. Human nature orientation. Is man's innate human nature good or evil?
2. Man/nature orientation. Is man's relation to nature one of harmony, subjugation, or mastery?
3. Time orientation. Is the time focus of human life past, present, or future?
4. Activity orientation. Is the mode of human activity being, being-in-becoming, or doing?
5. Relational orientation. Is man's relationship to his fellow man one of lineality, collaterality, or individualism?

Despite differences within a culture, cultures can be identified by their ranking of these value orientations. The American white middle class from which many professional counselors come has the following order of choice.

1. Man is considered evil but perfectable.
2. He is seen to have mastery over nature.
3. He is future oriented in relation to time.
4. He is oriented to doing.
5. He values individualism.

The degree of assimilation and the amount of value conflict of any sub-culture in America are dependent on the degree of goodness of fit between what that culture values and what the dominant white middle class values.

In order to provide mental health services to high risk populations, to persons living at or below the defined poverty level, or to those who are racially or culturally different from the norm prevailing in the United States today, it is appropriate to know how these subcultures rank themselves in relation to the five universal value orientations.

The Culture of Poverty

Until the 1960s virtually no official attention was given to the poor of this nation. For all practical purposes they were invisible until social scientists began to call attention to the fact that 25 percent of the total population lived at or below a defined poverty level.

Poverty, in the sense that it is experienced in this country, can be defined as the denial of minimal levels of health, housing, food, and education that our present stage of scientific knowledge specifies as necessary for life as it is lived in the United States. And, psychologically, poverty places people in society so that they become internal exiles. The poor develop patterns of defeat and pessimism and are excluded from taking advantage of new opportunities. Poverty keeps people from participation in the larger national culture so that it, in effect, creates a subculture of its own.

Within the poverty culture there are four major subcultures: the aged, agricultural workers, ethnic people of color, and industrial rejects. In the total poverty culture, the major percentage is ethnic people of color, who suffer more intensely from concentrated impoverishment than any other group because of the added burden of racism.

The value orientations and range of variations in the poverty culture generally are as follows.

1. Human nature is considered evil. Religion often plays a large role in this orientation.
2. People in poverty see themselves as being somewhat helpless and subjugated in relation to nature. Luck is prominent in this orientation.
3. Poor people are oriented to the present with little concern for future events or anticipation.
4. The poverty group is oriented more to being than to doing.
5. They are more concerned with collaterality than with individualism.

The Effects of Poverty on Human Development

There is a complex and uneven relationship between poverty and human development. In addition, the relationship is different for the blue collar worker, who works regularly and has a correspondingly stable life, than it is for the manual laborer, whose work tends to be irregular and whose life is thus unstable.

Within both groups there appear to be certain people who are more "vulnerable" and those who are relatively "invulnerable" to the effects of poverty. Coles [1], in his extensive study of black poor people living in stressful situations, finds an amazing amount of stability and resiliency. He also notes how often the role of adversity can also foster growth and strength. Garmezy [2] suggests that there is a need for basic research regarding who is "vulnerable" and how it is that some children are "invulnerable." He further recommends that research be focused on families and mothers in high risk groups who do produce "invulnerable" children, in order to analyze what they do and how they do it.

Within these variables, however, there are well-documented facts [3] regarding the poverty group that do affect the development of one-fourth of the nation's children and youth. In the group there is a higher incidence of

school failure and dropouts, drug usage, juvenile delinquency, unemployment, and family breakups;
lack of prenatal care and premature births and a subsequent high rate of handicaps;
mental retardation without organic etiology;
physical disabilities;
malnutrition;
emotional disturbance;
cumulative educational retardation.

Minority Cultures

Besides the culture of poverty, there is a wide variety of racial and ethnic cultural variations in our society. Although not all persons in these minority groups fall into the poverty class, the largest percentage of poor people are from minority groups and carry the double burden of poverty and racism. Because of the fact that a large percentage of minority people are poor, they share many of the common characteristics of the poverty culture, but each minority group carries its own unique characteristics and value orientation.

All minority groups are victims of racism. Racism, in essence, holds that a group of people are inferior because of their racial or ethnic heritage.

Racism is so pervasive in this country that the Joint Commission has called racism and its effect on the minority and the majority populations the no. 1 public health problem in this country [3]. The effect of racism on minority people is such that it removes incentive or motivation to improve their situation. In spite of their best efforts they are often relegated to jobs far below their capacity and education. The effect of racism on the development of self-image, which has been widely documented in the literature, is reflected in feelings of helplessness and hopelessness.

Each minority culture has positive values that can be encouraged and emphasized, but the overall effects of racism are difficult to overcome when racism influences people's lives in the following ways.

1. Poor environmental conditions (housing, malnutrition) that lead to illness and lack of services to treat and prevent illness
2. Poor educational experience that leads to educational deficits
3. Prejudice that leads to exploitation (underemployment, low wages), feelings of powerlessness, and insecurity

STRATEGIES FOR NARROWING THE GAP IN VALUE VARIATIONS

First, the counselor needs to be aware of his own cultural values and to acknowledge that his clients may have different value orientations. He must make every attempt to understand what the differences are, respect the differences, and make appropriate adjustments in his counseling interventions. The counselor also needs to be aware of how his clients react to people of the dominant culture. For example, the black child is taught to be suspicious and to mistrust the "honky." It is this healthy mistrust that often protects this child from being hurt, and in some cases accounts for survival. This child cannot be expected to move quickly into a trusting relationship with a white counselor.

By developing a theory and a process for counseling, the counselor can reduce the chances of imposing values on others by helping the client to master his own life, facilitating the client's own problem-solving abilities, and helping the client rethink values that have become self-defeating and developmentally harmful.

If the client speaks a foreign language or a distinctive dialect of English, communication difficulties can become insurmountable if the counselor does not understand it. The counselor can do a great deal to break down the barriers between himself and the client, and can facilitate trust, by accepting and understanding the client's language or dialect.

The counselor should function as an authority (but not be authoritarian) and with warmth and informality. His interventions should be direct and action oriented, including the whole family whenever possible, and accepting the client's orientation to external causation as well as the fact that the client's main goal may be relief of symptoms. With children, the natural methods of play, activities, and role play are particularly suited to meeting these expectations, but these methods can also be used as vehicles for family and parent counseling.

In planning counseling sessions, the counselor may also want to keep in mind the possible difference between himself and the client in time orientation. The counselor may assume that an appointment made a week in advance will be kept because he has a future time orientation. His client, however, may have an orientation that does not value future planning. The result is that the child may not appear for the appointment. In this situation the counselor can help the client to get to the appointment by providing reminders and by accepting the fact that they may have a very different orientation to time.

The counselor also needs to adjust his therapeutic style to coincide more closely with possible cognitive differences related to poverty groups. Because visual and physical modes of learning predominate among these groups, he should select these rather than verbal and auditory methods of communication. Similarly, he should keep the content of his communications problem centered rather than deal with abstractions, and he should pursue important problems one at a time.

Finally, the counselor must constantly try to understand others and vary his therapeutic strategies on this understanding. If he does not genuinely respect others' differences, his clients will know this and his therapeutic usefulness will be limited.

The strategies mentioned for narrowing the gap in value variations are only substitute measures for larger solutions. One solution is to have more counselors and clients with similar backgrounds working with one another, but the larger solution is a sociological one — the eradication of poverty and racism in our society.

SUMMARY

Each counselor brings his own set of values to the counseling process. At times these values may differ greatly from those of the child — particularly if the child is from a culture which is different from the counselor's. The counselor must be aware of these differences, avoid imposing his or her own values on the child, and develop strategies that narrow the gap of difference.

REFERENCES

1. Coles, R. *Children of Crisis.* Boston: Little, Brown, 1967.
2. Garmezy, N. Vulnerability research and the issue of primary prevention. *Am. J. Orthopsychiatry* 40:217, 1971.
3. U.S. Congress, Joint Commission on Mental Health of Children. *Crisis in Child Mental Health: Challenge for the 1970s.* New York: Harper & Row, 1970.
4. Kluckhohn, F., and Strodtbeck, F. *Variations in Value Orientation.* Evanston, Ill.: Row, Peterson, 1961.

(4) Stages and Influences in Personality Development

In order to provide effective counseling, the counselor should know the child's personal history and be able to relate it to the normal stages and the influences on child personality development. The counselor can then better assess the child's level of development and strengths and weaknesses, plan appropriate interventions, and evaluate their effect. This chapter presents selected theory and research related to personality development in infancy and childhood.

PRENATAL AND BIRTH INFLUENCE

Current research indicates that there are two major factors in prenatal development that makes an impression on the infant's personality: genetic factors and environmental factors.

Genetic Factors

Genetic factors have a number of known influences on personality development, for they influence the development and functioning of the autonomic

This chapter is adapted from P. Pothier, Developmental Reactions in Infancy and Childhood, in M. Kalkman and A. Davis (Eds.), *New Dimensions in Mental Health Psychiatric Nursing.* New York: McGraw-Hill, 1974.

nervous system — the part of the human nervous system that accounts for awareness of many emotional states. There is also a relationship between genetic composition and a tendency toward social introversion and inhibition, and social extraversion and activity level. Studies [9] also indicate that genetics has the following effects on human behavior.

1. Intelligence is influenced by the strong genetic controls related to numerical, verbal, and spatial ability.
2. Motor skills are influenced by genetics in relation to hand dexterity and balance.
3. Personality development is influenced by genetics in the areas of activity level, vigor, impulsiveness, and sociability.

Genetic irregularities are also known to be etiological factors in certain birth defects and physiological syndromes such as Down's.

Environmental Factors

Prenatal environmental influences also have their effect on the developmental functioning of the infant. Nutritional deficiency influences the neuromuscular development during the vulnerable period of myelinization in neurological growth. Viral infections at the time of myelinization also influence the development of the neuromuscular system. Rubella is identified as a specific causative agent in many birth defects. Further studies indicate that certain drugs, such as thalidomide and the psychedelic drugs, may affect the development of the fetus. Studies regarding the emotional state of the mother indicate that prolonged emotional strain has an enduring influence on the child. Other studies suggest that if the mother's age is under 20 or over 40 years there is a significant increase in the incidence of birth defects. The teenage mother has been especially studied in relation to having a high incidence of premature births, birth defects, dietary deficiencies, and frequent drug usage.

The birth process itself has been the subject of much study and theoretical debate in relation to its influence on the infant. Excessive drug usage during birth can exert permanent influence on subsequent personality development. Greenacre [3] states that the whole birth process exerts an influence on future psychophysiological patterns of the child, particularly in regard to distribution of energy and strength of drives. She further states poor antenatal conditions and abnormal birth produce a state of chronic tension and a susceptibility to excitation that she characterizes as a predisposition to anxiety. Although anxiety, as we know it, exists only with a dawning ego sense, some of the individual psychological content exists in the irritable responsiveness of the organism. This responsiveness is organized loosely in reflex responses, and exists as somatic memory traces which later exert psychological pressure. Abnormal and painful birth add to this store of psychological content.

Individual Differences

The composite of genetic and environmental influences, both prenatally and during the birth process, accounts for the wide variety of individual differences which have been studied in great detail. Lourie [6] draws attention to the need to begin to inventory these differences in vulnerabilities, and to devise methods of handling infants and children which are aimed at prevention of poor solutions to children's individual differences. Such problems as deviant arousal patterns, sleep deviations, high and low energy levels, variant sensory threshold, and inadequate ability to protect self or summon help from the environment are examples of individual differences that can be noted in infants. Research is needed that will categorize these differences and that will also test methods of successfully handling these special problems. Research data could then be computerized, and would be available through retrieval systems as a base for planning and programming for effective handling of individual differences at an early stage. This type of intervention is particularly important because of the concept of critical or optimal periods of development. Each stage has a developmental time limit in which appropriate stimulation is needed in order to foster optimal development. If individual differences are not taken into account in handling the child during these optimal periods, that child's developmental needs will not be met for that particular period. The child whose needs are not met at one stage carries over this deficit to the next stage, thus affecting all future personality development.

INFANCY

Infancy is the period of living that starts with birth and proceeds to the emergence of the capacity for communication through speech (approximately 1.5 years). This is a stage in development in which the human being is completely dependent on others for survival. He is particularly vulnerable to external influences because he cannot protect himself either physically or psychologically. Influences can strongly affect all future personality development. The most important relationship of this period is with the mother or mother substitute.

Developmental tasks and their concomitant anxiety are seen as basic personality organizers. Freud [2] stated that the ego is the "seat of anxiety," and that anxiety has a physiological base in the birth process and in infancy; physiological responses are then pressed into service to alert the organism to danger. Freud further stated that there is a later transition of the physiological conditions to an emerging psychological structure in which ego formation can be identified. According to Greenacre [3], these physiological tensions are carried over as psychological traces that are experienced as a predisposition to anxiety.

Adaptation between the mother and infant in each developmental stage involves an issue. How well these issues are resolved influences the infant's development. The first phase, undifferentiation (0–8 weeks), is a stage of imprinting socialization through the process of attachment, a process that ensures the life not only of the child but of the entire species as well.

Before the studies of the Harlows [4], it was thought that attachment was strictly a learned response, with the reward being the gratifications that the infant receives by having his needs met by the mother. The Harlows [4] indicate that the infant monkey is born with the capacity to emit attachment behavior toward the person caring for it, including clinging, vocalization, smiling, scanning, and following. These findings have been postulated to be applicable to human infants also.

Although these studies indicate that there may be innate factors that lead to attachment, how well this process is accomplished is variable. The issue here is the specific appropriateness the mother is able to maintain in response to her baby's highly individualized cues regarding his state and needs.

The next phase is when true reciprocity in response begins to appear between the mother and infant (5–12 weeks). The mother smiles; the baby, who now has the ability to fixate on the mother's face, smiles back. This attachment or symbiotic period continues until around the ninth month. The way in which the baby expresses himself and imitates social exchange depends upon his individual differences and his mother's response to him. The issue again is related to the mother's ability to respond to the child's specific needs.

Sometime between 6 and 8 months of age, the baby develops the ability to differentiate his mother's face from those of other human beings. Infants at this stage fear novelty and experience unpleasurable responses at seeing another face. Brody and Axelrod [1] have called this process a basic onto-genic rather than phylogenic basis of anxiety. However, this does not negate the phylogenic effects of the mother's ability to continue to meet the child's needs during this process of separation and the child's insistence and persistence in having his needs met. It is during this stage that Brody and Axelrod see the infant developing anxiety preparedness, or a protective shield that, although having its base in physiological paths, leads to concomitant emergence of rudimentary ego functions and the affect anxiety. The protective shield allows for both active and passive accommodations to stimuli that infants express as a tendency to appeal for help when stimuli become excessive. Without the appropriate symbiotic imprinting of the earlier stage, the infant would not develop the ability to experience normal anxiety and also to develop attachment to other objects later.

The infant without impediment from constitutional or environmental factors continues to grow in separation from his mother and in his beginning self-identity. This growth leads quite naturally to the next stage, in which the infant continues to develop autonomy. The issue here is how the individual style of self-assertion by the child is dealt with, especially when he is opposing his mother's wishes.

CHILDHOOD

At the end of the infant period, in which separation from the mother has been relatively smooth and the child begins to assume a separate identity, there is a solid foundation for a continued, broader socialization. The main purpose of the parents' attempts to socialize their child is to guide him in acquiring personality characteristics, behavior values, and motives that the culture considers appropriate.

For the child, this is the period of living that begins with the capacity for communication through speech and in which separation-individualization has been well established. The child begins to form relationships with people of his own level who share his attitudes toward authority and activities, and continues to expand this association with peers until the satisfaction and security of another person become as significant as his own.

Variables in Personality Development of Childhood

Kagan and Moss [5], in a longitudinal study of development during childhood, were able to identify four child behavior variables related to personality development: motive behaviors aimed at attaining cultural goals; sources of anxiety and conflict; defensive responses to anxiety situations; and modes of interpersonal interaction.

Motive behavior is overt goal-related behavior that has been learned by the child to attain specific goals. The common goals are social recognition, task mastery, nurturance, appropriate sex interest and gratification, and affiliation with peers.

The sources of anxiety and conflict in the preschool child are around fear of loss of parental love as the child moves away from the parents toward more independence; anticipation of physical injury; and expression of aggressive, sexual, and dependent behavior. In the school-age child the main sources of anxiety are fear of failure to master socially valued skills; intellectual incompetence; personal inadequacy; and deviations from sex role standards. As in infancy, the intensity of the anxiety is a function of the child's basic constitution and environmental interaction. The previously stated anxiety sources provide the motives for learned defensive behaviors aimed at the specific goal of diminution of unpleasant states. The major defenses of childhood are regression, denial, projection, aggression, withdrawal, and development of psychosomatic symptoms.

The fourth factor in child personality development is the mode of social interaction. Individual children vary in social interaction through the quality of interpersonal interactions, in approach or avoidance patterns, in the amount of spontaneity or tension, and in the amount of domination or submission.

Murphy [7] looks at the way children cope with new normal and abnormal stresses of life. It is through experiences in coping that the child develops a patterned way of dealing with newness. New and strong situations have different meanings for different children, and cause different reactions based on the children's individual differences, on infantile experiences to newness, and on the mothers' ability to meet specific needs in relation to newness. The child develops a repertoire of coping strategies that allow him to control the direction of his attention and interest, to control his anxiety, and to manage stress so that negative or anxiety reactions are balanced with positive gratification. Kagan and Moss [5] found that these behavioral variables, which have their foundations in infancy, become crystallized during the childhood period and continue through adulthood.

PRESCHOOL INFLUENCES

During the first year of life, the parents are usually seen by the infant as supporting persons who gratify needs as they are identified. In the second year, the parents, recognizing the need and readiness of the child, begin the process of socialization, which includes delaying gratification of the child's desires. This process is the first normal source of friction between the parent and the child. There is little solid research data on the best way to socialize a child, but the major goal is to minimize the friction and conflict that arise naturally.

Part of his readiness to participate in the socialization process depends on how well the child was socialized as an infant. Normally the infant learns to please the parents, and thus ensures affection and protection. In this process he also avoids unpleasant feelings generated by punishment and rejection. If the infant has not experienced gratification from his parents and the desire to please them, the next stage of development, in which he is expected to delay or curb gratification, will be more difficult. The child may have the physiological but not the psychological readiness to give up pleasurable behaviors.

To develop a sense of autonomy, the child must have a feeling of confidence in his ability to deal effectively with his environment and to develop mastery over bodily function and skill in manipulation. In this process he also must face the reality that there are rules connected with these functions. For example, in developing a sense of autonomy, the child needs to gain control over bowels and bladder; but at the same time he learns that there are rules regarding elimination that are imposed by the parents. The child's response to the rules or limits is negative behavior that may take the form of aggression toward the parents.

Anxiety Influences

In the preschool age, anxiety often accompanies specific behaviors: aggression, sex-related behaviors, and dependency. The source of anxiety seems to arise from a conflict between the child's desire to exhibit these behaviors and the attitude of his significant adults to these behaviors.

Aggression in childhood is universal, and the tendency or capacity for it has some innate components. How aggression is expressed, its nature, form, and control, are learned. The child may learn that he can get what he wants through aggressive behavior, and may become skilled in using this method of controlling others. The child also learns from his parents that some types of aggression are rewarded and some are punished.

Frustration is a major factor triggering aggression in preschool children. When the child is blocked or curbed in goal-seeking behavior, he experiences a threat to his self-esteem. He may be blocked by external barriers, internal conflicts, feelings of inadequacy, or anxiety inhibiting goal-seeking behavior.

There is a wide range of individual differences at this age in how much or how little frustration children can tolerate, and also in the ways that children respond. Some children regress to a level of more comfort; others may be overtly aggressive in gaining control and in reducing the anxiety of not being able to control the environment. The amount of conflict and anxiety in the expression of normal aggression in the preschool child is related to the way parents are able to accept and support the child in his developmental response.

In the preschool years, the major sex-related behaviors are masturbation and sexual curiosity. The major methods of dealing with these behaviors in American families are to restrict and redirect sex-related activity and not to label it. These actions quite possibly lead to anxiety, which is minimized if parents handle sexual curiosity and behavior realistically and without embarrassment or punishment. They should also answer children's sexual questions with content that is appropriate for the child's level of understanding.

The dependency motive is the wish to be nurtured, to be comforted, to be close emotionally, and to be accepted. This motive, which is still very strong in the early preschool period (3—4 years), may be expressed in a variety of individual ways. When dependent needs are met in the early preschool years, the child develops a feeling of security and is then able to move into more independent behavior as a 4- or 5-year-old and on into the later childhood years. When the mother is inconsistent in relating to dependent behavior (that is, sometimes rewarding and at other times punishing), the child is ambivalent about expressing both dependent and independent behavior, and experiences an increase in anxiety.

Influence of Play

Throughout childhood, play is the natural medium of self-expression. It is the method used for self-mastery, coordination, and mastery over objects. From play the child is able to form images and patterns of relatedness which form a whole out of parts.

Play activity is recognized as a complex assortment of the child's conscious and unconscious expressions. Through play, the child is able to act out areas of concern that he is unable to verbalize. Play is the language and work of the child, in which he often uses objects to act out conflicts; this activity also may have the effect of catharsis that speech has for adults. The child who, because of external or internal motivation, is unable to engage in active play limits his ability to use a tool that fosters mastery of developmental tasks.

Role Identification

Identification is the process that leads the child to incorporate the characteristics of another person within his own personality. It is neither a conscious
process nor the result of training. In the development of identification with
another person, there must be motivation to be like the model. There must
also be some characteristics in the child that are similar to those of the model.
The child sees his parents as having the abilities he would like to possess, such
as control or power over others, mastery over the environment, and the ability
to give or withhold love, and he identifies with these abilities.

A concept that is interrelated with identification is sex typing. In the ideal
situation, appropriate sex typing occurs through identification with the parent
of the same sex, who is seen as nurturing and having desirable characteristics.
Ideally, both parents consistently reward sex-appropriate behavior and discourage sex-inappropriate behavior. In the process, the child is able to adopt
the behavior, values, attitudes, and interests of his own sex.

Kagan and Moss [5] state that sex role identification is central to selective
adaptation and maintenance of behavior. The expressions of aggression,
competition, passivity, dependency, and sexuality are in part determined by
the child's assessment of the congruence of the behavior with cultural sex
role standards. Children are motivated to behave in many ways congruent
with hypothetical ego ideals and models of masculine or feminine qualities.
In addition, most human beings need to act in ways that are congruent with
standards affecting their ego ideals. Any behavior or belief that increases the
discrepancy between the child's evaluation of himself and his idealized model
provokes anxiety and is avoided, whereas any behavior that decreases the
discrepancy between the self-evaluation and the model of the self is rewarded
and repeated.

Development of Conscience

There is evidence of beginning conscience formation in the preschool years.
The child develops a set of standards of acceptable behavior and acts according to these standards. He feels guilty if he violates them. The process of
conscience development at this stage is also closely related to identification
with the parents. Anxiety about punishment or loss of love may be the major
motivation to acquire the standards that please the parents. Optimum superego development is closely related to the parents' ability to arouse in the
child unpleasant feelings about his misbehavior — feelings that are independent
of threats and that encourage the child to take responsibility for his actions.

Defects in beginning superego development are due to inadequate identification with significant others that may be based on the fact that the child does not experience his parents as being nurturant or having enough positive similarities with which to identify.

Extrafamily Influences

As the child grows older and begins to move away from the family, new socialization agents compete with the parents, most importantly for pre-schoolers, peers and teachers in nursery schools or day care centers.

The nursery school program has been the focus of many studies, which indicate that the nursery school child makes rapid gains in social participation compared with nonattending peers. They are less inhibited and more spon-taneous, independent, self-assertive, self-reliant, curious, and interested in their environment. Individual attention by nursery school teachers may reduce a child's maladaptive behavior and strengthen adaptive behavior. In this process, there is an increase in the child's self-confidence, frustration tolerance, and ability to persist in a task.

Peers also act as reinforcers for behavior in preschool children, becoming new models for imitation and identification. In the peer group the models are usually the most friendly children, who engage most often in cooperative play, tend to reinforce others, and are the least dependent on adults.

INFLUENCES ON THE SCHOOL-AGE CHILD

Entrance into school is one of the major adjustments in a young child's life, forcing the child to deal with three separate tasks: separation from the mother, or consistent mothering figure, for most of the day; establishing con-tact with a new adult, the teacher; and developing a meaningful relationship with peers.

Beyond this period of adjustment, the school child must accomplish five major developmental tasks: to develop academic skills, to maintain a high level of motivation for learning, to crystallize sex role identification, to continue the development of moral standards and conscience, and, finally, to learn to deal appropriately with anxiety and conflict.

There are a number of factors that influence the child's ability to cope with these normal developmental tasks.

Family

Although the family becomes a less important influence in the life of the older child, the effects of family interactions, morals, and values are still strongly felt.

If a school-age child's earlier developmental needs have been met, this child will be able to expend his energy in working on age-appropriate developmental tasks. He will have ego development that allows him to be in control of his aggressive, sexual, and dependent behavior. The child who has not had prior developmental needs met may not have the full amount of energy to pursue and accomplish age-appropriate developmental tasks. Current life experiences also influence how well he is able to develop during the school-age period. He may have had good family support in the preschool period, but a crisis such as death of a parent or divorce can severely influence the child in further development.

Family patterns also influence a child's academic achievement. The children with high levels of anxiety related to academic activity are often found to have unmet dependency needs related to their preschool development, which results in such high levels of anxiety that they cannot achieve up to their level of ability.

Teacher Personality

An important factor in the child's ability to accomplish developmental tasks is the personality of the teacher. Mussen, Conger, and Kagan [8] summarize their research on the relationship between teacher personality and teacher effectiveness: "Most children do best under well-trained, democratic teachers who know their subject matter, are interested in their pupils and are not overly concerned with their own problems. Such teachers encourage the students to actively participate in the learning process while maintaining leadership, direction and when necessary, reasonable discipline. In contrast, optimal academic and personal growth will not be stimulated in most students with a teacher who is either rigidly authoritarian, hostile, or unresponsive to students' needs; or by the teacher who is indecisive, uncertain, poorly trained, or too occupied with her own anxieties." Children function more effectively with teachers who have similar personality patterns and similar social, economic, cultural, and racial background to their own.

Peer Relationships

Yet another important influence on the school-age child is peer relationships. Whether a child adopts significant peer-group relations depends a great deal on whether he can identify with his peers by wanting to gain their acceptance. When the values of peers, teachers, and parents are somewhat related, there are fewer conflicts, but often the behavior that the peer group demands is in conflict with the wishes of teachers and parents. In this situation, the child has to decide whether adult or peer approval is more important.

The peer group becomes a major socializing agent for the child in teaching him how to interact and how to handle conflicts and anxiety regarding aggressive and sexual activities; and it also provides an opportunity to develop a realistic concept of who he is in relation to others his own age. During middle childhood, children often form into small informal groups — the "neighborhood gang." The activities and interests of these groupings are usually strongly sex typed and very influential.

Physiological and Mental Disabilities

Although physiological and mental disabilities do have some influence on the personality development in the preschool-age group, they are not the major influence that they become when a child enters school. Because the major focus on development of the school-age child is acquiring academic skills and related social activities, the child with physical or mental disabilities is severely impaired in his efforts to accomplish normal developmental tasks.

SUMMARY

It is essential that the counselor have a basic knowledge of normal child personality development and those factors that influence it. He uses this knowledge to assess the child's level of development, to plan specific counseling strategies, and to evaluate progress.

Although personality development proceeds through stages, each of which builds on and influences the next, there is also not only overlap in stages but also a great deal of individual difference from one child to another.

REFERENCES

1. Brody, S., and Axelrod, S. *Anxiety and Ego Formation in Infancy.* New York: International Universities Press, 1970.
2. Freud, S. Inhibitions, Symptoms and Anxiety. In J. Strachey (Ed), *The Standard Edition of the Complete Psychological Works of Sigmund Freud* London: Hogarth, 1959. Volume 20.
3. Greenacre, P. *Trauma, Growth and Personality.* New York: Norton, 1952.
4. Harlow, H., and Harlow, M. H. Learning to love. *Am. Sci.* 54:244, 1966.
5. Kagan, J., and Moss, H. A. *Birth to Maturity: A Study in Psychological Development.* New York: Wiley, 1972.
6. Lourie, R. The first three years of life: An overview of a new frontier psychiatry. *Am. J. Psychiatry* 127:33, 1971.
7. Murphy, L. B. *The Widening World of Childhood.* New York: Basic Books, 1962.
8. Mussen, P. H., Conger, J. J., and Kagan, J. *Child and Personality.* New York: Harper & Row, 1969.
9. Vandenberg, S. G. Genetics of Human Behavior. In J. Segal (Ed.), *The Mental Health of the Child.* Washington, D.C.: National Institute of Mental Health, 1971.

(5) Anxiety and Defensive Behaviors

In the preceding chapter, it was noted that anxiety is a natural human phenomenon that has its rudimentary beginnings prior to birth and in the birth process itself. Throughout the stages of child development, anxiety is seen as a major factor in personality organization. The chapter also indicated that there are unfavorable influences related to anxiety that are deterrents to development. It did not, however, discuss the dynamics of anxiety and how children cope with it or develop defenses against it. The defensive behaviors that children develop to relieve or avoid anxiety often bring them to the attention of mental health workers, teachers, and parents. This chapter will discuss the nature and dynamics of anxiety, child behaviors and symptoms related to anxiety, and implications for counseling (see Perls [4], May [2], Peplau [3], and Hilgard [1]). Strategies related to specific defensive behaviors are found throughout the book.

THE NATURE OF ANXIETY

Perls [4] sees all of life as essentially made up of unfinished situations. Before one situation is completed, another comes up to be coped with. Because human beings are constantly striving for balance or homeostasis, there is a motivation toward completion of situations. Perls states that excitement is the dynamic energy that propels us into each new situation and toward resolution. Others (May [2], Peplau [3], and Hilgard [1]) see this energy as normal or first-level anxiety. This excitement in the here-and-now situation enhances perception and the ability to cope with new situations.

Higher level anxiety occurs when the excitement is dammed up and cannot be released through motor responses. If the person is not able to release the excitement, it becomes locked in and is experienced as anxiety.

Perls also sees anxiety as related to the future, and similar to stage fright in that the person becomes afraid of what response he will receive as he is forced to move into new life situations. This hesitation to experience fully in the here-and-now, because of fear of responses to him, causes the blocking of normal discharge of excitement and the consequent building of anxiety.

The anxiety that the new counselor often experiences during early interviews, and in subsequent specific situations during the counseling process, seems directly related to the stage fright concept: "Will I be therapeutic?" This phenomenon may also be particularly true of the child in the early stages of counseling. In fact, the major goal of counseling is to help the child who lives most of his life being anxious about future consequences to experience himself and to appreciate himself in the present.

An explanation of this stage fright may be found in the contributions of May [2]. Anxiety is caused by any threat to the security of a person's biological integrity or self system, for example, expectations of the person that are not met or that are not in accord with the reality situation, or unmet need for prestige and status. The person becomes anxious because he has learned in the past that in experiencing a specific situation his security was threatened. When a new situation arises, he generalizes that the threat may occur again, and he experiences the previously felt anxiety.

Excitement, or first-level anxiety, is the major motivation for normal behavioral expression that is satisfying and growth-producing. Anxiety at higher levels, however, leads to behavior that is not self-fulfilling or satisfying. The person experiencing anxiety will have biochemical and physiological changes that may cause increased heart rate, rapid shifts in body temperature and blood pressure, urinary urgency, dry mouth, cold sweats, loss of appetite, and dilatation of the pupils.

The anxious person will also have his perceptions distorted. With excitement, a normal person is alert, seeing, hearing, and perceiving with his total self focused on the present. The anxious person's perceptual field is narrowed and, as anxiety levels increase, there is a corresponding restriction and distortion of perception. Anxiety destroys self-awareness. In these more severe stages of anxiety, the person finds himself unable to solve problems or cope with the situation being presented. The subsequent behavior of the anxious person is aimed solely at reducing the anxiety.

RELATIONSHIP OF ANXIETY TO ANGER

Every child who is referred to counseling is angry at something. Anger is an emotional response to anxiety or to frustration. Because all of life involves anxiety and some degree of frustration, anger is a familiar and common emotion. Children learn to discharge angry feelings through verbal and physical actions, either appropriately or inappropriately.

The child who is referred for counseling often has received more than his share of frustration and anxiety. He also suffers from the inability to express angry feelings (the withdrawn or regressed child) or else he expresses them inappropriately (the hyperactive or aggressive child).

BEHAVIORS RELATED TO ANXIETY

A child with mild to moderate anxiety may be observed to go to the bathroom frequently, or seek frequent drinks of water. If one watches the child's body closely one might see a tensing of muscles, especially those of the neck and shoulders. At this stage the child may have his perception narrowed, but he is still able to act to relieve the anxiety-provoking situation. However, part of his problem-solving procedure can involve the processes of denial and projection.

If the child has a high enough level of anxiety, he may attempt to cope with it by aggression, hyperactivity, or withdrawal. Some children develop physical symptoms such as headaches and stomachaches. These coping behaviors, normal during childhood, become harmful when the child finds it necessary to use them constantly to defend against high levels of anxiety caused by unmet developmental needs and external stress such as physical illness, divorce or death of a parent, addition of a sibling, or entrance into school.

The child who has previously used aggression or hyperactivity as a mode of behavior to relieve anxiety may find himself engaged in these activities constantly and with little relief of anxiety. His activity has become counterproductive. The withdrawn child finds himself immobilized and unable to engage in any activity that will foster growth or relieve anxiety. The child who was likely to develop headaches or stomachaches may develop even more severe syndromes in attempts to avoid feeling anxiety. These are children who are in need of mental health counseling to help them develop self-esteem and age-appropriate skills, physical, social, and emotional, to decrease their level of anxiety so that they will not feel the need to engage in patterns of self-defeating behavior.

Aggression

The child who has converted his anxiety to angry feelings has an increase in bodily tension that can be discharged by physical and verbal action often aimed at injuring either directly or indirectly, termed *aggressive acts.* This action may be toward the original person or object causing the anxiety situation, toward a substitute person or object, or toward himself.

Expression of Aggression

There are constitutional and biological factors that are available in all human beings to support aggression, which takes on different forms of expression as the child develops. In infancy, aggression may first be expressed by biting, spitting, vomiting, or making contempt noises. Later, feces or urine may take on aggressive significance by their expulsion or withholding. As he develops more motor skills, the child acquires other methods of hurting: hitting, kicking, pushing, throwing, screaming, and swearing. Later he learns that he can also cause harm by destroying the property of others by stealing, or by bothering or distracting others in the performance of their tasks or goals. An even more indirect form of expression of aggression, and perhaps the most damaging to the child, is failure to use abilities or skills to hurt the parents.

It is within the context of relationship with other persons that the child learns specific means to express aggression. The child learns from his parents, and from the norms developed by society, when, where, and how to express or not to express aggression. Numerous studies validate this thesis by showing a high correlation between aggressiveness in parents and that found in their children.

It is often found that a child who is hyperaggressive at school is not aggressive at home. The child may have learned to express aggression by imitating his parents but is afraid to express it at home because of fear of punishment or loss of love. He will have learned that there is some positive reinforcement for aggressive behavior through observing his parents, but he has also learned that for him the positive reinforcement of aggression occurs away from his own home setting.

Implications for Counseling

As stated previously, aggressive behavior is a normal coping behavior that is a necessary part of development. The child is referred to counseling for his aggression when it interferes with his development or goes beyond the acceptable societal norm. The goals of counseling are twofold: to increase the child's self-esteem so that inappropriate aggressive acts are not necessary, and to teach the child acceptable forms of expression of aggression.

In the beginning stage of counseling, the child who has been referred for aggressive behavior may not reveal any of it to the counselor. The reasons for this may be similar to those expressed earlier in relation to parents. The child does not know how the counselor will respond, and the fear of punishment or rejection inhibits the aggressive behavior. As trust and acceptance develop more firmly in the relationship, the child may feel more free to expose his "bad" side to the counselor in order to test his acceptance by the counselor.

Hyperactivity

The hyperactive child is one who attempts to reduce his level of anxiety through bodily and verbal motion. His actions differ from those of the aggressive child in that they do not aim at injury to himself or others, although they may do so inadvertently. As an infant, this child may be extremely restless, have irregular sleep patterns, and cry frequently. In his preschool and school years he continues these patterns, but as he is able to ambulate his activity becomes more varied. In a classroom he is easily identified as the child who wanders about the room, talks aloud to others or self, and makes frequent trips to the pencil sharpener. This child has a very short attention span and is constantly moving and making noise. His movements are short, jerky, and usually nonproductive. Although his activity is aimed at reducing anxiety, it often has the opposite effect.

Some hyperactive children are found to have a physiological basis for their behavior. These children need specific types of medical, physical, and educational therapy. They may also need mental health counseling because of the anxiety involved in their interpersonal relationships.

Implications for Counseling

The hyperactive child is hard to cope with at home, at school, and in counseling. Because he is constantly moving and noisy, he is an annoyance to almost all adults and to his peers. In the counseling situation it is necessary to set many limits on him to prevent harm to himself and to others and the purposeless destruction of objects. The overall goal of counseling is to decrease anxiety by increasing self-esteem and by helping to channel body movements in more growth-producing ways.

Withdrawal

Withdrawal behavior means that instead of acting out to relieve his anxiety, as the aggressive child does, the child reduces his contact with the outer world and thus the chances of being involved in anxiety-provoking situations. Some children who overuse withdrawal become almost immobilized and mute. Withdrawal behavior takes on different forms of expression as the child develops, but basically it is related to a reduction of body movement and verbalization. The infant may lie very quietly wherever put and seldom cry or babble as other infants do. The older child may sit in a corner of the school yard and not talk to or play with peers. He may behave more normally at home than in a school setting because he feels more secure there.

Implications for Counseling

The child who uses withdrawal behavior as a defense against anxiety will not engage in enough activity to develop mastery over the tasks of childhood. He is not referred as often as the acting-out child because he often does not cause anyone else any problems. At times it may fall to the counselor to interpret to teachers and parents that withdrawal behavior can be as harmful to the child as is aggressive behavior.

These children are difficult in counseling because they expose so little behavior to work with. It usually takes a long time in both individual and group counseling for these children to trust enough to be able to risk interactions with new people. In group counseling, the child may watch more active children and, when he is feeling more comfortable, may model his behavior after a more active member of the group. The goals of the counselor are to accept the child's behavior at whatever level he is able to function, and to offer positive reinforcement whenever the child is more active physically or verbally.

Regression

Regressive behavior occurs when a child goes back to a stage of development that is more comfortable for him than the current stage in order to reduce anxiety. The effects on the child are similar to those of the withdrawn child in that he does not engage in age-appropriate activities. The preschool child who is toilet trained may begin to wet himself as well as to use language that is more appropriate for a younger child. The school-age child may cease to take responsibility for himself that he had previously taken, such as dressing himself and going to school by himself. A certain amount of regression is expected in normal child development and may occur at the time of illness, birth of a sibling, or family crisis. The difficulty arises when the child does not resume his normal developmental activities in a reasonable length of time.

Implications for Counseling

The child who uses regressive behavior to an extreme is often referred for counseling because those around him cannot tolerate regressive behavior in a child who should be able to function at his normal age level. Parents and teachers are concerned about a school-age boy who needs his mother to dress him and walk him to school, and who may find thumb-sucking comforting.

Psychosomatic Symptoms

Another group of children who are frequently referred for counseling are those who experience physical symptoms for which there is no apparent physiological cause. The origin of specific symptoms is a highly complex interaction of physiological and psychological factors. It can be hypothesized that these children convert their felt anxiety to physical symptoms. These are children who have frequent colds, headaches, and stomachaches. Some common psychosomatic syndromes in children are ulcerative colitis, rheumatoid arthritis, asthma, obesity, anorexia, enuresis, and encopresis. In each of these syndromes there has been demonstrated to be similar types of psychodynamics between the child and the family.

Implications for Counseling

Perhaps one of the most difficult concepts that counselors have to relate to parents and teachers is the need for mental health counseling for children with physical symptoms. Referrals often come from medical sources, after a regime of medical treatment does not seem to be helpful in relieving the symptoms. Counselors can point out that the child's symptoms do not seem to be decreasing, and suggest that the child may be using the symptoms for self-protection.

Through counseling, these children learn to accept themselves, gain in self-esteem, and work through distorted interpersonal relationships. With progress in these areas, there is usually a decrease in their physical symptoms.

SUMMARY

The basic concern that brings children to counseling is anxiety. To cope with anxiety the child may use aggressive, hyperactive, regressive, withdrawal, or psychosomatic symptoms to an extent that these behaviors interfere with normal personality development.

The aim of counseling is to reduce the child's anxiety level and to help him use these defensive behaviors in a way that fosters development rather than impedes it. Examples of how to counsel children with specific defensive behaviors are found throughout the book.

REFERENCES

1. Hilgard, E. *Theories of Learning.* New York: Appleton-Century-Crofts, 1956.
2. May, R. *The Meaning of Anxiety.* New York: Ronald, 1950.
3. Peplau, H. *Interpersonal Relations in Nursing.* New York: Putnam, 1953.
4. Perls, F. *Gestalt Therapy Verbatim.* Lafayette, Calif.: Real People Press, 1969.

(6) Selected Systems of of Psychotherapy

Each counselor has a theoretical framework on which he or she bases his or her practice, selecting from a variety of systems of psychotherapy those that he or she finds most effective. This chapter discusses some of the theories and treatment processes on which counseling with children can be based.

In order to facilitate the reader's understanding of this chapter, the following definition of terms is offered.

1. *Psychotherapy* — any treatment process related to emotional disorders
2. *System of psychotherapy* — a well-accepted method of psychotherapy that has a theoretical base and specific techniques or strategies for conducting therapy
3. *Nondirective therapy* — the main focus and pace of the treatment is directed by the patient
4. *Directive therapy* — the main focus and pace of the treatment is directed by the therapist
5. *Techniques* — specific operations that the therapist uses in a system of therapy. Can be used interchangeably with *strategies*
6. *Theory* — a generally acceptable principle or body of principles

ANALYSIS OF SYSTEMS OF PSYCHOTHERAPY

There are many systems of psychotherapy and counseling, with a variety of theoretical bases and techniques for practice. At first view they seem quite divergent, but on closer examination there are similarities and commonalities, some of which Frank [3] was able to identify. The first common factors relate to selection of patients and success. Psychotherapy and counseling reach but a small proportion of those who are in need of help, each system claims to treat all diagnostic categories, all systems have about the same rate of success. Frank further identifies those clients for whom treatment is most successful: those who have good ego strength, whose complaints are linked to environmental stress, who can express feelings and problems well, who relate well to others, and who are strongly motivated to change.

Common techniques can also be identified in the practice of psychotherapy and of counseling. First, there is a relationship in which the helper is trusting as well as accepting. The setting is often very different from the client's daily living, and is seen as a safe place for expression of self. Some forms of psychotherapy and counseling, however, are accomplished in the child's natural environment. All techniques are based on a theory or rationale that also explains the causation of the client's problems. They all encourage new ways to think and feel, and all require client involvement.

A review of the research on child counseling reveals little controlled research except by behaviorists. There are a great number of psychotherapy studies with the child as his own control that indicate significant gains in symptom relief and in normal developmental progression. This research, however, does not shed much light on how this process is helpful, nor does it answer the question of whether the child would have made similar changes and growth without the treatment intervention. What is missing are controlled studies that demonstrate

that desirable changes in personality and behavior come about concomitantly with counseling;
that these changes would not have occurred in the absence of counseling;
that the consequences of counseling are long-term.

Researchers should investigate the variables that control the effectiveness of the therapeutic process. There is a specific need for research into the covariation in specific counselor-client interactions in which identifiable and measurable behavior of client and counselor interaction are analyzed. Two of the reasons why such research has not been carried out more extensively are the difficulty of controlling the many variables involved, and the problem of obtaining a large number of subjects whose parents are willing for them to be involved in such an undertaking.

For many years numerous case histories have, nevertheless, documented the effectiveness of mental health counseling and psychotherapy with children,

particularly in relation to developmental crises. There is also much validation
in these cases for early intervention as a method of preventing later, more
complicated emotional disorders.

The therapists and counselors reporting these case histories have a variety
of backgrounds and theoretical bases. Frank was, however, able to identify
common characteristics in the successful therapist, regardless of theoretical
rationale or techniques. The successful therapist personally participates in
the therapeutic process with warmth, genuineness, empathy, and zeal. Perhaps
those personal qualities have more to do with therapeutic success than training
in a particular method. Research has yet to unravel the mysteries of healing
through the therapeutic process. The treatment processes and theories that
are included in this book are among a number of those widely accepted. These
selected theories and treatment processes have proved to be effective in practice, and are particularly applicable to mental health counseling with children
and their parents. They include relationship therapy, gestalt therapy, and
behavior therapy.

The major theme that runs through these theories is that a child is capable
of growth and change. The theories also emphasize that the helping process
focuses on strengthening positive aspects of the child's personality. There is
also agreement that social-behavioral deficits in the child are due to personal
interactions with that part of the social-personal environment that in the past
did not support the positive, creative growth of the child's total personality.
This conviction does not, however, necessitate that counseling dwell on past
interactions but rather that it focus on current behavior and responses in the
here-and-now. Other basic tenets are the importance of the parents' involvement in counseling, and the inclusion of family counseling, when possible,
in the total treatment for the child.

Through experience, the individual therapist selects the theories and treatment process that he finds most successful in practice. I believe, however,
that whatever theoretical base the counselor chooses, he needs to have the
basic qualities that Mayeroff [4] describes of a "caring" person. He brings
himself to the relationship with another, acknowledging the self-limitation
of who and where that other *is,* rather than who or where he thinks that other
should be. He is as honest and authentic as his limitation allows. He has
courage to take risks, recognizing that growth goes into unknown areas. He
experiences the other person as having potentialities and a need to grow, and
he cares to help in that growth. He recognizes his own need to be needed.
He does not impose his will on the other, but facilitates the other's becoming
more himself and helps him care more for himself. He has patience, is willing
to wait, has trust, and hopes for changes and growth. And for those who

relate to children, perhaps a double dose of each of these qualities is necessary, in addition to an empathy for the vicissitudes of childhood.

NONDIRECTIVE SYSTEM OF PSYCHOTHERAPY

 ### Relationship Therapy

Principles and Assumptions

Relationship therapists assume that the child has resources within himself for growth, and that these resources have been restrained or placed beyond the availability of the child because of a variety of circumstances. The goal of relationship therapy is to help the child become aware of these resources, the lost parts of himself, and to use them for himself instead of for self-defeating, esteem-destroying activities.

Forerunners in the development of this treatment process were Alfred Adler and Otto Rank. More contemporary relationship therapists are Jessie Taft, Virginia Axline, Fredrick Allen, and Clark Moustakas.

The relationship therapists' philosophy of the treatment process includes the following tenets.

1. The determining aspect of the process is the *relationship*.
2. The emphasis is on experiencing emotional dynamics rather than on insight or interpretations.
3. The focus is on the dynamics of the here-and-now relationship rather than on past relationships.
4. There is another focus on strengthening creative, positive parts of the personality.
5. Therapy is adapted to the unique individual needs of each patient and to changes in the patient.
6. A major goal is to help the patient take over constructive management of himself in both therapy and life situations.
7. Resistance in the patient is viewed as a positive statement of a will striving for independence and a force to be encouraged, strengthened, and directed.
8. There is recognition of the individual as a social being who needs another person or persons for self-realization and development.

Techniques

In relationship therapy, the main role of the therapist is to be with the child in the sense of paying attention to him in a way not usually possible in the child's daily life at home or in school. The child leads or directs the focus and pace of the therapy. The therapist follows and responds to the child's direction.

The relationship therapist occasionally makes some internal connections with the child's past and his present activity, verbal or nonverbal, but that is not a major tool of the therapist. The relationship therapist considers it more important to be "with" the child in his activity and to empathize with the child's feelings in the here-and-now situation. In addition, the therapist communicates to the child what he sees the child doing, and how he sees the child being involved in his activity. In a sense, the therapist is able, through this process, to give the child immediate feedback on what the therapist sees happening with the child in the here-and-now situation. The purpose of this type of intervention is to build awareness of self in the child and to help the child begin to talk about what he is experiencing. It is a step-by-step process of building self-esteem in small increments, and involves using the current relationship to rebuild and remedy previously damaging interpersonal encounters.

DIRECTIVE SYSTEMS OF PSYCHOTHERAPY

Gestalt Therapy

Principles and Assumptions
The major principles and assumptions underlying gestalt therapy are similar to those of relationship therapy. The major difference lies in the direction of the treatment process itself. The relationship therapist focuses mainly on supportive, guiding, "being-with" activities, whereas the gestalt therapist focuses on more directive and confronting interventions. In both procedures there is a focus on verbal and nonverbal communication; however, in gestalt therapy there is a more intrusive, active direction on the part of the therapist in guiding the patient to experiences that develop awareness.

These more directive and confronting interventions are particularly appropriate for use in short-term counseling related to developmental and circumscribed problems. Because these techniques are powerful and are aimed at breaking through defenses, extreme care needs to be taken in using them with severely disturbed children. Children whose consistent behavioral response is withdrawal usually do not benefit from or involve themselves in these interactions until they feel secure in the counseling relationship. The major contributor to the development of gestalt therapy is Frederick S. (Fritz) Perls [5]. His followers have been numerous, and many have adapted his confronting techniques to fit their own individual therapeutic styles.

Techniques

The gestalt therapist also works with his clients in the here-and-now situation, focusing attention on whatever material the patient brings to the session to work on. This material may originate in verbal expression, such as a dream, or in nonverbal expression such as a body posture or gesture. Because the importance of both dreams and body posture or gestures are usually beyond the awareness of the patient, the role of the gestalt therapist is to bring the underlying feelings into awareness. The techniques that the gestalt therapists use often include some aspects of acting or perhaps the use of graphic media to aid the patient in the awareness of his own feelings.

One example of the use of acting in gestalt therapy relates to the treatment of dream material. When a patient begins to relate a dream verbally, the therapist asks him to act the different parts of the dream. The purpose of this technique is to encourage the patient to explore and experience parts of himself that have been hidden from conscious awareness. The underlying assumption is that each part of the dream is in fact a part of the person's personality, and as he acts the parts he is able to reclaim these parts of himself.

Graphic material can also be used in relation to dream material. When children or adults are not emotionally ready to act the parts of a dream, they can be directed to draw them or model them with clay. Because art products are held to be an extension of the personality, this type of action also aids the patient in his awareness of self.

An additional technique related to gestalt therapy was developed by followers of Fritz Perls, Eugene B. and Juanita B. Sagan;[1] one unique aspect of this approach is the integration of therapeutic experiences. For example, if the patient has expanded his self-awareness through therapeutically acting the parts of a dream, he is encouraged to take time to integrate the experience through writing, talking, drawing, or sleeping. The therapist makes a deliberate effort to encourage the patient to follow up on an awareness experience. The therapist may suggest integrative activities to the patient, or he may choose to incorporate integrative activities into subsequent therapeutic sessions. For example, if a patient drew a dream in one session, the therapist might encourage him to discuss the experience with others and, in a subsequent session guide the patient in acting the dream.

Behavior Therapy

Learning Theory Principles

The behaviorist starts with the assumptions that all behavior is learned, and that both prosocial and deviant behavior can be accounted for by a single

[1] Institute for Creative and Artistic Development, Oakland, California.

set of social learning principles that is applicable to child rearing practices and to therapy. Initial application of learning theory to issues concerning behavior, such as the research of B. F. Skinner, Bijou and Baer, and Dollard and Miller, was somewhat limited in its application to human situations because this research was based on studies of animal learning. An expansion of knowledge of human social learning is possible, however, by incorporating studies such as those done by Bandura and Walters [2] on modification of human behavior in dyadic and group situations.

Basic research in learning with animals has revealed that learned behavior can be controlled by its consequences. More specifically, the research indicates that if a behavior is emitted and is followed by a stimulus that the subject experiences as rewarding or reinforcing, there is a better than chance probability that the emitted behavior will be repeated or increased. The amount, rate, or intensity of that response can be regulated or controlled by the amount and type of reinforcement that is given. A corollary to this basic law of learning is that, if an emitted response is ignored or not responded to in a manner that the subject experiences as rewarding, the emitted behavior will not be repeated, or will decrease to the point of extinction. Most of the activities on which we conduct our daily lives incorporate these basic principles, although they are not sufficient to explain all our behavior.

Social Learning Principles

One of the crucial phenomena in social learning that is not accounted for by the previous postulates is the acquisition of novel responses through observation. The followers of operant conditioning procedures account for this phenomenon by the process of successive approximations, or shaping, whereby small increments of a total behavior are learned until the total behavior is learned. For example, the process of teaching a young child to put on a shirt is broken down into small steps with appropriate assistance and reinforcement until he can do the whole task. The child has learned a totally new behavior. Bandura [1], however, was able to produce evidence that learning may occur through observation of the behavior of others even if the observer does not do what the model does or receive any reinforcement; the observer may, however, receive vicarious reinforcement through the reinforcement given to the model. It is conceivable that the child learns a great number of novel behaviors and understands their consequences through observation of the environment. Besides the daily observations of his family and school, both of which environments are fairly controlled, one wonders about the potential influence, both positive and negative, of observer learning through the medium of television. After the initial learning of a novel behavior through imitation, the new behavior would have to continue to be reinforced in order to continue. In the counseling situation, the child may learn new behaviors through counselor or peer modeling.

Another phenomenon that accounts for social learning is generalization. A learned pattern of response tends to generalize to other situations that have elements or cues similar to those present in the original learning situation. Learning new behavior would be very difficult without being able to build on prior experience. Almost of equal importance is discrimination learning. The child must learn when and where certain behaviors are acceptable and rewarding, and when and where they are not.

In addition to these external factors related to learning and differential reinforcement, there is also the child's personal history of reinforcement that influences what and how reinforcement is experienced. For one child a spanking may be experienced as a punishment that deters specific behavior, whereas for another child the spanking may be seen as a positive reinforcement. If a child receives little or no attention for any behavior, he may resort to behaviors that he has learned will elicit some attention, even a spanking.

Techniques of Behavioral Therapy

The therapist can apply the principles of social learning and positive reinforcement throughout his contacts with children. In both individual and group therapy, imitation and modeling of new, more adaptive behaviors is an essential therapeutic dynamic. The therapist can also be involved in setting up behavior modification plans which either he or a teacher or parent can implement.

In developing a behavior modification plan, there are prescribed steps that need to be followed. First, the therapist, in cooperation with the child's family or teacher, and in some instances with the child, decides on the behavior that needs to be changed. Usually a plan for children includes decreasing a maladaptive behavior and increasing an adaptive behavior. Data are then collected on the occurrence of these behaviors in regard to frequency and association with antecedent and consequent events. The counselor also needs to decide the type of reinforcement that is appropriate for the child and the schedule for administering the reinforcement. After these decisions, interventions are made for a stated period of time. At the end of this period data are again collected on the occurrence of the desired behavior. The data are then compared with the baseline data in order to evaluate if the program has successfully decreased maladaptive and increased adaptive behavior. If there has not been significant behavioral change, the therapist and mediators begin to problem-solve with their plan until they find a solution that is successful.

SUMMARY

There are a variety of theories on which counselor and therapists base their practice. The choice of theoretical orientation is based on the background and experience of the counselor, who uses the theoretical framework that is most effective for his practice. This chapter has presented both directive (gestalt and behavioral) and nondirective (relationship) theories on which counseling can be based.

REFERENCES

1. Bandura, A. *Aggression: A Social Learning Analysis.* Englewood Cliffs, N.J.: Prentice-Hall, 1973.
2. Bandura, A., and Walters, R. H. *Social Learning and Personality Development.* New York: Holt, Rinehart & Winston, 1963.
3. Frank, J. D. The demoralized mind. *Psychology Today* 6:22, 1973.
4. Mayeroff, M. *On Caring.* New York: Harper & Row, 1971.
5. Perls, F., Hefferline, R. F., and Goodman, P. *Gestalt Therapy.* New York: Delta, 1965.

(7) Communication in Counseling

Because communication, verbal and nonverbal, plays such an important part in developing both healthy and unhealthy relationships, it is important for the beginning counselor to have a firm grasp of the processes by which it is effected. Fostering and facilitating healthy communication in children and their families is a crucial factor in promoting optimal child development. This chapter focuses on the nature and dynamics of communication; the three following chapters discuss in more detail its forms most common to children: movement, play, and art.

THE NATURE OF COMMUNICATION

Human communication can be defined as encompassing all modes of behavior that an individual employs, consciously or unconsciously, to affect another — not only the spoken and the written word, but also gestures, body movements, and somatic signals. The implication of this definition is that all behavior has communicative value and therefore has meaning. Human communication has two major components: the content or information-giving message and the process message. The process message, or metacommunication, provides a statement about the relationship between the communicants and also about the nature of the content message. For example, a little boy may say to his mother, "I am hungry." This statement relates to the content. How he says it, and what tone he uses, gives further information about the content. The tone may be whining or pleading, which says something about the relationship between the child and the mother and about the child's expectations in relation to his "I am hungry" statement.

The nature of communication is such that it takes place within a system, and the system is related to all parts of the individual and his interactions with others. A shift in one part of the system affects all parts of the communication system.

Successful Communication

Although there is communicative value in all behavior, certain criteria must be met to have successful, satisfying communication among people. First, the means of communication and the message must be at the appropriate developmental level for the receiver. Second, there needs to be feedback by which the sender can understand the effects of his message on the receiver. Third, communication must be efficient. Language should be simple and delivered at an appropriate time. Last, communication should be flexible so as to allow opportunities for participants to comment on discrepancies between the content and the process. It should also allow for differences in expression.

Effects of Unsuccessful Communication

Children who have not experienced successful communication patterns in their early lives have not had the opportunity to experience satisfaction through the communication process, resulting in a buildup of anxiety in the child and a continued reinforcement of disturbed patterns. Ruesch [5] states that the tangential response is one of the most powerful ways to discredit the perception of the sender. A tangential response bears an incidental relationship or no relationship to the message it supposedly replies to. In other words, the receiver disregards the interest of the sender. For example, the child says, "I'm hungry" in a pleading tone meaning, "Feed me." The mother responds, "I have a lot of work to do today." She disregards the child's message and gives a tangential response: "Don't bother me." Another type of disturbed communication arises when there is a discrepancy between verbal and nonverbal communication. The mother may say, "I love you" to a child, and in the message say: Trust me; come close to me. Yet when the child comes close he feels a rigid, rejecting body, and becomes confused as to what he should do.

Bateson et al. [2] describe a form of disturbed communication termed the double bind. In this pattern the sender gives a primary negative injunction followed by a secondary injunction conflicting with the first at a more abstract level and, like the first, enforced by signals that threaten survival. The third injunction prohibits the victim from leaving the field because of survival needs and/or a promise of loss of love. The double bind can be illustrated in the following sequence. A mother, in talking about her son, expresses a fear that he will be a sissy; however, the message she gives her son is: "I won't love you if you are a sissy. Sissies don't fight when someone hits them. But I don't want you to fight because you might get hurt." The response to this kind of repeated communication is anxiety, confusion, rage, and pain.

NONVERBAL COMMUNICATION

Perhaps the most important type of communication in child counseling is nonverbal communication. In child counseling the main focus is often on activity such as play, art, and movement, not on verbal communication.

Nonverbal messages are received mainly through visual perception. These messages are sent in a variety of ways, and include one's relationship to others in space and the particular movements of the body within that space. The body communicates in many different ways through movement, especially that of arms, hands, feet, facial expression, eye contact, and body posture.

Even when there is no verbal communication, nonverbal communication continues. Verbal behavior is mostly under conscious control, but nonverbal behavior is not as controlled by the conscious defense system, and may provide more accurate and authentic statements regarding the communication being sent.

Body Movement

Ekman and Friesen [3] indicate how nonverbal behavior can provide information that differs from verbal. Their studies show that differences in neuroanatomy and cultural influences combine to produce specific types of body movements and facial expression that escape conscious repression and emerge as "leakage" or "deception clues." They found that the face sends off the most nonverbal messages, but it is also equipped to be closely controlled. People are aware of facial gesture and are practiced in deceiving in this way, for example, by a card player's "poker face." For the skilled observer, however, the face can give "micro" types of displays that serve as leakage and deception clues.

Hand movements send off more messages than legs or feet but less than the face. However, they cannot lie as well as the face. With awareness, hands can be hidden or inhibited more easily than the face, but there is less general awareness of hand gesture than facial ones, so there is correspondingly more leakage. A person may be smiling and speaking happily while holding on to himself with his arms.

Legs and feet do not have the repertoire of message sending that the face and hands have, but at the same time they are also further out of awareness and inhibition. When legs and feet send messages they are significant indicators to leakage and deception. Such messages may be reflected in changes in tension or movements like kicking or crossing legs.

Using this kind of information, the counselor receives data regarding the child's internal state that may be very different from verbal content. The counselor can comment on this behavior and ask the child if he can talk about what he feels. The child may not be able to respond, but the counselor's intervention is a step toward helping the child become more aware of internal states and accepting responsibility for them.

Space

Another aspect of nonverbal communication that is important to therapeutic work with a child is the child's place in space in relation to the counselor. It has been hypothesized that the closeness or distance the child chooses is related to his degree of comfort in the situation. Each spatial move the child makes in relation to the counselor has some meaning that the child is not willing or able to express verbally. These changes give clues to the tone of a verbal communication. At times the clues accent the verbal communication, but at other times they may deny it. The child who states that he really likes the counselor while backing away is making a clearly ambivalent statement.

Hall [4] has classified distances between individuals and also assigned meaning to them: intimate distance (0—18 inches), which combines several physical sensations to indicate involvement with another body; personal distance (18 inches—4 feet), which most comfortably separates individuals; social distance (4—12 feet), which reduces involvement; and public distance (over 12 feet), which minimizes the opportunity for meaningful personal involvement. In relation to the therapeutic process with a child, the counselor can use this scale of spatial distance to evaluate where the child is in relationship to him. The counselor can also assume that some shift of feeling is going on if the child suddenly shifts from one type of distance to another. Verbal reflection of this shift by the therapist can give an opportunity to pursue its meaning with the child.

Besides physical distance, children may also develop an emotional distance. A child may be sitting close to the counselor at what one would assume is an intimate distance, but be emotionally distant. It is as if the child had a wall around him. If the counselor tries to break through the wall, for example, by touching the child, the child will move away if he is not ready for this closeness.

Eye Contact

Communication with the eyes indicates not only the social role a person is assuming but also deeper, more permanent aspects of his personality. Argyle and Dean [1] have developed theories based on a series of studies and related to the variety of functions that eye contact may serve, and list the following main functions.

1. Information-seeking for needed feedback
2. Signaling that the channel is open for further interaction
3. Concealment (fear of being seen) or exhibitionism (desire to be seen)
4. Establishment of recognition of a social relationship
5. Conflicting messages in which both approach and avoidance are communicated

They also suggest that intimacy has several interrelated variables: physical proximity, eye contact, the nature of conversation, and the amount of smiling. They found that altering one of these components can cause a shift in some of the other components used to maintain equilibrium in the relationship.

It can also be noted that severely disturbed children have very little or no eye contact. A sign of improvement in these children is increased eye contact.

IMPLICATIONS FOR COUNSELING

Nonverbal data give a great deal of information for the counselor to use in helping the child become more aware of himself, his feelings, and his behavior. The counselor too is constantly communicating nonverbally to the child. The child is very sensitive to the authenticity of the counselor's verbal statements and checks them out with nonverbal statements. Although it is not often practical, video feedback is one of the most useful methods for the counselor to become aware of his own nonverbal behavior and how it affects the therapeutic process. The counselor also has the responsibility to facilitate successful verbal communication by consistently utilizing the criteria for successful communication himself and for facilitating it in the child.

The counselor can also position himself in a way that facilitates communication, seating himself on the floor or a low chair so that he is physically level with the child. He should also dress in attire that communicates his readiness to participate in child activities.

SUMMARY

This chapter has presented some of the basic concepts of communication, the criteria for successful communication, and the effect of unsuccessful communication, both verbal and nonverbal. It also stated some implications for counseling before proceeding to the next three chapters on movement, play, and art in child counseling.

REFERENCES

1. Argyle, M., and Dean, L. Eye contact, distance, and affiliation. *Sociometry* 28:289, 1965.
2. Bateson, G., Jackson, D., Haley, J., and Weakland, J. Toward a theory of schizophrenia. *Behav. Sci.* 1:253, 1956.
3. Ekman, P., and Friesen, W. V. Nonverbal leakage and clues to deception. *Psychiatry* 32:88, 1969.
4. Hall, E. *The Silent Language.* Garden City, N.Y.: Doubleday, 1967.
5. Ruesch, J. *Disturbed Communication.* New York: Norton, 1967.

(8) Movement in Counseling

GEORGIANN M. GIELOW

Movement and dance concepts contribute to the understanding of nonverbal communication in children and form a framework for planning therapeutic interventions in child counseling. Case studies of movement and dance in counseling can be found in Appendix A.

BASIC MOVEMENT AND DANCE CONCEPTS

In the study of dance, simple and direct concepts are used to describe movement. All these concepts may be observed on a continuum, with the outer ends representing the extremes and the middle representing a balanced use.

Space

The space continuum is from limited to expansive. Each person has his own feeling of comfort in space and his own response to territory. He can stand changes in the amount of space available at any given time, and tolerate the closeness of others, even seeking to be close to others. He does not feel a sense of drifting or being lost in a large space, but rather goes about defining the boundaries of the space so that he can control it rather than letting it control him.

Range of Motion of Body Parts

A normal range of movement would include the ability to use all body parts to their full range or to confine body parts when necessary. For example, in walking there is an interplay between relaxation and tension in all joints from the neck to the toes. In order to understand his environment, an individual must reach out into the environment or the space around him. He must also be able to move away from those things in the space around him that might be harmful.

Time

Normal movements involve an interplay between fast and slow. There is usually not one movement to the exclusion of the other; however, sometimes the whole body moves quickly. At other times one part, say the hands, is moving fast while the torso is still. There are many combinations possible, and the individual chooses the paces that are comfortable for him after he has experienced the variety possible.

Tension or Force

The tension continuum is between strong and weak. Sometimes the situation calls for the individual to marshal all energy to react to the situation; at other times he needs to hold back the expenditure of energy. At times one body part must be used as an outlet for energy rather than letting the whole body explode: for example, pounding fists and clenching teeth rather than coming to blows.

Attitude

A person does not walk erect every minute of the day. He sits, kneels, lies, stretches, and bends. All this movement provides additional stimulation from the environment. The person reacts to those things in the space around him, and thus acquires knowledge of his environment.

Interpretation of Movement

These are the terms by which pure movement can be analyzed and used to interpret feelings or moods being communicated nonverbally. Movement indicates the person's self-image and how these self-feelings are communicated in affective attitudes toward the people around him. Following are some examples of movements people commonly use when they are in touch with reality.

With sadness of depression, the facial expression is not alert. The face seems to have a dropped appearance. The mouth is not turned up into a smile, and the eyes are not held open. Everything seems to be falling down. Even the head seems to use less space as it goes down near the chest. Movement is slower, and the force is pulling down in the center of the body rather than out into the extremities. The shoulders are pulled into the center of the body. There is less use of body parts. Possibly there are some weak hand gestures as the arms are held close to the body.

The opposite of sadness would be a state of excitement. The body seems to bounce or generate energy outward. The space that is utilized is much more expansive in terms of reaching out toward others. The body parts all seem alive and in motion. The timing is usually much faster than that found in sadness. Energy is being expended. The idea of bouncing gives a change in attitude.

In fear the body presents itself with a different observable base. The body parts are drawn to the center for protection, but they are very much alive and ready for reaction, in opposition to the state of sadness. The person's use of space is minimal, but he is aware of space and what is in that space rather than not being aware of the space around, as in sadness.

These are examples of normal feeling states which everyone experiences and moves in and out of. The counselor must know the normal use of movement in order to determine what movement patterns are not productive, for children's movement is a natural expressive outlet. It is fun. Children need to move in order to expend energy. By moving they get to know who they are and what they are capable of achieving. By experiencing space they learn such concepts as tall, small, high, low, heavy, light, slow, and fast. Moving involves their whole organism and is an outlet for fantasies and other tension producers. When children learn a great repertoire of movement responses, they develop a facility for expressing themselves and adjusting to their environment. Their movements of bouncing, dropping, swinging, and stretching have inherent muscle-relaxing qualities. With this relaxation of muscle tension, energy is released and channeled into investigation of the environment.

THE IMPORTANCE OF DANCE CONCEPTS TO COUNSELING

In normal children feelings may be expressed through muscle movement, which is a natural outlet and a way to expend energy. In troubled children anxiety builds up and is displayed in forms of bodily tension. The stimuli that produce the tension vary with the individual, and can be quantitatively measured in muscle tension, blood pressure, and chemical process. Tension can also be observed in movement patterns which in emotional disturbance tend to be consistently on the extreme ends of the continuum rather than in the middle or balancing area. The child uses moving or not moving to reduce anxiety tension.

Range of Abnormal Movement

The extreme range of movement is from hyperactive and aggressive behavior to withdrawn and passive aggressive behavior. The child either is in a constant state of hyperactivity or withdrawn behavior, or he resorts to this movement pattern only in times of high anxiety, depending on the disturbance.

The Hyperactive Child

The hyperactive child displays facial mobility rather than facial concentration. He is constantly looking at things and people around him, and he is moving out in space, exploring and falling over or bumping into people or things. Gestures are of a frantic nature, accomplishing little in a constructive way. Locomotion takes him into the territory of others, which instigates annoyance. He finds it difficult to sit still. Some part of the child's body is constantly in motion. The tempo is fast or moderately fast, and the child finds it difficult to slow down. He explores many levels as he is on the move, and there seems to be an inner tension that is quite strong. His movement appears as an impulsive fling through space.

The Aggressive Child

The aggressive child has a similar movement pattern. His gestures and body stance of alertness and available energy for attack serve as a warning to people who approach his territory. Locomotion is directed outward. The child takes the offensive position, which causes others to take a defensive position. Movements are quick but with more direction than those of the hyperactive child. The tension level is quite strong and is maintained because of the constant preparedness to fight.

The Withdrawn Child

The withdrawn child represents the extreme opposite of the hyperactive or aggressive child. This child is concerned not with the environment but with his own inner responses to the environment. Some parts of the body, however, are concerned with what is going on around him in order to maintain protection. The body posture is usually low, and the back or side is presented rather than the frontal, visceral area. When someone approaches a withdrawn child's territory, the child moves away either into space or into self.

The range of motion of body parts is quite limited. The movement is all inward directed. The shoulders droop. Sometimes the hands will move as if in a motor overflow, but usually not more strongly than in a tic-like movement. The manner of locomotion is as if to see if the water is cold before the child moves into the new environment.

These three extremes of abnormal movement patterns do not productively release energy. Because of their interaction with the environment, they may even increase anxiety and tension. It is as if the child is caught in stereotyped movement patterns and has not had the experience with other movements to be able to try a new approach to the environment. A child has to feel safe in order to trust himself and to be able to explore the variety of movement experiences possible in expressing his feelings. With the emotionally disturbed child, the first step is to accept the movement patterns that the child uses to communicate nonverbally. The counselor then helps to change these patterns into new movement patterns which result in new feelings and moods. The counselor effects change by reducing, replacing, expanding, or extinguishing those identified patterns that keep the child from interacting productively with the environment. Progressing at the child's pace helps to develop a trusting relationship and a willingness by the child to risk learning new and better coping techniques in tension-producing situations.

COUNSELING STRATEGIES

Using movement interventions with emotionally disturbed children is sometimes difficult, for these children are overly conscious of themselves and their deficits. They are asked to move. They resist because they are already feeling inadequate and will not risk opening themselves up to more ridicule or feelings of inadequacy. The counselor needs to expend more energy, showing how to have fun and that movement is fun. The counselor models fun by smiling, laughing, swinging his arms, slapping his knees, running, making contact with others by touching and holding. Many times this overdramatization is necessary in order for the child to feel that if adults can do it, he can do it too. At these times, when the counselor is not getting the typical expected response from the child, he tends to want to draw back from the situation; but it is only with repeated dramatizations and demonstrations that the child finally learns how to let go appropriately.

Sometimes the counselor needs to share his ego with the child. This may be accomplished by just being near a child. The counselor stands next to him or in his range of vision, so that when the child is feeling insecure or having some difficulties accomplishing a task, he can look up and see the adult who is available to help, or touch the adult and feel the warmth of the helping adult nearby.

Touching

Touching can be used to calm a child, to show positive feelings of approval and affection and also increase the child's self-image, to obtain eye contact, to desensitize a child who fears contact, and to gain attention.

To calm a frightened or withdrawn child the counselor should use soothing, long strokes or rocking kinds of movements. He can put his arms around the child's shoulders or chest as in a hug. This helps the shoulder muscles to relax the tension in head, neck, and shoulders.

To calm an aggressive child the counselor needs a firm approach. He again has contact with the shoulders, arm, or hand, and calmly holds it in place (not incapacitating movement, just externally controlling) while verbalizing ("Slow down. Easy. Cool it.") to help the child regain control. This must be in the first stage of an aggressive movement, when verbal comments can replace the need to ventilate physically. The aggressive child can be calmed if the counselor's movement can be effectively firm and slow without being threateningly abrupt and fast, and if the counselor controls the tone of his voice to a low, soft pitch. He does not present his body to the child as a challenge or force that cries to be attacked, but rather as a controlling aid outside the child's self. He also tries to help the child verbalize the feelings that have surfaced.

To show positive feelings of approval and affection, the counselor can pat the child's head, shoulders, or hands, along with such comments as "Good job. Well done!" This praise is not only a boost to the child's image, but also it tends to make the child want to reexperience the desired feeling of approval, thus becoming a paired positive response.

To speak to a child, the counselor should avoid calling across a room but should go to the child and get the required eye contact that indicates that the child is listening. This can be accomplished by gently and slowly lifting under the chin to raise the head. If the child resists by not focusing, the counselor can put two fingers in front of the child's nose and draw him back to the counselor's eyes. Once the counselor gains eye contact it should be maintained until the verbal message is given. This can be done by gently holding the child on both sides of his head and getting down to his eye level. The child is also held by his shoulders to keep his hands off other objects. By keeping the child from his usual distraction techniques, such as moving around the room or into another room, the chances of the child's hearing are increased.

Desensitizing the Withdrawn Child

To desensitize a child fearing contact with either an adult or peers, the counselor can very slowly, briefly, and at every opportunity possible come near the territory the child has established as his own. The cues as to how fast or slowly one advances or retreats rest upon the observation of the child's movement cues of anxiety, such as drawing body parts into himself, or moving away. The counselor moves closer to the child as his anxiety decreases and the fussing and squirming give way to a conditional acceptance. This is, of necessity, a slow process which involves first decreasing spatial distance, and then increasing the time and amount of body contact. The counselor may start by briefly and slowly brushing the child's skin, possibly on fingers or hand. Being near and reaching out, but without touching, permits the child to decide to touch. These first short contacts are gradually lengthened by patting the head or shoulders as the counselor walks by, by standing near the child so that he feels the adult's body warmth, and by placing hands on his shoulders and then moving on. A handshake gives a brief but positive contact.

If a child fears another child but trusts an adult, the other child and the adult can approach the vicinity where the first child is playing, getting closer and closer every day until a situation arises or is arranged in which the two are involved in a group game.

For Impulse Control

Another problem that emotionally disturbed children often have is impulse control. To practice losing control and regaining control is very important to these children, because this is often the area that is causing them difficulty. If the child can practice in a safe environment, then he is not so likely to be overwhelmed and not know what to do when conflict situations arise. Swinging movements with drops and releases and returning to normal position are useful in helping the child find out that he can control movement. He can "give in" and then regain equilibrium, a skill that many times the child does not know he possesses. He can find a productive outlet for tensions in practicing this skill.

Movement games are particularly helpful in dealing with the dependence-independence struggle with adults because, in movement games, both the child and the adult take turns giving directions and having control. A typical example of an activity game would be the statue-making game in which the child is spun around to lose control and then drops into a position or shape that he has to hold and that becomes the statue. The child really enjoys spinning the adult. With older children, this activity is not so much a game as an exercise. These children are challenged to be competitive and do things as well as or even better than the adult.

Another activity that children try on their own is leaning forward as far as they can before falling down to the ground or putting their foot out to catch their balance. Children, during the process of growing up and interacting with peers, normally test themselves in activities to see what their bodies can do. Disturbed children do not do this consistent testing because they are convinced that they will fail, and other anxiety concerns consume their time and energy. These common ways that children test themselves can be used as games to teach emotionally disturbed children how to safely test themselves.

The one thing that children can control very easily is their own breathing. The counselor can ask the child to close his eyes and concentrate on his breathing to the point of breathing audibly. Then the child is told to move any body part on inspiration and bring the body back to its resting place on expiration. Various rates of breathing can be experimented with, each rate being under the total control of that child's breathing. The goal is to help the child to understand that he is capable of controlling movement.

For Body Image

Another area of concern in emotionally disturbed children is body image. Because of the lack of movement experiences there is a rigidity about these children's movements, a lack of knowledge of what they can do. With this lack of experience comes a feeling of: "I'm not like other kids. I can't do things. I walk funny. I stand funny." Many times children have to start at the beginning by finding out what movement each isolated body part is anatomically capable of achieving. With the accomplishment of skillful manipulation of body parts comes increased control of body movements and a more positive self-image. They find that they can now do what their peers are doing. Simple accomplishments, like cartwheels and somersaults, are important to children who compare themselves to peers in gym class or on the playground. Many times the child uses his body as a whole and does not see his parts as being able to move separately. An exercise that fosters this understanding is making shapes with the body. When a child is making shapes the adult can observe which parts are seldom or never moved, and then ask the child to make a shape which includes that neglected body part.

By knowing how to coach children in the effective use of their bodies in sports, the counselor can motivate them to play with peers. Disturbed children often do not know how to play the games that other children play. They need to practice such basic play skills as throwing, catching, and balancing as in rollerskating, skate-boarding, and batting. Through learning a motor skill the child has an opportunity to experience success.

For Hyperactivity

When a person moves he increases the number of external stimuli, which in turn lead to increased awareness of the environment, which leads to growth from these new learning experiences. The hyperactive child already has increased stimulation and needs to decrease movement in order to benefit from activity. Hyperactive children often have limitations in fine and gross motor coordination. The counselor's task is to express his expectation of the child to perform movement patterns the way other children do, and to help this child change his movements. The child can be helped to obtain some control over his body by repeating the movement pattern over again to show that he can do things better when he slows down and lets his thinking catch up to his body. After he successfully repeats the movement, he should be strongly rewarded with verbal praise. Invariably the second time around is more satisfying to the child.

The counselor can provide body contact to model slow, calm movements and to confine the child's unproductive movements. This process helps relax the child, who also can be relaxed with rocking movements. The counselor stands behind the child with arms around shoulders and shifts his body gently from side to side. This helps the child deal with transitional waiting times, for example, waiting in line with the class.

For Aggression

The aggressive child poses problems similar to those of the hyperactive child. He is constantly moving and needs to learn to control that movement. He can also be challenged into hitting the air around him rather than hitting people. Punching bags and "Bozos" can provide a useful channel for aggressive, impulsive hitting. In addition the aggressive child can be encouraged to use verbal rather than physical forms of aggression toward others.

It is also important to help the aggressive child to learn other forms of tension release, such as fist pounding into a pillow or palm of one hand; clenching and unclenching fingers; shifting from one foot to another; or concentration on deep breathing. The aggressive child should also be provided with physical activities at regular intervals for the productive release of tension and energy.

DANCE AND MOVEMENT IN COUNSELING WITH GROUPS OF CHILDREN

The techniques and concepts of dance and movement also apply to the group setting. Some of the issues that arise as group members interact lend themselves to activities that involve movement and dance.

Movement Games

One issue that may arise in children's groups is irritation by one member because another member is modeling or imitating him. This negative response can be changed to a positive one by a movement game. A child is asked to start a movement. The group members copy that movement, then another child is asked to demonstrate how to change the first movement in a small way. Again, the group models the second child. This can proceed until each child has had a turn to be the one to be "copied." Variations in movement can be in terms of space, time, attitude, body part used, and tension. The children are able to explore these dimensions of movement and to make a choice as to how they want to vary movement.

Folk Dancing

Folk dancing is another way in which movement expression can be introduced to children. Moving as a group creates an atmosphere of group accomplishment and an experience with taking turns. The children learn to listen to instructions in order to learn to dance, and they move close to and touch others. These processes help build a close group feeling.

The counselor structures the dance experience to the ability of the children. Simple footwork and floor patterns can quickly be mastered and experienced as successful dance forms. A simple dance can be expanded by the children themselves by using the variations of movement as previously described. Initial experience in dance should be short, simple, successful, and fun.

Pantomime

Children enjoy the process of pantomime, in which others have to guess what or whom they are imitating. The subjects for the pantomime can come from the children's ideas, or the leader may structure suggestions by writing names of people, things, or animals on slips of paper to be drawn from a paper bag. The suggestions can be issues that group members have expressed: "mean teachers," "bossy parents," or "that bully." Even very withdrawn children often become involved in the guessing process and then find themselves acting too.

Structured Exercises

Another form of movement for a group is structured group exercises. These movements provide an energy outlet, an opportunity for practice of body control, and an opportunity to listen and follow directions. The children may take turns leading the group in exercises or in an obstacle course. The counselor can form an obstacle course, and then a follow-the-leader process can be initiated. Boys seem to particularly enjoy this type of movement and the competition in physical prowess.

Music and Musical Instruments

Other activities that are fun and that release energy productively use music and musical instruments. One activity is to have the group tell a story, in movement, that is related through music. This activity stimulates creative thinking and gives an acceptable outlet for fantasies. For example, in acting out "Jack and the Beanstalk" the children use the cues from the music to stimulate movement. The "giant" music stimulates heavy movements, whereas the "Jack" music stimulates lighter, airier movement.

Musical instruments have inherent movement qualities which give children auditory, tactile, and kinesthetic feedback. For example, cymbals have a sustained quality which means movement is continuous and smooth, and occupies time. A tamborine is vibrating in quality, and stimulates continuous, jerky movement. Musical instruments can be paired to meet a child's movement needs within this group. For example, the aggressive child will feel comfortable with percussive sounds, and should be guided to try more sustained kinds of movements that involve inner control, like those inspired by a cymbal.

Tension-Relieving Techniques

After a very active or tension-filled experience, the counselor may want to reduce the level of activity by introducing relaxing techniques. The children may be asked to lie down without touching another person. The leader then asks them to get into positions that are comfortable to them. The children can then be led to relax various parts of their bodies or to concentrate on their breathing. These relaxing experiences are helpful in preparing the children for leaving the group session, particularly when they are expected to return to controlled settings such as classrooms.

SUMMARY

Nonverbal communication through body movement provides a base for understanding a child and for planning intervention in maladaptive behavior. Dance and movement concepts provide a base for interpretation of the child's self-image and emotional state. Specific nonverbal techniques can be developed for children who are hyperactive, aggressive, or withdrawn, to help them with impulse control and body image.

(9) Play in Counseling

Play activity is as important in child counseling as verbal communication is in counseling with adults. Play is a vehicle that children use to communicate with the counselor and with other children, as well as an arena for children to work out internal conflicts in which the counselor can intervene therapeutically. The play activities described in this chapter are suitable for both individual and group counseling. Case studies of play in counseling may be found in Appendix B.

DYNAMICS OF PLAY ACTIVITY

Play activity can be categorized into three basic types: mastery activity related to the development of specific skills; activity based on rules, such as checkers and cards; and make-believe activity — the imaginative or symbolic part of play. Although these activities may be engaged in separately, there may also be overlap. For example, a child may engage in a skill-development activity with a fantasy theme. In counseling the three areas may often be blended, but major therapeutic play activity is in the realm of make-believe or fantasy. Play activity can be summarized as a complex assortment of the child's conscious and unconscious expression, and it is the natural medium of authentic self-expression for children.

Play for emotionally disturbed children may differ from the norm in intensity and focus. Children in counseling may be more fearful, anxious, or angry than are normal children. Through play these children are able to concentrate on specific persons and incidents in relation to their fear, anger, and anxiety.

They may project these persons or incidents from the past onto the counselor so that whatever they do or say relates also to what is going on in the here-and-now situation with the counselor.

From watching and participating in their play, the counselor can learn how these children view their world and how it is unique and different for them. The children also learn how the counselor's reactions differ from those of other adults they have known. The counselor provides a steady, constant background for the children while maintaining his own integrity in spite of the roles the children may assign to him.

Disturbed children often use play and fantasy to work through anxiety-laden experiences. If in play activity they come so close to the content material that their anxiety becomes uncomfortable, they will usually stop the activity and turn to something else. The counselor can acknowledge out loud that this is the way that they can protect themselves from experiences that hurt too much. The counselor can further state a positive expectation that at a future time the children may be able to explore more of their feelings about the anxiety-producing situation. When they can tolerate more anxiety they will return to the play activity that revolves around the conflict area. The children are able to act out, through play, those concerns that they cannot verbalize. Later on they may be able to verbalize their feelings.

The children who have the best opportunity to use play therapeutically are the children who have a high fantasy level, who use make-believe in their natural play settings. Young children may use dolls or a dollhouse setting to act out real-life situations as make-believe. The older child, if asked to tell a make-believe story, can readily tell something that is clearly not based in reality, and may even act out the story. These children have parents who are interested in and accept imagination, act as models for identification, and provide opportunities for the child to practice fantasy. Children with a low fantasy level will look at the dolls, dollhouse, puppets, and dress-up clothing, but will not see any value in using them and will avoid even picking them up. Such children, when asked to tell a make-believe story, will often be blocked completely or will tell something obviously based on fact.

Because a large part of the therapeutic play process depends on children's ability to engage in fantasy play, children who have limited ability to fantasize will be able to benefit least from the therapeutic play process. However, children with low fantasy levels need not be excluded from play counseling automatically. The counselor can work with their parents to help these parents value and encourage imaginative play in their children, and he can teach the children to fantasize by demonstrating story-telling, playing imaginative games, and playing roles with dolls and puppets. The counselor acts as a role

model for imaginative play, and gives much positive reinforcement to the
children for any fantasy play or verbalization. At first the counselor may
have to take almost all responsibility for initiating the fantasy play, but
gradually he gives more and more responsibility to the child. In storytelling,
for example, the counselor may initially tell a make-believe story and then
try to engage the child in dialogue about the story. At another time he may
tell part of a story and have the child finish it. Still later the child may be
able to initiate and complete a whole make-believe story.

The counselor may also need to consider the child's fantasy level when
encouraging the child to express aggression. In the child with a high fantasy
level, acting out aggression in the counseling sessions often leads to a decrease
in aggressive acts in daily life. However, for the child who has difficulty using
fantasy, the effect may be reversed. This child may be more likely to act out
aggression in daily life following fantasy aggression in the counseling sessions.

ROLE OF THE COUNSELOR

For the disturbed child, playing alone does not have the same therapeutic
value that playing has with the counselor present. The therapeutic process is
not automatic in play but it becomes possible in counseling when the counselor responds with consistent sensitivity to the child's feelings, accepts the
child's attitudes, and conveys a consistent and sincere belief in and respect
for the child. This kind of "being with" a child conveys to him a high degree
of empathy and an attempt to express verbally and nonverbally, "I understand."

In nondirected or spontaneous child play, the counselor functions as a
participant observer. The child and the counselor are in a room together with
a variety of suitable toys and equipment. The child is told that he can use
any of these things in any way that he wants. The counselor maintains an
attentive concentration on what the child does and gives verbal feedback
about what he sees. He participates in the play only when the child actually
invites him to engage in a play activity.

There are times, however, when the counselor may take a more directive
role in play counseling. One example was given previously for the low-fantasy-
level child; another situation is with children who are withdrawn. The counselor may also initiate play activity that is directed toward helping a child
work through a specific therapeutic problem or guiding him to increased
awareness of self.

The Setting

The counselor may be in a setting in which a therapeutic counseling room is provided; if not, he may have to improvise and equip one. The room should be located in a place where there will be a minimum number of interruptions and where noise coming from the room will not disturb others. Spilled paint and water should be acceptable and easily cleaned up, and there should be only a minimum number of breakables or untouchables. This room will take on a unique quality for the child as a place that is a refuge from some of the pressures of his world; it will have a constancy and a sameness that are predictable. The child will recognize that play in the counseling room always has a purpose because he is there for his emotional problems.

For groups, the ideal would be to have a large room for activity and a smaller room for discussion periods. If two rooms are not available, a part of the large room can be set aside for group discussion. This area can be equipped with table and chairs or with pillows and rugs for sitting. The activity area should be equipped with a variety of toys and equipment meeting the needs of children ranging in age from 5 to 12 years. By having a wide range of equipment and toys, the children can select the activity or material that is appropriate for them.

PLAY ACTIVITY AND MATERIALS FOR YOUNG CHILDREN

Young children (3–9 years) need play materials that stimulate fantasy development, expression of aggression, sensory input, physical coordination, and skill development.

Fantasy Development

A playhouse corner can be one area where make-believe can be enacted. Children like to dress up in adult clothes and then assume the roles assigned by the clothes. A trunk full of clothes might include women's dresses, high heels, purses, hats, jewelry, veils, scarves, men's suits, wallets, and shoes. It might also include firemen's and policemen's uniforms, hats, and badges. The playhouse corner may have small beds, blankets, dolls, baby bottles, dishes, and brooms.

A dollhouse is also the scene of much fantasy development in the playroom. It should be equipped with a complete family including father, mother, and siblings. This construct may not directly reflect a child's family but it does provide an opportunity for him to react to the doll family from his own experience. For example, a boy from a fatherless family may express resentment, through play, that his father does not live at home; or an only child may look longingly at the sibling doll and express loneliness and desire for a sister or brother. Ethnic doll families should be used, when appropriate, in order to further assist a child in being able to identify with the dolls.

Puppets, of a variety of types, are very useful to children in expressing fantasies. There are manufactured hand puppets representing families and animals, but simple hand puppets can be made of paper bags. Large paper bags can be used, also, over the head just as hand puppets are used. Puppet play is particularly useful in counseling because the child often assigns the counselor a part. The counselor in this part can intervene and confront the child in a way that might be quite threatening to the child if done directly.

Playroom equipment does not need to be expensive; in fact, the less elaborate the equipment, the more the child is in a position to improvise and make the material fit his own fantasy needs. A simple box may become a bed, a car, a house, or a boat as the need arises for these props as a part of the play. Well-sanded blocks of various sizes and shapes can also provide unlimited possibilities for fantasy play. Blocks may become objects such as those listed above or they may be used in constructing buildings and walls.

Expression of Aggression

Because many children undergoing counseling need to learn the appropriate expression of aggression, care is taken to include toys that children can use in aggressive activity. Punching bags, boxing gloves, and plastic "Bozo" figures all encourage such activity.

Other types of toys that aid children to express aggression are soldiers, cowboys, and guns. Children who are inhibited and not ready to hit a punching bag may act out battles and wars with these toys before they are able to engage in physical aggression.

Sensory Stimulation

Water and sand are excellent vehicles for providing a variety of sensations and feelings. They provide vast opportunities for the child to explore and experiment, encouraging and stimulating an inhibited child, and at other times acting as soothing agents for disruptive children.

Physical Coordination and Skill Development

Active sporting activity is useful in channeling children's energy and in helping them to develop mastery over their bodies. In individual and group counseling the children and the counselor can engage in such activity as playing
catch, shooting baskets, and running races. In individual counseling these
activities can be adapted to two-person activities that provide opportunities
for the counselor to coach the child. Many children in counseling have disturbances in coordination, and this type of instruction also helps children
learn how to use their bodies more appropriately and with a more satisfying
release of energy.

PLAY ACTIVITY AND MATERIAL
FOR THE PREADOLESCENT CHILD

For children in the preadolescent age group (9–12 years), the previously
mentioned play activity and materials may not be appropriate. Although the
materials suggested for the younger age group should be available, additional
age-appropriate materials should be added. Preadolescent children are often
too young for verbal interview methods but too old for toys. The play
activity of the older child may provide an opportunity for skill development
but, more important, it provides a vehicle to stimulate therapeutic interactions
between the child and the counselor, and among children in groups.

Appropriate activities include manual tasks, sports, and board games. It
is important that the counselor have some experience with the materials or
activities available. Although the child may initiate an activity, the counselor
may be called on by the child to help with it; however, the counselor needs
to guard against overhelping. He should use a problem-solving approach to
help the child think through the process and to encourage the child to accept
responsibility for completing an activity. In order to accomplish this process
he needs to know how to complete the activity himself.

Manual Tasks

Older children have the skills to use tools, and can gain satisfaction from using
real tools to make objects to take home or to use in the playroom. Scraps of
lumber can be easily and inexpensively obtained, and may provide for a wealth
of creative activity. A nail-pounding board or stump may also serve to build
skills and release energy.

Crafts are a less active form of manual activity that older children find interesting. There is a large variety, including making leather and bead objects, candles, and pottery, and assembling models. Scouting manuals provide a number of suggestions for activities that are appropriate for this age group.

Other types of manual tasks include sewing, weaving, and cooking. Both boys and girls enjoy engaging in these creative activities.

Active Sports

Older children usually have the skills to engage in such activities as kickball, baseball, basketball, badminton, and table tennis. For those children who still have poor coordination, coaching in specific skills can be provided.

Board Games

There is a variety of board games that appeal to preadolescents: cards, checkers, chess, and Monopoly are among the classics. With these games the focus is away from physical skill development and more toward using the activity as a bridge for verbal communication or to stimulate interpersonal interaction. For example, most children have strong responses to either winning or losing a game. A child's response can then become a base for therapeutic exploration by the counselor.

DIRECTED PLAY ACTIVITY

In contrast to nondirected or spontaneous play, the counselor takes a more active, intrusive role in children's activities. The goal of directed activity can be to help children with specific therapeutic problems, to expand awareness of self, to provide an opportunity for inhibited children to engage in play activity, or to stimulate interactions between the child and the counselor or among children in groups.

When planning directed activities, the counselor should take into consideration several concerns. First, what type of activity would suit the child's psychological and developmental needs? Then, what is the most appropriate time in the counseling relationship to introduce the activity? Because these more intrusive, directed activities may raise the child's anxiety level, it is best to introduce them when the child's personal environment is fairly stable and the therapeutic relationship is well established.

Some of the more popular activities include mutual storytelling, role play and psychodrama, and simulated games.

Mutual Storytelling

Historically, values and insights have been transmitted through the telling of fable, myth, and legend. Storytelling in child counseling has proved effective in helping children develop more flexible and adaptive behaviors without the anxiety of direct confrontation [1]. This method uses the language of the child and provides the opportunity to bypass conscious inhibition with humor and drama. It can be used alone as a major therapeutic tool, or in combination with other types of child counseling activities. It is particularly useful with children who are verbal, who have active imaginations, and who engage in storytelling. For short-term counseling, it often proves invaluable in effecting behavior change in short periods of time.

The counselor asks the child to tell a story about something that happened to him, or to someone else he knows, into the tape recorder. The process can be made to sound exciting by pretending that the story will be broadcast to an audience over the radio. The counselor instructs the child to make the story interesting to the audience by including a beginning, a middle, and an end. And he asks the child to state the moral of the story at the end. For younger children, he can ask, "What can we learn from the story?"

When the child has completed the story, the counselor tells another story using similar characters and setting and involving more health-producing types of behavior. The counselor's story is based on his interpretation of the symbols in the child's story revealed through the child's psychodynamic history. The counselor also ends with a moral that is appropriate for the therapeutic aim of his story. After they have both told their stories, the counselor offers the opportunity to listen to the tape, allowing further integration of the new material and insights. Some children even take their tapes home in order to listen to them between two sessions.

To use this method effectively, the counselor needs to be excited, imaginative, and involved in the process. He may need to help the child to start (Once upon a time there was a little boy who . . .) or to continue if he gets bogged down in the middle. If the child does not respond to these activities, the counselor should drop the intervention and perhaps try another time. The counselor must pay close attention and remember the details of the child's story in order to accurately base his improvised story on that of the child. He must, of necessity, have a great fund of knowledge of psychodynamics in general, and as much knowledge as possible about the child's psychodynamic structure in order to provide a therapeutic story for the child.

Because this method breaks through to the child's unconscious material, it is a very powerful tool and must be used with great care. After the child has told a story, the counselor may be aware of what the child is saying, but he may decide that the child cannot face the total revelation. The counselor would then gear his story to help the child deal with the parts he thinks the child can integrate. In subsequent storytelling sessions the theme the child raises will probably recur. There is time to work through the problem material at a pace the child can assimilate.

The kind of story the child tells varies with the stage of the counseling process. In the beginning stages, the child's stories may not have very "heavy" symbolic content. The counselor does, however, learn something of the child's internal feelings and responses. These data are stored for future use. In the working stage of counseling the stories reflect more of the conflict the child is experiencing. A theme may be carried over from the beginning stage and be dealt with in more depth. As the counselor gets to know the child better he can improvise stories that more appropriately relate to the child's problems. In the terminating stage the child's stories have less disturbed content, and also incorporate the morals or insights that the counselor has developed. In addition, the child is able to carry out alternative behavior patterns outside the counseling setting.

For a less verbal child a variation of the storytelling method is to encourage the child to draw pictures of certain situations in his life and then tell stories about the pictures.

Role Play

Role play with children is a natural method of interaction in play. The children act "as if" a situation were actually occurring. Directed role-play activity encourages children to work on problem areas through activity that involves thinking, feeling, and doing. Role play facilitates awareness and understanding of self, and provides opportunity to practice social skills, to develop empathy for others, and to increase communication skills.

In directed role play the counselor sets the stage and describes the situation to be acted out, then asks the child to play the part. A girl who is frightened of her teacher can be asked to first act out a scene between herself and the teacher, with the child playing herself. Then the counselor can ask the child to play the part of the teacher. Through this process, the child may become more understanding of her own behavior and develop empathy toward the teacher. Inhibited children may have some difficulty engaging in direct role play, but they may be able to act out directed scenes by using puppets and dolls.

Psychodrama

Psychodrama is similar to role play, but the focus is on the child's internal feelings. Appropriate for the preadolescent age group (9—12 years) and in group counseling, the use of psychodrama facilitates work on interpersonal experiences and conflicts. It should be used with caution and only by a counselor who is experienced with the technique. In the practice of psychodrama one person is representative of the group. He explores an experience in his life under the direction of the counselor and with the support of group members in group counseling, using both verbal and nonverbal activities. The counselor may also instruct another member of the group to play different parts of the individual's personality. The other person can do and say things that the individual's own ego will not let him do and say. The individual in the "hot seat" is able to expand awareness and insight into himself, and try different behaviors. In addition, the group as a whole has a vicarious experience of awareness and insight.

In psychodrama with children in group counseling, an incident that has been painful, fearful, or otherwise difficult for a member is selected for re-creation. The acting of the incident as it occurred helps the child reexperience the original feelings that were aroused through the incident. The child is encouraged to set the scene and to pick the players. After the scene has been acted out, the child may be asked to set it again so that he comes out feeling better. Other members of the group may give him suggestions and ideas, and may even themselves act out different responses to the situation. The goal is to help the child who had the original experience develop a wider repertoire of responses to a difficult situation.

Simulated Games

Simulated games are similar to role playing in that the child is involved in an "as if" experience. Games can be used to develop self-awareness, fantasy, interpersonal interaction, and communication skills, and can be used in both individual and group counseling with children from preschool age through preadolescence. Only simple experiences should be used with young children (3—9 years).

In a simulated game the counselor directs children in a series of activities that guide them in a step-by-step "as if" experience. Following the experience, the children have an opportunity to talk about what the experience meant to them. The following are two examples of the many simulated games that can be used with children in counseling (see [2]). An experienced counselor can use his or her creativity to develop similar experiences that lead children to growth in awareness and to resolve specific problems.

Animal Fantasy Game

Animal fantasy is one game that can be used with young children to develop awareness of self and empathy for others. The children are told that animals have something to teach them and that by getting into the skin of an animal, its movements and its rhythm, they can discover parts of themselves. Then they are given a series of verbal instructions such as: Think of a slow animal; choose an animal that you want to be; get in a position of that animal resting quietly; now move very slowly as that animal might move. The experience can be varied by focusing on different types of animals — fast, big, small, fierce, or gentle.

Happiest Time Game

This experience can be used with older children to encourage fantasy development. The counselor gives the child sentences to respond to in writing, such as: Imagine the happiest time possible; state what would happen; state what you would feel like. After writing his response the child shares his writing with the counselor or, in groups, with other children. The experience can be varied by focusing on saddest or angriest experiences.

Planning Special Activities

Planning special activities provides opportunities for children in individual and group counseling to decide what they want to do and then to think through how they want to do it. In groups, this type of activity is particularly helpful in facilitating cooperation and interaction among group members. Activities can be planned around birthdays, holidays, and terminations. In older age groups, planning and carrying out special activities can be one of the major procedures in counseling.

In both individual and group counseling it may be appropriate to have a regular snack time (juice-crackers-popcorn). This activity gives the child or children an opportunity to plan what they want to eat, participate in its preparation, and engage in social interaction around eating. In active groups, this may be the time when the group is most together.

SUMMARY

Play is one of the most important activities for children. It allows them to develop mastery of self, to communicate, and to work through conflicting feelings. In counseling, play may become the major vehicle for establishing a therapeutic relationship and for the child to engage in therapeutic activities. Play materials and activity should be presented that are appropriate for the child's stage of development. The child may engage in nondirected play, or the counselor may direct the child's play for specific therapeutic purposes.

REFERENCES

1. Gardner, R. A. *Therapeutic Communication with Children — The Mutual Story Telling Technique.* New York: Science House, 1971.
2. Otto, H. *Group Methods to Actualize Human Potential.* Beverly Hills, Calif.: Holistic Press, 1970.

(10) Art in Counseling

Spontaneous and directed art are important activities in counseling because not only is art expression closely linked with the child's self-concept, but also it is a natural form of self-expression in children. By understanding its nature and value, the counselor can use art both as a diagnostic and evaluative tool and as a therapeutic vehicle. The art activities described in this chapter are appropriate for individual and group counseling. Case studies of art in counseling may be found in Appendix C.

Art is a language of symbols that communicates feelings and ideas that might not be expressed verbally, because art expression is not as subject to defense mechanisms as is verbal expression. Self-expression through art is more likely to be an authentic, natural expression of the total child at the time he is making his art product. When a child draws, he usually draws himself, his own experience, or that of someone with whom he identifies. He draws from his mental perception, which includes his ideas and feelings rather than just his visual perception. His art expresses his unconscious tensions and feelings. Art is also a form of communication that has no barriers of time and space.

Besides communicating his personality to the outside world, art also provides the child with an activity that is cathartic in nature. It provides a natural method of working through both conscious and unconscious feelings.

INTERPRETING CHILDREN'S ART

The basic assumption used for interpreting children's art is that children's drawings have something to tell about the children who drew them. There are some universal concepts that are applicable to the interpretation of all children's art, but superimposed on the universal concepts is the child's own individual, unique personality.

Some counselors interpret children's inner feelings by the colors they use. This technique may be valid if the counselor knows these children well and is familiar with the colors they use to express different emotions; however, the counselor must be careful not to make interpretations if he does not know the children. Although the meaning behind the use of colors may be highly individualized, there are a few universal associations that may be found in children of all cultures. These include red for fire, anger, and the setting sun; blue for water and deep things; and yellow for sun and flowers.

Throughout the chapter various observations are made relating children's art processes to personality. The observations are clues that must be viewed in relation to a child's total development.

It is important for the counselor to be aware of the normal development of art expression so that he can be sensitive to deviations in development, can use art as an assessment tool, and can plan art activity that is developmentally appropriate.

STAGES IN THE DEVELOPMENT OF ART EXPRESSION

The Scribbling Stage

The scribbling stage occurs normally in children from 2 to 4 years of age. At first there are random marks and later, more controlled scribbling. At this stage, the child's scribbles do not take on any discernible representation. The focus is more on the muscular or kinesthetic process of involvement in the activity. Scribbling may be viewed as an extension of the child's motor play. This does not mean that the drawing does not have some meaning for the child when he did it, but that the content is more likely to be derived from less cognitive processes. These scribbles are influenced by the child's physical and emotional makeup; although there are similarities in all scribbles, each child develops and expresses himself individually, as seen in differences of pressure, continuity of stroke, impulsiveness, area of stroke, and pace of activity (fast-slow). These differences can provide clues to a child's beginning personality development. Most children engage in scribbling with delight and with the pleasure of movement and of making something appear on paper that was not there previously. Even in scribbles they express a variety of emotions: anxiety, fear, anger, and delight.

Preschematic Stage

This stage starts at around 4 years of age and extends to approximately 7 years. The change from scribbling to beginning representational drawings may seem to occur quite suddenly. A little boy may make a circle and call it a "mommy." If Mommy is around she may reinforce this behavior each time the child makes a circle. Children in this stage usually attempt to make representations of persons and familiar objects from their environment. They move from a chance form to being able to reproduce forms and create images. Although they may still use some scribbling, they develop increasing control over their ability to express true representation. The children may comment on what they draw, but it is not appropriate for adults to ask or to interpret to children what they think the drawing looks like.

The most frequent beginning representational drawings are of persons who are important to children and of articles of clothing, houses, trees, and vehicles (cars, airplanes, boats).

Schematic Stage

This stage occurs in children between 7 and 9 years of age. At this stage the child has developed a definite and consistent concept that is highly individualized. His drawings are descriptive of the environment, and usually each one makes up a whole representation.

The drawings are of the world as the child sees it, and as such they are not what adults would term reproductions. There is little concern for perspective, and the drawings usually include a base line, perhaps of green grass, and a top sky line of blue. Yellow suns often predominate in the sky. The child draws those things from the environment that he thinks are most important.

Realistic Stage

At around 9 years of age, children's art takes on a more realistic form. The sky comes down to the ground, and the base line is not as definite as in the previous stage. In this stage there is more concern for proportion and depth. The drawings tend to be smaller and to contain more detail. Content of the drawing is often related to the society as a whole and less to the egocentric focus of the younger child. The child at this stage is also likely to be more critical of his ability in art expression. He may be inhibited in his willingness to engage in art activity, and if he does draw he may attempt to hide his drawings.

Fluctuation in Stages

Normal development always has its digressions that need to be viewed in a broad context. Stages may not be as discrete as described, and age levels are certainly not firm. A child who has had an illness or an emotional crisis may regress to a previous stage, but the regression does not become of concern unless the child stays in the regressed stage for a prolonged period of time. One must also bear in mind that there is a broad range of normal individual differences.

ART IN THE ASSESSMENT OF CHILD PERSONALITY

There are innate and environmental influences on some children that make their development different from that of the normal children previously described. In normal emotional growth children are able to identify clearly and easily with their art, which contains personal statements and which is flexible and creative. Children with emotional disturbances often draw stereo-typed, rigid drawings. The context of their drawings may be detached and nonpersonal. They may draw houses or animals, but state that these objects are "not mine." Highly anxious children may also repeat meaningless patterns and figures as a way to reduce their anxiety.

Children's art is not only valuable in assessing a child's level of physical, intellectual, and emotional development, but it is also a useful evaluation tool. Drawings made at the beginning of counseling can be compared to later draw-ings, indicating progress or no progress. These data can be used with other data in decision making regarding when to terminate counseling.

Projective-Diagnostic Techniques

Drawing a Person

The child's drawing of the human figure also develops in predictable stages and is one index of developmental level and self-concept. In the beginning figures of the 3-to-4-year-old the head predominates, eyes appear as goggles, and arms and legs are usually appendages of the head. Later the trunk appears as either a smaller circle or a stick line. Children do not draw the human figure in a profile until the stage of realism; however, they may draw mixed front and profile pictures before this time.

The following technique is suitable for children beyond the scribbling stage. A child can be presented with a piece of construction paper, a crayon, and a space to work on that is comfortable and appropriate for his size. The counselor then asks the child to "draw a person." Usually children will be eager to draw, but some will say that they "can't." These children can be encouraged to draw without giving them any specific instruction about how to draw. The counselor should avoid making interpretive statements to the child about the drawing, or asking, "Who is it?" He can, however, ask if the child can tell him anything about the picture.

Figure drawings can be interpreted in a variety of ways. The Goodenaugh Draw-A-Man test [1] can be used in this manner. It provides a valid indication of the child's level of intellectual development. In this test the child is given IQ credit for the amount of detail included in his drawing compared to children of his own chronological age. A rough judgment of level of development can be made by comparing the child's human figure drawing to the normal stages of development.

Some clues about emotional development can be gained by means of the child's omission or overemphasis. The child who overemphasizes hands and arms may be an aggressive child or may have been the recipient of aggressive acts. The child who omits or draws small arms and hands may be a timid, withdrawn child. The emotionally unstable child may draw figures with their feet off the ground, no feet, or small feet. The disturbed or depressed child may draw a very small head at a time in his development when normal children draw large heads. The accentuation of certain body parts, not exclusively genitalia, may be an indication of problems in the sexual area. For example, a boy may focus on chest and muscle development or facial and underarm hair; a girl may emphasize breast development, facial makeup, or hair style.

Drawing the Family

The same procedure as described previously can be used for "drawing your family." This technique is suitable for use with children over 4 years of age. Children's responses are highly colored with their feelings about themselves and their families. These drawings should not be judged by the criteria of levels of development or intelligence, but by the following: size is equivalent to importance; order of development is equivalent to most to least impressive; position of child is equivalent to expression of his status in importance. Additional information can be gained by exclusions, parent preference, who is placed next to whom, indications of sex, extra ornaments or clothes, accentuated or omitted parts, additions other than persons (trees, houses, animals). Each of these criteria has something to say about how a child views his family and his place within this most important social system.

The child with low self-esteem may leave himself out, be very small, and be last in order of importance. The child with sibling rivalry or jealousy may omit the rival or make himself larger than the rival. Family drawings may also clearly reveal an oedipal conflict. These projections can be used by the counselor to understand the child and to form a basis for future therapeutic interventions.

Further Diagnostic Observations

Additional observations may be made that are relevant to children with emotional disturbance. If a child consistently fails to include people in his drawings, one might hypothesize that the child has difficulty with interpersonal relationships. Most children reflect joy, sadness, fear, or anger in their drawings. If these emotions are absent or overemphasized consistently, this may be a clue to emotional disturbance. One might also look at the size and placement in drawings, erasures, and shadings. If a child consistently draws very small figures and uses a small portion of the paper, this may be indicative of restriction of personality development. The child who attacks drawing with vigor, has a great deal of muscular movement, is noisy, and has difficulty confining himself to the paper may be hyperactive or aggressive. The child who makes innumerable erasures may be one who is constantly striving for perfection and who is never pleased with what he does. Shadings in drawings also have significant emotional meaning for the child that is highly individualized. A boy might draw a figure of a boy and shade in the hair, pants, or shoes with no significance attached. The disturbed child may shade in unusual parts, such as the hands, one arm, or a side of the face.

The selection of color may be indicative of emotional disturbance. Most children color the sun yellow, the sky blue, and the grass green. If a child beyond the scribbling stage consistently uses colors that are not natural, this may be indicative of disturbance. This is also true for the child who consistently uses one color or an unusual color — for example, black — in all his paintings.

These observations must be made over a period of time, and be viewed in the context of the child's total development in order to understand fully their relationship to the child's personality.

THERAPEUTIC APPLICATION OF ART IN COUNSELING

Motivation

Because one of the basic problems that emotionally disturbed children have is identification with their art, the counselor needs to use strategies that motivate optimum involvement. The motivation provided must be suitable for a child's developmental level.

The inhibited or young child may need modeling or shaping by the counselor. The counselor can draw or paint and then ask the child to try this activity. If the child still cannot participate, the counselor may place a crayon or brush in the child's hand and actually start the movements. The counselor may also shape more expansive movement for the restricted child, or use fantasy to encourage the child, or ask the child to pretend that he is running around the playground and then to trace his movements on the paper.

The motivation that the counselor provides for the older child is in the form of support and encouragement. The counselor can help to stimulate the child's art activity by asking questions — when, where, what, and how — related to objects or human figures. The counselor can also comment on what the child is doing and how well he is doing his art activity.

For the child in the schematic stage, the motivation for art activity often has its basis in action. The child has the opportunity to use concepts as a living experience and to explore different ways of expressing concepts. The motivating subject matter may be action (climbing a tree); profile or front view (talking with friends); time, space (trip to a farm); private world (fantasy, dream); or the material itself (exploring clay).

Children in the realistic stage need to be encouraged to use art as a form of expression without undue concern for how the product looks. Because they have a critical self-consciousness that is often inhibiting to free expression, the counselor can use a strategy that helps overcome this problem. He can ask these children to engage in their art activity with their eyes closed and to use their unaccustomed hand. This process often frees children from the critical restrictions they place on art and may lead to an even more authentic artistic statement, for the unaccustomed hand is less subject to restrictions that are common to the accustomed hand.

For all stages of development the counselor can also provide motivation by talking with the children about their art, mounting selected pictures, and taking photographs of the children's art products.

Art Materials

Art materials should be appropriate to a child's developmental ability. In the scribbling stage, the child should have large pieces of paper (construction, newsprint, butcher), large crayons, chalk, felt pens, finger paints, and ceramic clay.

In the preschematic, schematic, and realistic stages the materials should include large paper as indicated above, tempera paint, brushes, pencils, crayons, chalk, collage material, finger paints, wire sculpting material, and clay.

The room in which art activity takes place should also have a supply of water and sponges for cleaning up, and smocks to cover clothing.

DIRECTED ART ACTIVITY

Art activities can be planned by the counselor to help children with specific behavior that arises in counseling, to increase self-awareness, and to stimulate interpersonal interaction.

When planning a directed art activity, the counselor should select a medium with which both he and the children are already familiar. Earlier exploration of the material may be the first stage in an art experience that will be directed toward a specific therapeutic focus at a later time. The activity should also be suitable to the children's stage of development. The counselor should plan a time after the directed art activity for children to talk about their art product and also the process of making it. In groups, children can share their art product and their experience. They have opportunities to observe how their art is both similar to and different from that of others. The counselor may ask older children to write about their experience and then to share it with others in the group. The counselor may also want to plan future sessions with the same focus, but using different media. For example, in one session children can be asked to draw "how they feel inside" and in a subsequent session use the same focus, but use clay for expression.

When preparing a child or a group of children for a directed art experience, the counselor can tell them the purpose of the experience (get to know yourself better, get to know your group members better, work on specific problems). He can then explain what the focus or topic of the activity will be (drawing yourself, drawing the group, drawing yourself when you're angry). Then he can guide the child or children in activities that prepare them for the experience. (Find a comfortable place to work where you won't bother someone else, relax your body, close your eyes, begin to think about what you're going to draw, get in touch with the materials you will use, feel the texture and size of the paper, feel how the chalk is different from the paper in size and texture.) With this kind of preparation the child is more ready to move into a deep exploration of the focus of the activity.

The activities that will be described are appropriate for children from 5 to 12 years in both individual and group counseling. The young child will develop the focus at a less complex level than the older, more skilled child.

Counselors should be constantly thinking of other creative ways that they can use art in their counseling with children.

Focus on Individual Growth

Activities that focus on a child's individual growth or awareness in either individual or group conseling can include the following: portraits of self and family; drawing self at specific times (under stress, angry, sad, happy, fearful); how he feels inside; what he wants to be when grown up; a safe place to be. The media for expression can be collage, drawing with crayon or chalk, painting with brushes, finger painting, paper constructs and sculpture, and ceramic clay.

Focus on Group Interaction

In order to help the group interaction process and to help group members understand one another better, group art projects can be proposed: group impressions of their world, their neighborhood, their school, or their group itself; a specific holiday theme. All of the media previously mentioned can be used for each focus.

Focus on Evaluation

Directed art activities can also be used for evaluation. Self-portraits or family portraits can be drawn at the beginning and ending of counseling. The child can compare them and observe differences in himself. The counselor may also ask a child to make a chart or a picture depicting his growth from the beginning of counseling. In groups, the evaluation focus can be on the individual children and/or the group as a whole. The group members can be asked to make individual charts or pictures that indicate group growth or changes. This type of evaluation helps children more clearly identify their growth areas and to integrate the growth into their self-system.

Focus on Problem Behavior

At times a child in individual or group counseling may need to release energy or express aggression. Art can provide an appropriate channel for this expression. A child can be directed to punch and pound clay or to draw with crayon, chalk, or paint on large paper with large, sweeping gestures. He can also be directed to draw pictures of what is bothering him. Tearing paper can also be a method of reducing individual and group levels of tension.

As mentioned previously, the inhibited or withdrawn child may need a great deal of direction, support, demonstration, and even shaping to begin to engage in the use of any art materials. These children also need a great deal of praise for any activity they initiate.

Art activity can also be used to focus on and resolve problems as they arise in groups. For example, if a clique has formed within a group, making a group picture will often clearly illustrate to the members what their behavior is. From this point the counselor can lead the group in exploring ways to work together.

SUMMARY

Art activity is another natural form of communication for the child. Art processes and products provide unique insight into the way children feel about themselves and about their developmental stages. Children's art progresses through stages from simple scribbling to complex representational drawings.

Art materials and activity should be presented that are appropriate for the child's skill development. Children may engage in spontaneous art activity, or the counselor may direct them in art activity that has an evaluative or therapeutic focus.

REFERENCE

1. DiLeo, J. H. *Young Children and Their Drawings.* New York: Brunner/ Mazel, 1970.

(11) Preparation for Beginning Counseling

The two methods of direct counseling for children are group and individual counseling. The decision about which method or combination of methods is most appropriate for a child is ideally made by a mental health team after an initial evaluation that includes interviews with the child, his family, and possibly his teacher. The decision is made primarily on the basis of the child's psychological needs.

COUNSELING MODALITIES

Group Counseling

The basic criterion for placing children in group counseling is that each child has "social hunger" and the ability to use others as role models.

The major value of group counseling to the child is learning alternative forms of behavior from peer models. In group counseling, the effeminate boy learns from a more masculine boy how to behave more like a male; the hyperactive child learns from the less active members to be more controlled; and the withdrawn child learns to be more active from members who are more outgoing. The group also provides opportunities for children to experience giving and receiving, catharsis through play and talk, self-knowledge and awareness, reality testing, and trying out different behavior in a safe setting. Particularly in the older age group, norms of acceptable behavior are developed and the group exerts pressure on those who do not abide by these norms.

The counselor provides a role model of warmth and acceptance of each group member by providing activities and strategies that meet individual needs.

He recognizes achievement of desirable behavior in individual group members, and helps to develop group norms of what is expected, what behavior is allowed and not allowed, and what rewards and punishments will be operating in the group. In a well-balanced group, the members will eventually take major responsibility for implementing the norms, and the counselor becomes the "gate keeper." The counselor also assures the physical and psychological safety of group members. In the beginning stage of counseling with children 9 to 12 years of age, and with younger children throughout counseling, the counselor will need to be much more active. With young children, the counselor will need to be in authority, and to provide support and security.

Children who seem to gain the most value from group counseling fall into the following categories.

1. The immature child
2. The withdrawn child
3. The child with phobic responses to specific objects or activities
4. Effeminate boys and masculine girls
5. The child with "pseudo-assets" (who acts too good)
6. The child with habits such as overeating, temper tantrums, thumb sucking
7. The aggressive child

Individual Counseling

Some children do not have a desire or need to be accepted by other children, and the effect of the group process is not beneficial for them. They are not able to use their peers for role models, and they may not be suitable role models for other children.

The value of individual counseling for these children lies in establishing an accepting, supportive, consistent relationship with an adult. Through individual counseling, the child has similar types of opportunities for growth as the child in group counseling, the major difference being that the corrective relationship is with one adult rather than with a group of peers. The counselor alone has the responsibility for setting and reinforcing limits in individual counseling.

Children who benefit most from individual counseling fall into these categories.

1. The child with an early maternal deprivation or loss
2. The child who has intense sibling rivalry and who hurts others in the group, whom he sees as siblings

3. The child who appears to have no conscience, cannot give to others, and is cruel to others
4. The child with accelerated sex drives, or one who has been exposed to sex perversion
5. The child who steals habitually
6. The extremely aggressive child
7. The child who has recently had a gross stress reaction

Although these children are found to benefit most from individual counseling, children who are included in the categories for group counseling can also benefit from individual counseling. At times the choice for group or individual counseling of these children may depend on the availability of resources for each. Some children may be involved in both individual and group counseling.

Referral of Children for Counseling

Children who are referred for counseling are often initially brought to the attention of mental health workers by teachers, physicians, nurses, and social workers. Parents may be aware that something is "wrong" with their child but are often not able to take a step toward seeking help without professional assistance. Some of the problems encountered in overcoming the parents' resistance to the helping process will be discussed in Chapter 14.

After a child has been referred, members of the mental health team interview both the parent and the child. The data from these interviews provide a base for choosing a treatment for the child.

THE ASSESSMENT PROCESS

Initial Interview with Parents

The first step in interviewing parents is to explain what they can expect in the initial diagnostic process, what will be expected of them, and the types of treatment programs available. Interviews with parents will be discussed in more detail in Chapter 14; the focus here is on what kind of data are collected from the parents in order to make a decision regarding the type of direct child treatment.

The counselor explains that besides the parent interview, their child and perhaps his teacher will also be interviewed, after which, on the basis of the information gathered, the mental health counseling team will make a decision about what treatment program they judge will be most helpful. Then there will be a follow-up interview with the parents to discuss the plan, the cost and duration of the treatment, and their own future involvement. The parents have an opportunity to accept or reject the proposed plan at this point.

The counselor then elicits some basic history from the parents, asking them to state what it is that concerns them about their child and when they first noticed it, and to relate a history of the child's physical and social develop-ment and of his relationship with his siblings, parents, and peers. He may also elicit some data from the parents about their own personal histories and their marital relationship. Finally, the counselor asks the parents what the parents think is the cause of their child's problems and how they think their child can best be helped to overcome these problems.

Additional information that is usually very helpful can be obtained by interviewing the parents with the referred child or with all the children in the family. Dynamics may appear with these groupings that are not observable in interviewing parents and children separately. Usually this type of interview provides a great deal of verbal and nonverbal data on which assumptions can be made regarding the origin of the child's problem and on which a hypothesis may be formulated for treatment.

Initial Interview with a Child

An initial interview with a child should take place in a child counseling room in which the child has an opportunity to use play and art materials that are appropriate for his developmental level.

Some children come easily to the counseling room, whereas others are quite resistant. Young children who resist leaving parents are usually anxious and afraid. The counselor can introduce himself in the waiting room and then invite both parents and child to join him in the playroom. After the child is in the playroom, the counselor can ask him if he is ready to let the parents go back to the waiting room while he plays for awhile. For some children this is sufficient support to allow them to stay, but other children may cry, kick, and scream at being left. These children may need more time and support to be able to stay in the counseling room without a parent. The counselor can offer assurance that he accepts the child, expects him to return, and will be waiting for him. For some very frightened or resistant children, direct inter-viewing and treatment may not be possible.

Once inside the room, the counselor can again say who he is and that the reason for the child's being there is that his parents and teachers are concerned about him and would like to help him. The child is encouraged to say anything he wants, and to play with any of the things in the room. The session usually lasts from 30 to 60 minutes, depending on the age and attention span of the child. The interviewer should take notice of the child's verbal and nonverbal behavior in relation to content, pressure, reality, and level of tension.

The interviewer positions himself in the room so that he is near the child, but not so close that he interferes with the child's activity. He joins in the child's play only if the child asks him to do so. The verbal child will often ask questions about different materials in the room by means of which he may be exploring the parameters of the room and the relationship with the interviewer, and indirectly asking permission to play with materials. Instead of answering the child's questions directly, the counselor can reflect his supposition about the child's underlying motive for asking the questions, and ask the child if he can make a statement out of the question. For example, if a child picks up a crayon and asks, "What is this for?" the counselor may say, "Can you tell me what you do with a crayon?" The counselor may also add: "It's okay for you to use the crayon if you want."

If a child is verbally responsive, the interviewer can structure part of the interview to gain further data regarding the child's personality. Some of the questions or statements that he might pose to the child concern the following areas of interest.

1. The child's reason for being there
2. The child's interests
3. The child's peer and family relationships
4. The child's fears or dreams
5. What the child wants to be or do

Data Collection and Organization

In addition to personal interviews with the parents and child, the counseling team may, with parent permission, interview teachers and obtain the results of physical and psychological examinations before making a decision. A member of the counseling team may also observe the child in a variety of settings — school, home, after-school activities.

The collected data from all sources can then be organized into an assessment of the child's strengths and weaknesses and an overview of his or her personality functioning. A guide for organizing data follows.

1. *Guide for Evaluation of Current Personality Functioning:* Name, age, sex, IQ, physical status, height, weight

2. *General Appearance and Behavior:* Describe in graphic terms, e.g., height (small, tall, etc.), build (slender, chubby, etc.), manner (nervous, morose, etc.)
3. *Symptoms:* Reasons given for referral
4. *The Child's Environment:* Family unit — number, sex, ages, physical aspects, sociocultural status — relationship between parents, parents to other children (sibs) and to patient, sibs to one another and to patient. School environment or treatment setting environment, learning problems
5. *Reality Adaptation:* General estimate of the maturational level of child's personality. Perception of external reality. Degree of mastery of developmental functions, degree of distortion of real experience. Use of body in mastery — active, passive, coordinated, play, speech, control. Use of fantasy as bridge of contact to reality
6. *Interpersonal Relations:* Degree of contact with others, adults, children, degree of closeness or separation, degree of dependence on adults, degree of control of another person, capacity for identification with others
7. *Attitude toward Self:* How stable is the child's self-identification; what are the bases of the child's self-esteem and self-confidence, reactions to failures; how does he compensate for feeling of inferiority; discrepancy between strivings and accomplishments; degree of self-absorption and self-understanding
8. *The Quality of His Affects:* Are his affects appropriate to the reality situation? Describe his affective responses qualitatively
9. *Anxiety:* What degree of anxiety does the child indicate? How is it manifested, under what conditions? How does he relieve his anxiety?
10. *Patterns of Control:* Indicate his general capacity for control of emotion, degree of impulsiveness, control of impulses, capacity for self-expression, for pleasure or displeasure in experience
11. *Defense Patterns:* As identified from above data
12. *Central Conflicts:* Conscious, unconscious, and discrepancies between. State how the conflict is manifested in the child's symptoms; trace the relationship between these conflicts and the type of anxiety and main defenses used to control anxiety. Correlate these conflicts with the developmental patterns and constitutional factors

Appendix D describes a child's evaluation based on this format.

INDIVIDUALIZED TREATMENT PLAN

Developing a Treatment Plan

From the detailed assessment, hypotheses can be made regarding the major areas in which the child needs help. The assessment indicates when the child is able to function at his developmental level (strengths) and when he is below the norm or has abnormal development for a child of his age (weaknesses). A treatment plan would then be tailored to build on the child's strengths, restore or correct the deficits or distortions, and provide for mastery of age-appropriate developmental tasks. This type of treatment plan would also indicate that different techniques and methods are needed within the counseling sessions for different children, and that a strategy that works for, and is appropriate for, one child may not be at all appropriate for another. For example, the hyperaggressive child needs to learn to control aggressive behavior and needs more limits than the inhibited child, who keeps all his anger bottled up inside and who needs to be able to experience a more permissive environment.

Treatment plan goals should include having the following basic needs satisfied.

1. The *need for affection* through a warm, human response and a genuine concern
2. The *need for security* through the provision of reasonable freedom from physical harm and of constancy of setting
3. The *need for belonging* through the therapeutic relationship as an extension of family and school ties
4. The *need for a feeling of personal worth* through identification with the counselor as role model

Appendix D describes a beginning treatment plan for a child based on the previous assessment.

After the mental health team has decided on the appropriate treatment plan and has selected the counselor to work with the child, the family is then consulted. Parents are asked if they agree with the plan of treatment and if they are willing to assume their own responsibility regarding involvement in counseling at the level suggested, and also financial responsibility for the counseling process. If all is agreeable with the parents, child counseling can proceed.

PLANNING TO BEGIN COUNSELING

Individual Counseling

Frequency and Duration
It is difficult at the beginning of counseling to determine the duration of treatment. Long-term counseling, in which the goal is for the child to work through all his conflicts, is an expensive process that is not open to many families. The

more current trends in counseling are toward short-term counseling related to specific developmental problems or developmental crises. As for a student counselor, the length of counseling is often guided by the length of time the student has available.

Usually, the younger the child the more open he is to the direct treatment approach. He has less ego damage, is more open to identification with counselors, and is more open to reeducation than is an older child. In other words, the young child has fewer years of built-up damage to his ego and, because of his natural dependency, can utilize the therapeutic relationship readily.

The age of the child is also considered in planning the length of time for each session and frequency of individual sessions. For the young and/or hyperactive child, it may be more appropriate to have frequent sessions lasting for short periods of time. This child may be seen for 20 to 30 minutes, twice a week. For the older child, weekly sessions of 50 to 60 minutes are appropriate.

Group Counseling

Frequency and Duration

In group counseling with children 3 to 9 years old, in which the focus of the group process is preventive in nature, 40-minute sessions weekly, for 3 to 12 months, is appropriate. However, if the focus is remedial in nature, the group should meet for approximately 40 to 50 minutes, two times a week. Group counseling with this age child is often termed individual counseling with children in a group setting. Although they do learn from observing one another, the group process and group cohesion are not as powerful factors as they are with the 9-to-12-year age group. The decision for the length of stay in the group depends on a child's behavioral change in the group, at school, and at home.

Composition and Size of Group

It is essential that the composition of the group be carefully considered. Without appropriate personality balance, the therapeutic forces of identification and modeling cannot come into play and the group may very well turn out to be harmful rather than therapeutic. There should be personality types that both differ and are complementary to one another. It is helpful if there are one or two "neutralizers," children who are less disturbed than the others, in the group to provide models and also stability to the group process.

Close friends or relatives should not be considered for inclusion in the group because the goal is to break away from old patterns of behavior, and this might be more difficult with close ties. There should not be more than two years of age or developmental level among the members. With boys, for whom physical activity and prowess are so important, the counselor also needs to keep in mind the physical size of the children. In children at preadolescence, there is a wide range of differences in physical growth and maturity. A very small child may constantly be intimidated by a much larger and stronger child, and the stronger child may be realistically fearful of hurting a much smaller child.

In regard to sex, in the younger age groups (3–9 years) boys and girls can be included together, for they still complement one another and are about the same size. However, in the age range from 9 to 12 years, it is desirable to separate the sexes. There are obvious differences in size and development at this stage. In addition, boys and girls at this stage usually have well-defined sex-appropriate activities that are not always compatible. This stage is one in which identification with one's own sex is very important.

The age of the child also affects the decision regarding size of the group. In the younger age group, the size should not exceed five, and for a beginning counselor three is a better number. The older age groups should not exceed seven, and probably five is best for the beginning counselor.

Open or Closed Group

The closed group is often thought ideal in order to work through group processes because members move to different levels of involvement through experience together. However, it is often difficult to maintain a closed group because children do drop out of groups for a variety of reasons. If the therapeutic force within the group is dependent on the balance of personalities, it may be beneficial to replace members when they leave. These changes do make an impact on the group. The leaving of a member should be considered with all the care given to any termination and, if possible, with time for group members to work through their feelings about the termination of a member. The leader should also prepare the group and the new member for the new member's entrance. The group will likely regress for a period of time to an earlier stage until the new member has been assimilated into the group.

Single or Conjoint Counseling

There are advantages and disadvantages in both single and conjoint counselor arrangements for group counseling; however, in some situations there is little or no choice. For single counselors, there is a disadvantage in having (1) no one with whom to check out reality, (2) no one for support in the group sessions, (3) no backup person for group continuity, and (4) only one person for the children to model. The single counselor arrangement does, however, have some advantages: (1) the counselor does not have to negotiate with another personality, (2) a child cannot manipulate between two people, and (3) the young child may be able to relate to one adult more readily than two.

The conjoint counselor arrangement has the advantages of (1) providing two different styles and models of adult leadership, (2) allowing for more adequate meeting of individual needs, and (3) providing continuity when one counselor is not available. The major disadvantage for the counselor in coleading a group is the time and energy that it takes to develop an appropriate and satisfactory coleading relationship.

Inclusion of Child Who Is in Individual Counseling with One of the Counselors
It is not appropriate for the child who needs a strong attachment to one person to be included in a group. Such a child may be one who has experienced early maternal deprivation or loss. Others to be excluded from a group are the children who have personalities that should be excluded from group participation as previously discussed.

Another criterion for inclusion of a child who is in individual counseling with one of the counselors is related to the counselor himself. Does the counselor have the ability to relate to the child in the group setting in an impartial manner that does not raise rivalry in other group members? Student counselors often find this kind of relationship very difficult to handle therapeutically. There is a tendency to overidentify with or overprotect the child.

There are, however, a number of advantages to inclusion of the child in the group. The child who is withdrawn or immature needs the stimulus of other children to learn how to use the therapeutic relationship more effectively. This child may need to learn to share adults with other children, especially a child without siblings. The group experience also provides the counselor with additional therapeutic material to work on in the individual sessions.

SUMMARY

Direct counseling with children may be either individual or in groups. Children are selected for each type on the basis of a detailed assessment of the child's personality.

In planning to start counseling, a number of issues must be considered. There are different issues and strategies to be considered for individual and for group counseling.

(12) Stages in Counseling

The counseling process is usually considered to have three fairly well-defined stages — beginning, working, and terminating. The stages can be identified by the type of behavior that is displayed by a child in individual counseling or by most of the children in a group. This chapter describes the characteristics of each stage, and counseling strategies that are appropriate. Two case studies illustrating well-defined stages in individual and group counseling can be found in Appendix E.

THE BEGINNING STAGE

The beginnings of both group and individual counseling have similar character-istics. First, there is anxiety related to a new experience, which is decreased as the child learns to trust the counselor and group members by experiencing the structure of the counseling process. The counselor helps to decrease initial anxiety by defining the nature of counseling and by stating basic behavior limits that are acceptable in counseling.

Group Counseling

The beginning of group counseling is usually characterized by two substages — the exploratory and the transitional.

In the exploratory stage, the counselor takes the responsibility to introduce the members to one another, and also reviews the goals, expectations, and ground rules of the group. In this stage the children will usually exhibit superficial behavior, not the type of behavior for which they were referred, or which the counselor may have observed either at home or at school. The children seem to be watching and feeling out each group member as well as the counselor. They seem to be deciding what roles they will take in the group, whom they can trust, and with whom they can identify. The leader is much more active at this stage than in later stages in terms of structuring the group activity, helping set norms, and limit setting.

After the initial "honeymoon" type of behavior of the first few sessions, the children begin to change their behavior. They may become more infantile, provocative, demanding, and unreasonable. This is the transitional stage. There is a contagion among the group members that finds them being caught up in hyperactivity or ganging up against the counselor. The group activity is scattered and individual rather than focused, cooperative, and productive. The counselor is tested to great extremity as to his ability and willingness to accept each group member. His goal at this stage is to convince the children of his acceptance of their behavior but at the same time to prevent the group from engaging in behavior that individual members cannot control.

The student counselor will need a great deal of supervisory support during this tumultuous transitional stage. The student may need to remember that this stage is necessary in order for the group to move into the working stage. The children will move into the working stage when they are convinced that they can trust the counselor, when they are convinced that the counselor accepts them in spite of their "bad" behavior, and when they are beginning to trust one another.

If the group does not begin to move into the working stage in six to eight sessions, the counselor should look at the therapeutic balance of the group composition. If there is not appropriate balance in behavioral types, or if there are members who are not ready for group counseling, then group progress may be retarded. If there are too many children with one type of behavior, for example, hyperaggression, the group will not be able to develop control from within the group, and the therapeutic dynamics of modeling appropriate behavior will be absent. In this situation the counselor would have to remove one or two of the hyperaggressive children and replace them with others who are perhaps less active.

Individual Counseling

The beginning stage of individual counseling is also a period of time when the child learns to trust the counselor and becomes convinced that the counselor accepts him.

It is through experiencing the structure of the counseling that the child learns the nature of counseling — what is his freedom, and what is his responsibility. From the beginning, a child will also set up social, emotional, and physical distance between the counselor and himself. The sensitive counselor will be aware of this and will not intrude, but will allow the child to set the pace. If the counselor makes a mistake and moves closer physically, socially, or emotionally than the child will allow, the child will not fail to let him know by a change in behavior — usually withdrawal. The beginning counselor may possibly misconstrue this action by the child as the child's not liking him. It is more likely that the child is delineating how close to be, but not saying: "Go away. I don't like you."

The beginning stage of individual counseling is a time when the child gets to know the counselor and the counselor gets to know the child. In their sessions, in whatever activity the child is doing, the focus of the counselor is to be "with" the child with all the attention that can be mustered. The counselor carefully watches how the child responds to difficult situations such as a block house that will not stay up. He watches the child's body musculature, facial expressions, and neck muscles for signs of tension. He watches for patterns of muscular activity in certain situations. The child will also be watching the counselor's kinesthetic activity even if he seems to be totally absorbed in play. If the counselor is feeling irritated or anxious about something the child is doing, the child will notice a change in the counselor's body tension, perhaps an increased swallowing, lip licking, or reddening in neck and face area. If the child does pick up these nonverbal cues in the counselor, then the counselor may expect that the child will let him know by a change in behavior.

The behavior of the child in individual counseling at this stage is usually similar to the exploratory stage of group work. The child is usually on his "good" behavior and it is not until he begins to trust the counselor that he allows some of the "bad" behavior to come out. Then the child may move into a transitional stage. He may function similarly to the children in a group at this stage, testing all the limits of the playroom in order to find out if the counselor will accept him even if he is "bad." Here again the counselor is called upon to be patient, accepting, and supporting as the child tests his ability to accept him consistently.

In both individual and group counseling the behavior of the transitional stage is the most variable. In some individual and group counseling relationships the children may move directly from the beginning to the working stage with very little or no transitional types of behavior.

THE WORKING STAGE

In both individual and group counseling the working stage has similar characteristics. Anxiety about the newness of the experience has decreased and a degree of trust is well established. With a climate of trust and acceptance the children can begin by means of directed activities in movement, play, and art to work through some of the problems for which they were referred for counseling and toward the goals they may have for themselves.

The dynamic of learning through modeling the behavior of the counselor or other group members becomes fully operative. One behavior that the counselor may model is confrontation by reflection of behavior, a focus on the children's here-and-now feelings, and disclosing his own feelings and responses.

In the working stage child behavior usually changes; consequently limits related to behavior may also change. In individual counseling and in group counseling with young children (3–9 years), the counselor will have to be very active in setting therapeutic limits on child behavior. In a well-balanced group of older children, the children will develop their own limits of acceptable behavior. The counselor becomes a "gate keeper," assuring the safety of group members and offering timely intervention.

The length of the working stage — usually the longest of the three stages — is variable depending on the goals for which counseling was initiated.

THE TERMINATING STAGE (SEE ALSO CHAPTER 13)

The goal of all counseling activities, both individual and group, is to end successfully. The ending ideally signifies a certain degree of behavioral change and a greater sense of self-worth in the child or children. The ideal termination, however, is not always accomplished, and feelings other than acceptance and pleasure may arise in the terminating stage.

Ambivalence

Even though the child may feel adequately prepared to terminate, he may feel a certain amount of ambivalence in terminating, some reluctance to let go of his old self and really to be able to trust his new growth. The child is able to work through this ambivalence in the actual terminating experience, in fact becoming even more aware of his strength, and being able to trust his ability to shed the past. The child may also feel a reluctance to give up this special relationship that is meaningful to him and to give up the use of the counseling room that is so different from any other setting.

Separation Anxiety

The child may also experience separation anxiety based on the threat or fear of anticipated desertion or loss of love of an important person. This anxiety is normal, has its origins in early childhood, and is experienced in everyday life.

Separation anxiety may become pathological if the separation occurs in early childhood and there is no acceptable mother substitute. It may also arise from threats of loss or desertion by a rejecting mother. For these latter children, each termination is very painful, and extra time and care must be taken terminating with them. Working through feelings of loss and separation at the end of counseling prepares the child for future experience in his life when this dynamic may again be experienced.

The student counselor may also have as difficult a time terminating as the child. He must also deal with his own separation anxiety. He must cope with the loss of a relationship that was rewarding and fulfilling, and in which he gave a great deal of himself.

Types of Termination

There are a number of different types of termination that occur in child counseling.

Ideal Termination
The ideal termination occurs when the child, his parents, and his counselor agree that it is time to terminate and there is sufficient time to work through feelings surrounding termination. This may occur in both long-term and short-term counseling as well as in group and in individual counseling.

Abrupt Termination
Termination sometimes occurs with very little notice and may be due to a variety of circumstances such as family or counselor moving away from the area.

One situation that occurs from time to time in the practice of counseling with children is withdrawal without notice. Both the counselor and the child are left with a sense of nonclosure. The counselor may attempt to explore, by phone or direct contact, with the child's parents the importance of a termination period for the child. Some parents will then allow a few sessions for ending the relationship; but there are parents who, for a variety of reasons, will not provide for this termination period. In the latter situation, the beginning counselor often experiences a great deal of frustration, resentment, and disappointment.

Termination Caused by Inadequacy

There are times when it is appropriate to end counseling because it is not found to be helpful. The counselor may find that he is not able to deal with a certain child in a manner that is therapeutic, usually because the counselor has unresolved conflict areas in his own life that are awakened by the child. Or the child may not be ready to be truly involved in counseling. The child who is initially very resistant may fall in this category. Another reason may be related to the parents. Some parents are not able to allow their child to become well, and sabotage the child's counseling in spite of the efforts of their own counselor to deal with this problem. Parents may also withdraw from their agreement to be in counseling along with their child; and without their involvement in their own behavioral change, child counseling may prove to be unfruitful.

Time-Limited Counseling

Another reason for terminating before the ideal time is when the original agreement is for a particular length of time or number of sessions. At times parents may be financially able to support only a stated number of sessions. Short-term counseling caused by developmental problems or crises also may be time-limited. Counseling by student counselors is often for a stated period of time because of the limitations of the students' training program.

Brief Separations

There are times during counseling when there are separations caused by vacations or illness. Whether caused by the counselor or by the child, the child usually resents the separation and may blame the counselor for its occurrence. This type of separation needs to be dealt with as carefully as a final termination. In fact, it may be the first step in working toward a final termination.

VARIABLES IN COUNSELING STAGES

The length of time for each stage is variable depending on the emotional needs of children; however, the working stage is usually the longest. In short-term counseling — four to eight sessions related to developmental crises — all the stages are shorter, more compact, and less easily distinguished. In open-membership group counseling, with members leaving and new ones joining, the stages are also less clearly identified.

Although there are normative types of behavior for each stage as previously discussed, each counseling group and each individual counseling relationship takes on its unique form and style. It is the uniqueness and newness of each counseling experience that is not only challenging but exciting.

SUMMARY

Counseling can be observed to have three fairly well-defined stages: beginning, working, and terminating. In the beginning there is anxiety about a new experience, exploration of what the experience will be like, and learning to trust through the structure of the counseling process. In the working stage, when trust is established, children can work on resolving some of the problems for which they were referred for counseling. In the terminating stage the child works through separation anxiety and ambivalence about giving up counseling.

(13) Strategies for Counseling

The previous chapter indicated that the three stages of counseling have different goals and elicit different types of child behavior. In order to accomplish the goals and to deal therapeutically with child behavior, the counselor needs to develop strategies for various types of behavior. This chapter discusses the strategies that might be appropriate for each stage and for the variety of behaviors that a child may display throughout counseling.

INDIVIDUAL COUNSELING

In beginning sessions the counselor can ask a child who he is, and why the child is there with him. If the child is able to respond verbally, the counselor then has an opportunity to validate or correct the child's perceptions. If the child does not respond, the counselor can take the initiative to tell the child who the counselor is and why the child is there. The child may or may not hear the counselor accurately or be able to give any verbal feedback that indicates that he understands; however, in subsequent sessions he may ask more questions about the process and who the counselor is. The child's anxiety often distorts his hearing and ability to understand in the initial sessions. The counselor can return to these topics in subsequent sessions, when the child is less anxious, in order to further clarify for the child why he is in counseling.

The counselor can use the same process for exploring what the activity in the counseling room will be, asking what the child can do and will be doing there. Some children who are counseled in a school setting think that this is a special kind of tutoring because the referral is often connected with the child's not being able to attend to his academic work. If the child does not answer, the counselor can tell him that this is a place where he can do and say what he wants, and that the equipment is for his use while he is in the room.

Initial Limits

Limits are experienced by the child as the need for them arises during counseling. A limit that always becomes a reality during the initial session relates to time. First, the child is told how long the individual session will be. He experiences this limit when the counselor tells him that the time for the session is over. The counselor can help the child accept this limit by notifying him five to ten minutes before the ending time. The counselor can also introduce a second limit regarding time by stating clearly his expectation that the child will return the following week, and also the approximate number of weeks or months that the child is expected to return.

Confidentiality

The counselor explains to the child that nothing that happens in the playroom will be shared with others, except the counselor's supervisor. The child is given free choice to talk about what happens in the playroom with his family, teacher, or peers; but the counselor will not talk about what happens unless given permission by the child. There are occasional times in counseling when a situation may arise when the counselor and the child need to talk together with parents or teacher. This meeting is planned ahead by the counselor and the child, who also decide mutually what will and will not be discussed outside the counseling room. If a tape recorder is being used, the counselor can introduce it to the child as being available for him to listen to at any time, reassuring him that only the counselor and the supervisor will listen to the tape outside the counseling session.

Contract with the Child

Although the child is usually involved in the initial decision-making process regarding treatment, the counselor also needs to talk with the child again regarding his willingness to engage in the counseling process. It is often difficult and inappropriate to expect a child to make this decision in the first interview. But it is appropriate to let him know that he does have a choice, and that the counselor will be talking with him more about it during the next sessions. This statement is made with a positive expectation of the child's returning for the next session.

Each of these topics is ideally brought up at some time during the first session, but this is not always possible. How much is dealt with depends on what the child is doing, and how he is reacting to being there. The student counselor should guard against a tendency to blurt out everything possible because of anxiety, and should be able to sense the child's readiness and to gear any statements to the child's pacing.

GROUP COUNSELING

Prior to gathering children together for their first group meeting, the counselor can meet with each child to begin to define the counseling process and the expectations that the counselor has for the child's participation. The same format and areas discussed for individual counseling are appropriate. In addition, the counselor can discuss issues related to the group process.

The counselor tells the child that there will be other children in the group with similar problems, and that they will probably like one another. The counselor also stresses that the group is a place for the child to work on his individual problems; that it is all right to talk about these problems in the group; and that what happens in the group will not be talked about by the counselor outside the group. The counselor also expresses the expectation that the child will attend regularly and will be on time; that all group decisions will be made by consensus only; and that the counselor may make the decision to remove the child from the group if this action is appropriate for the child's physical and psychological protection and search for mental health. The counselor may also ask how the child himself thinks he needs to change. Some children are able to respond to this question, and some cannot. If a child is not able to respond, the counselor can ask him to be thinking about what he wants to get for himself from the group.

ESTABLISHING TRUST IN COUNSELING

One of the major tasks of the beginning stage of counseling is the development of mutual trust. Without some degree of trust, there can be no counseling. Trust begins with early interactions between infant and mother. How well the mother is able to meet her baby's basic needs and establish a reciprocity in relationship determines in large part how difficult or easy the trust process is for the person in later life. At one end of the continuum, the autistic child, because of conditions which are not altogether known, is unable to be involved in the developing trust process, and is excluded in a world of his own. On the other end of the continuum there is the normal, open, actively trusting child. In between, there are all degrees of trust.

Definition of Trust

Although the concept of trust is often discussed as a base for relationships, definitions of trust are few and vary widely. One definition of trust is "reliance upon an object, event, or person in our attempt to achieve a desired but uncertain objective in a risky situation" [2].

In this definition one can identify components that apply to the counseling relationship. First there is a choice to trust or not to trust. There may be a variety of reasons for or against this choice, but the major factor appears to be how the child perceives the emotional climate. Second is the ambiguity of the outcome, because the child cannot know whether the counseling sessions will be pleasant or unpleasant. Third is the need for a demonstration of reliance in a person or situation. Fourth is the acknowledgment that there is an element of risk-taking involved in the therapeutic process. If the child has experienced rejection, ridicule, and betrayal, he leaves himself open to the possibility of a repetition in the new relationship. And finally there is a desired objective, that of the well-being of the child, which is the goal of the relationship.

Strategies for Developing Trust

Trust, in the sense of this definition and its identifiable components, does not just happen, but needs to be developed through a certain emotional climate that surmounts the fears and anxiety involved in risk-taking. It is through the living therapeutic relationship that the child learns to trust. The child learns that he can depend on the counselor to behave in a predictable way in a given situation. For example, a child who comes from a rigid, neat home will expect punishment if he spills paint on the floor. In counseling, he may expect to receive the same kind of punishment; but when he makes a mess with paint and water the counselor does not act like his mother. Through repetition of this kind of situation, the child learns that the counselor will react in a predictable, dependable way.

Another important component of trust is acceptance. For the child who does not accept himself, and who has lived in a climate that validates that nonacceptance, it is a major function of the counselor to help the child to improve his image of self. A climate of acceptance of the child can be developed by the counselor by means of allowing the child to express feelings freely without judgment, and by accepting negative attitudes. These two factors reduce the necessity for defensive behavior. The counselor can also use the following strategies to structure an accepting environment.

1. The counselor is ready when the child arrives and, if this is not possible, the counselor apologizes for being late.
2. Appointments are faithfully kept by the counselor. If it is necessary to break one, the child should be notified in advance.
3. The counselor maintains the confidential nature of the relationship.
4. The counselor demonstrates warmth, concern, and genuine interest in the child as a person of worth.
5. The counselor accepts the child exactly as he is.
6. The counselor accepts the pace and distance selected by the child.

The child thus experiences a degree of trust and acceptance by another person, a person whom he likes, a person who pays attention to him. Then the child begins to think: Maybe I'm okay. Maybe I can begin to trust myself and accept all parts of myself and use my energy for myself.

It is impossible to experience a state of complete trust or acceptance of oneself or of another. In fact, if it were possible it might not be advisable to trust 100 percent. Gibb [1] affirms that distrust is rooted in a lack of acceptance of self, and hence a consequent lack of acceptance of others; however, healthy mistrust is based on a person's acceptance of himself. Healthy mistrust is reality-based, and protects the individual from trusting people, objects, and events that are potentially threatening and harmful.

REDUCING ANXIETY

Initial Anxiety

It is hard to know, sometimes, who is more frightened or anxious at the prospect of an initial interview — the child or the student counselor. For both there is the risk of starting out on something that is unknown. For the student counselor the anxiety stems from not knowing what to do, fear of not being able to handle the child's behavior, and perhaps a fear that the child will not come to the interview room. For the child, the response may vary widely, depending on his personality, the seriousness and nature of his disturbance, and how well he is prepared for accepting this new activity. His anxiety may be somewhat softened if he has had the opportunity to see the counselor as a friendly, supporting person before this initial individual session. This might be accomplished during the initial assessment period. The child can meet the counselor with the support of the parents in an office or home setting. The counselor may also visit the child in the customary school setting.

The student counselor may be able to reduce his anxiety in anticipation of the first counseling session with a child by role-playing, under supervision, what he will do and say prior to engaging in counseling.

The fearful, anxious child may have difficulty going to the counseling room. The counselor may talk with the child in the waiting room or wherever they may be prior to coming for their initial counseling session. The counselor can describe the counseling room, the kinds of toys and activities it contains, and what the child can do, and may ask a parent or teacher to accompany the child to the counseling room. If the child still refuses to come, the counselor should go on to the room, saying to the child that he will be waiting there because this time has been set aside just for the child. This process may need to be repeated a number of times before a child is ready to join the counselor. If the child remains so anxious that he cannot freely come to the room, it is more appropriate to defer initial counseling until the child is less anxious.

The anxious child, once in the counseling room, may insist on having the door open. The counselor at first complies with the child's request, but as the child's anxiety decreases the counselor initiates sessions with the door closed.

Transitional Stage Anxiety

In individual counseling, the child who begins to exhibit some of the behavior for which he was referred for counseling may experience anxiety related to expected responses by the counselor. The counselor may observe that the child's body is more rigid; the child may laugh inappropriately, ask for a drink of water, or to go to the bathroom. The child may reduce his anxiety by moving to another activity, withdrawing, or regressing; however, some children may not be able to do this for themselves. In this situation the counselor should redirect the child into another activity, perhaps verbalizing that the child looked and acted uncomfortable with the other activity, and seemed to need help changing to a new activity.

In group counseling, the scattered and provocative activity of the transitional stage may raise anxiety levels. To reduce anxiety the counselor can remove equipment and activities that might be misused or dangerous, such as tools, paints, or clay. He can also reassess the activities provided for the group as to their appropriateness for the group members' skills and abilities.

In addition, when the group activity level becomes high, the counselor may change the pace of the session by directing the group to another activity such as a walk outside or by offering refreshment time. If the group anxiety remains high in spite of these interventions, it is appropriate to terminate the session early rather than to allow the group anxiety to go beyond therapeutic bounds.

Counselor Anxiety

The counselor may use his excitement or normal anxiety to bring spontaneity to counseling. If, however, he experiences within the relationship a threat which produces an anxiety reaction at higher levels, he must attempt to endure or bind this anxiety, recognizing that his perceptions and observations may be distorted and also that he is communicating anxiety to the child. To minimize the amount of anxiety communicated, and to maintain the relationship as therapeutic, the counselor who becomes aware of his anxiety should utilize withdrawal behavior, for example, by becoming less active in a session. If he cannot contain his anxiety, he should terminate the session early, taking great care not to let the child feel guilty. The counselor may simply state that the session will end early because of how he feels and not because of anything the child did or said.

LIMITS IN COUNSELING

Counselors and therapists generally concur that limit setting is an essential and important technique. Moustakas [3] believes that without limits there would be no therapeutic benefits in counseling. Children who are referred to counseling often are children whose parents have difficulty setting appropriate limits. In the counseling relationship, when the child exhibits behavior that necessitates limit setting, the counselor has the opportunity to limit a child's behavior in a way that is different from that which the child has previously experienced.

Limits are necessary to define the boundaries of the counseling relationship and also to tie it to reality. They provide a structure within which the child can grow. At the beginning of counseling, the structuring begins through which the child learns the nature of the counseling process.

Many children who are referred to counseling lack self-control. They have high levels of anxiety that are partially relieved by impulsive behavior but that at the same time may result in discomfort, disorganization, and lowered self-esteem. Well-defined limits that are set and enforced in a consistent manner give support to a child who does not have the ego strength to control his own behavior. The counselor becomes the child's external control until the child is strong enough to control his behavior from within.

Because impulsive behavior is not only self-destructive to the child but also unacceptable to society, setting limits on unacceptable behavior is a therapeutic learning experience. The child learns in counseling that his thoughts and wishes can be accepted, but that his actions will be controlled. The child is encouraged to verbalize his thoughts and wishes and to act them out symbolically. If the child is angry and attempts to hit the counselor, the counselor restrains the child from hitting, and encourages the child to verbalize; the counselor may suggest that the child release his energy by means of hitting a pillow or a punching bag.

A final rationale for limits has to do with the counselor rather than with the child. In order to remain accepting of the child, the counselor may have to set limits on behavior that raises his own anxiety. Because acceptance of the child is basic to the therapeutic relationship, the counselor must be aware of what behaviors are likely to be anxiety-provoking to him and must plan to set limits on these behaviors.

Setting limits on specific behavior evolves through the counseling process, but there are basic limits that provide boundaries and structure for the total counseling process.

Time

The amount of time for the counseling session may be the first limit that the child encounters. The child needs to know the length of each session. Counselors can help children accept this limit by reminding them when the time for ending is nearing. It is helpful to have a clock available so that the child can check the time for himself. When the stated time has elapsed, the counselor says that it is time for the child to leave. Some children will try to extend the time by bringing up important material, but the role of the counselor is to be firm and insistent on the ending time. The final limit in counseling also relates to time: the termination of counseling.

Use of Toys and Materials

Most counselors agree that the child should not be allowed to take toys and other materials away from the counseling room. The child is allowed and often encouraged to take home his art products, crafts, and constructions, but he cannot take the toys or the materials used to make the art products. The child needs to understand that the toys belong to the room, are used by others, and would not be there if he took them away.

Staying in the Playroom

After the initial stage, during which the child may have some difficulty getting to and staying in the counseling room, it is expected that the child will stay in the room. If he leaves, the child must understand that he cannot return. Some children will try leaving to manipulate the counselor, whereas others may leave because they are too anxious about something that happened in a session.

Safety

The counselor does not allow behavior that is a danger to either the child or himself. This limit increases the child's feelings of security. It also prevents the child from feeling the guilt, anxiety, and fear that may arise if he is allowed to attack the counselor.

Cleaning Up

Counselors are in some disagreement as to whether children should be involved in cleaning up the counseling room before leaving. In deciding whether this limit is appropriate for a child, the counselor should refer to the treatment goals for the child. An excessively controlled, neat child who is being encouraged to be messy might be discouraged from cleaning up, whereas another child needs to be encouraged to be more controlled and neat. If handled well, cleaning up can be an experience that brings the child and the counselor closer together.

Strategies for Setting Limits

The two major factors which must be considered in setting limits on children's behavior are (1) what are the therapeutic goals for the child and, within this framework, (2) what limits can the counselor implement most therapeutically.

The key to successful implementation is to clearly state each limit in behavioral terms, to state the consequences for breaking each limit, and to intervene with consistency and a minimum of ambivalence. In addition, the counselor also recognizes the child's feelings and wishes, and points out other channels through which feelings can be expressed. He also helps the child to express the resentment that often occurs when behavior is restricted, but avoids power struggles with the child.

The counselor does not state all the limits at the beginning of counseling, but allows the limit setting to evolve as the child experiences the structure of the counseling process.

When setting limits with a child, it is helpful for the beginning counselor to understand that the child does not often recognize him as a particular person but as an extension of a significant adult in his life. The child is often not able to identify the counselor's face or project either good or bad onto him as a person. The child's acting out in relation to limits is usually toward the projected or extended significant adult rather than toward the counselor as an individual.

Broken Limits

When the counselor sets a limit he is creating a structure. When the child breaks the limit, the structure is changed and the limit no longer has meaning in the relationship. This produces feelings of uncertainty and anxiety in both people, and their relationship is in jeopardy. If another limit can be set which both can share, then the structure can be restored and the growth process can continue. Sometimes the counselor must set a number of limits before finding one that is accepted and that restores the structure. This process may involve much struggle, but stronger bonds emerge and new feelings of intimacy and relatedness are experienced.

At times it may seem impossible to find a compromise that is satisfactory. The counselor may have to institute a "time out" period for the child. The time out provides an opportunity for the child to calm down and also restricts all activity in the counseling room for a period of time. The time out may prevent having to impose the ultimate limit of having the child leave the counseling room. Children in counseling have usually experienced enough rejection, and do not need further rejection by being sent out of the counseling room. There may be times, however, when it might be more therapeutic to end a session than have the counselor completely lose control of a session. Appendix F presents a case study on setting limits in child counseling.

STRATEGIES FOR PROBLEM BEHAVIORS

Aggressive Behavior

In handling aggressive behavior, the counselor should prevent the child from harming himself or the counselor. The counselor should also verbally support the child by accepting the behavior and the worth of the child. The counselor can also redirect the behavior into other channels such as hitting objects, fantasy play, drawing feelings, and verbalizing feelings.

For some children the imposition of limits elicits rage that is expressed in tantrum behavior. These children are out of control and need external control to keep from harming the counselor or themselves, or to reduce their anxiety at being out of control. If a child is small enough, the counselor can hover over him in a controlling and protecting manner. This approach offers closeness, affection, and protection. A larger child can be held on the floor with his arms, legs, and face away from the counselor but with the counselor's body against the child's back. For the very active child, the counselor may have to restrain the child's arms with his own arms and the child's legs with his own legs.

When the child begins to cease struggling and to relax, then the counselor can begin to talk while still holding the child at least around the waist. The counselor verbalizes about the child's behavior, being careful to keep comments away from right or wrong, and with a focus on the child's worth as a person. The counselor acknowledges to the child that it is all right to be angry but that a person cannot be allowed to hurt another person or himself.

Often, after the child has experienced a tantrum and the safety of external control, he feels a great relief and closeness to the counselor. A child may want to be held or wrapped in a blanket after such an experience.

When these strong emotions, which have been bottled up inside a child for a long period of time, are released, there is often a simultaneous release of tears as tension is reduced. The counselor can acknowledge the value of tears to the child. Because tears are often not valued in our society, particularly in males, the counselor may have to provide special encouragement to the child to experience his tears and the accompanying feelings of relief.

Withdrawal Behavior

The child who withdraws from others as his major method of coping with anxiety is often more frustrating to relate to than the hyperaggressive child. The counselor has the opportunity to relieve by action or counteraction the anxiety of an acting-out child, but with the withdrawn child the counselor must move very slowly and patiently until the child feels anxious and more secure about the relationship. The counselor can tell the child about his frustration at not being able to relate to the child, and may suggest that other people whom the child knows may feel the same way. Some withdrawn children can be reached by the counselor's talking to or approaching the child indirectly through a doll or a puppet, and through body movement as described in Chapter 8.

Regressive and Dependent Behavior

Some children respond to felt anxiety by means of regressed behavior. These children will return to a stage of development which is more comfortable for them. Here again, if they resort to regressed behavior quite consistently to cope with anxiety, they will not be able to engage in age-appropriate developmental activity.

Some children have very strong dependent needs because they have never experienced unconflicted affection. These children may need to be held, rocked, and petted, as do much smaller children. Because they may be too anxious to receive this affection directly from the counselor, a first step may be for the counselor to hold and rock a pillow, with the child being able to receive some feeling of affection vicariously. Later the counselor may be able to have the child hold a pillow in the same manner or allow the counselor to tuck him into a blanket as if the child were being patted and petted.

Some children may also need to satisfy their unmet dependency needs by going back to sucking a baby bottle. The counselor can verbally acknowledge the child's needs and reassure him that this behavior is all right, at least in the counseling room.

Sexual Behaviors

Sexual feelings and behaviors are often a great source of anxiety to both the child and the counselor as they emerge in the counseling relationship. There are some children who have conflicts in the sexual area that continue to emerge in sex-related behavior in childhood. Masturbation in public is normal for the preschool child, but it is not a usual occurrence during later childhood. The child who masturbates in the counseling session, either openly or discreetly, may be doing it for a variety of reasons, such as to attract attention, to test limits, or to indicate lack of control. In any case, the counselor needs to think through how he will handle this behavior therapeutically. First, it is appropriate for the counselor to comment or reflect on what the child is doing, and to try to elicit some type of verbal response from the child about the behavior. If the child is unable to respond verbally, the counselor may again restate that he accepts the child and that this behavior is allowed in the counseling session. The counselor also may state that masturbation is not usually allowed in other places, but may be done privately.

Another sexual behavior that the child may engage in is curiosity about the counselor's body parts, or seductive types of behavior. Boys may place their hands on a female counselor's breast or look up her skirt. Little girls may touch the male counselor's genital area or otherwise flirt with the counselor. In both instances, it is appropriate for the counselor to remove the child's hands without criticism or undue attention and to say, "I don't want you to do that." If this type of curiosity or seductive behavior persists, the counselor should look at his own behavior for signs of provocation.

PRAISE

The counselor must be careful about offering praise to children. Praise should realistically reflect a child's accomplishments and efforts. A child may not be able to accept praise of his character or personality because of his image of self, but he is usually able to accept realistic praise of his behavior. Praise statements should be stated clearly to reflect the child's behavior. If a child is able to control his impulse to hit out at the counselor, the counselor can offer praise by reflecting realistically what happened: "I notice that you were able to control yourself today. Instead of hitting out at me you hit 'Bozo' instead."

Children who have a poor self-image may feel a great deal of anxiety and mistrust at the counselor's attempts to praise or encourage their behavior. The counselor can acknowledge the difficulty but at the same time offer honest praise for desirable behavior. When the children become more comfortable and accepting of praise, the counselor may offer them a pat on the back to help them further appreciate the fact that they have done something worthy of praise. The counselor may also keep a jar of hard candies to offer during or at the end of a counseling session to children who have earned a reward.

REFLECTIVE CONFRONTATION

In the working stage of a relationship, when trust is well-established, a therapeutic strategy that is available to the therapist is reflection of what the child is doing or saying. The counselor acts as a mirror for the child, reflecting back what the child sees and hears, in order to bring this behavior more into focus. Another purpose is to convey understanding and acceptance to the child. The reflection may free the child to make more direct statements about the behavior and the underlying feelings.

It is best to keep interpretation of possible inner dynamics to a minimum. The counselor may have sufficient data on which to make an assumption about the psychological dynamics behind a behavior, but the assumption may not be correct. The child may withdraw in this situation because of the added threat of a misunderstanding on the part of the adult. Another danger in interpretation is that the counselor may be absolutely correct regarding the dynamics. In this situation the child may endow the counselor with magical thinking. Interpretation may also be a source of resistance in the child, whose self-esteem and survival depend on how his behavior is labeled. An interpretation of behavior can be a threat to the child's whole structure and seen only as criticism.

Strategies for Reflective Confrontation

From observations of behavior and data collected about the child, the counselor knows that there is a problem that the child needs to face. In making the decision regarding when and how to confront the child with his behavior, the counselor should consider the type of child, the goal of counseling, and the stage of the counseling relationship. For example, if a child is quite immature and anxious and the goals are to help the child to be less anxious and more mature in his behavior, the counselor would not initiate confrontation until the child begins to indicate that his anxiety has abated. Usually the beginning stage is not the time to initiate this type of intervention. If the time does not seem right for confrontation of a behavior, the counselor need not worry about missing an opportunity, because the behavior will undoubtedly repeat itself so that the counselor will have a chance to plan a strategy and choose an optimum time for the confrontation to be of therapeutic value to the child.

In planning a strategy for confrontation, it is appropriate for the counselor to review past clinical notes to ascertain when progress has previously occurred, choose a time when the child is experiencing support from his environment, and manipulate a play situation so that the child can work out the conflict through fantasy (doll play, puppets, or mutual storytelling).

The student counselor may tend to resist confronting the child with unacceptable behavior for a number of reasons — fear of rejection by the child or of causing distress to the child, or of spoiling the child's play. By means of support from his supervisor, the student can become aware of and work through his own feelings that retard the use of therapeutic strategies when the child appears ready for them.

The counselor reflects what he observes in the child's verbal or nonverbal behavior in an attempt to make the child aware of this behavior. He may ask the child to make a verbal response to the reflection. If the child is not able to do so, the counselor does not make the connection or interpretation that he has made, but waits until the behavior occurs again, and then repeats the process. For example, a child from a very neat, controlled environment may spill paint purposefully and then look to the counselor for some type of response. The counselor reflects what he sees the child doing, and asks the child to talk about his thoughts or feelings. "I notice that every time you paint you spill some on the floor and then look over to me. Can you tell me what you're thinking about when you do that?"

The student counselor should avoid any tendency to nag the child. He may feel that he has failed if the child does not respond. Here again, the counselor needs to deal with his own feelings of urgency. If he is sensitive to the child's needs, he will be aware that the child sets a pace that the child can cope with. If there is a solid basic trust in the relationship, a few mistakes by the counselor will not hinder the therapeutic process.

DIRECTED EXPERIENCES

As stated previously, it is in the working stage that the counselor initiates directed experiences in play, art, and movement with children individually and in groups. Because the purpose of many directed activities is to break through defenses and to facilitate authentic responses and communication, extra care must be taken in planning these activities so that they retain their therapeutic purpose. The student counselor should particularly think through each of the following recommendations before implementing directed experiences.

First, the counselor should have previously had experience with the process or medium to be used (role play, clay structure). Second, he should develop a plan for the activity and discuss it with his supervisor. The plan should answer the following questions: Is the activity psychologically appropriate both for the children and for the counselor? Is the group process or the child at a stage where this activity will facilitate the therapeutic value of other experiences? Are all the children in the same place in relation to the group process, and how are allowances to be made for those who are not yet ready for this activity? What are the possible positive and negative consequences of this activity?

If there are children in a group for whom the activity may be psychologically harmful or physically inappropriate, there should be alternatives to active participation, such as observation of the group or participation on a less involved level than the others. The decision of whether or not to participate fully is one which the counselor may have to make for a child, or help a child to make for himself.

Some student counselors become quite enthused with using a variety of media in counseling. However, they should move slowly, by introducing only one technique or experience in a single session. And before presenting another, they should give the child or children ample opportunity to review and discuss the first experience. Directed experiences presented in this manner have the optimum opportunity to be useful in behavioral change.

A final consideration is related to the counselor himself. The counselor should involve the children only in activities with which he is comfortable and, as mentioned before, with which he has had some prior experience. It is also very helpful to have a coleader in groups when using these activities. If there are children who need additional support, there is someone available for them while the rest of the group continues at a faster pace.

STRATEGIES FOR TERMINATING COUNSELING (SEE ALSO CHAPTER 12)

Evaluation of the Child's Progress

Throughout child counseling there is a constant analysis and reassessment of data and rethinking of goals and strategies. It is these data, gathered from session to session, that may provide cues as to the appropriateness of ending counseling. Some criteria to consider in evaluation of data are posed by the following questions.

1. In relation to normal growth and development, is the child now at age-appropriate levels?
2. Has the child corrected deficits or distortions in development that he had at the beginning of counseling?
3. Do the child, his parents, and his teacher now feel more comfortable with one another?

In addition to these criteria, the child may also bring material to the sessions that relates to termination, such as dreams regarding separation from the counselor. A child may even verbally state that he is ready to stop coming.

General Considerations

The major goal should be to minimize the child's feelings of rejection, and termination should be planned to fit the child's needs, age, developmental

level, and personality. In the ideal termination, which is planned in collaboration with the child and the parents, reasons are discussed and a period of
time is set for working through responses. When a student counselor must
leave at the end of a training period, he should clearly state the reasons for
leaving and try to keep ambivalent feelings to a minimum: "I'm sorry that I
have to go, but I have to go. I am finished with school now and I have to take
a job somewhere else."

Method of Presentation

Based on the counselor's judgment of the child's concept of time as a reality
factor and on the child's potential level of separation anxiety, the counselor
introduces the idea of separation prior to its occurrence. The younger and
more disturbed child will probably need a calendar or other device that
graphically illustrates the number of sessions remaining. The counselor may
say: "After three more sessions you will not be coming here any more."
    The child may not make any response or acknowledgment of the coun-
selor's statement. He may not believe that the statement is true, or the meaning of the words somehow does not penetrate to his reality. The child may
deny or block out the message about termination. The student counselor is
often upset by this nonresponse, feeling that if the child does not respond he
does not care. However, as the time moves closer to termination and the
message is repeated both verbally and graphically by the counselor, the child
gradually accepts the reality of termination. Some children, however, respond
immediately with anger and aggressive behavior. Others may openly deny or
rebel with statements such as: "I'll come even if you're not here." Even
though efforts are made to minimize the rejection of the child, the child will
often feel rejection, a loss of self-esteem, or frustration, and a resultant angry
response. A child may express anger by aggression or regression in order to
punish the counselor.

Review of Counseling Process

During these final sessions no new material should be introduced or worked
on with the child, so that the major energy can be used for preparation for
termination. It is, however, helpful to review some of the things that have
happened during counseling. How this is done depends a great deal on the
age of the child, and on his ability to be involved in the process. An older
child may be able to verbally review incidents and progress, whereas a younger
child may draw pictures illustrating what he remembers. To help the child

take credit for growth and changes, the counselor might plan a directed evaluation experience such as described in Chapter 9.

Celebration

In the final session it may be appropriate to plan a celebration of the child's "graduation" from counseling. This may take the form of a small party and the giving of gifts. The counselor may ask the child what he would like to do – another step in helping the child realize the growth and changes he has made, and to reduce his ambivalence about ending counseling. Sometimes a counselor will give the child a gift at the final session so that the child has something tangible to remind him of the counseling relationship. This gift may be a duplicate of a favorite toy or art material. The child sometimes brings a gift for the counselor. The gift may be of his own initiation, or it may have been directed and supported by the child's parents.

Introducing a New Counselor

If another counselor is to continue working with the child, the new counselor may be introduced during the terminating sessions and gradually take over a more active role. For some children and counselors this transition period may not be appropriate and may interfere with the termination of the original relationship. This decision should be made conjointly by the child and the counselor.

Terminating Group Counseling

Often groups are set up on a time-limited basis so that members know how long the group will be together. In this case the counselor has ample opportunity to deal with the dynamics and strategies of termination as previously described. When groups are terminated on the basis of sufficient behavioral change in group members, it is essential that the group members be involved in the evaluation of their behavioral change and the decision to terminate.

The group experience can be evaluated by both individual and group progress. For the individual child, an evaluation can be made of behavioral change in relation to the child's individual goals for himself and by his increased use of developmentally appropriate coping behavior in the group, at school, and at home. The group progress can be evaluated by the ability of the group to pass through the beginning stage into a working relationship in which the therapeutic dynamics for growth come into play.

In an open group, in which members leave for a variety of reasons and are replaced with new members, the termination must also be dealt with in the group. The counselor again should utilize all the strategies involved in individual termination, but with the group members having the opportunity to work through their responses to the leaving member. As in individual counseling, there are times when members terminate abruptly, with no notice to the group counselor. The terminating member does not have the opportunity to work through his emotions about leaving, but the group may want to talk about how they feel about the leaving member. Some members of the group may feel responsible or guilty because a member terminates; others relieved but also guilty. These feelings need to be brought into the open and talked about.

The entrance of a new member in the group may lead to regression in members' behavior. The counselor needs to be alert to this possibility and to plan to initiate interventions that were appropriate in the transition stage, in order to continue the climate of acceptance and to prevent group disorganization.

SUMMARY

This chapter has described in detail the type of strategies that are needed for different stages of counseling, including establishing trust, setting limits, reflective confrontation, and termination activities. It also describes strategies for specific types of child behavior — aggressive, withdrawal, regressive, sexual, and credit-taking.

With these strategies in addition to those described in the previous chapters, the student is supplied with the basic tools with which to begin the exciting, challenging, and at times frustrating process of child counseling.

REFERENCES

1. Gibb, J. R. Climate for Trust Formation. In L. P. Bradford, J. R. Gibb, and K. P. Benne (Eds.), *T-Group Theory and Laboratory Method.* New York: Wiley, 1964.
2. Giffin, K. The contributions of studies of source creditability: A theory of interpersonal trust in the communication process. *Psychol. Bull.* 68:104, 1967.
3. Moustakas, C. E. *Psychotherapy with Children.* New York: Ballantine, 1959.

(14) Working with Parents and Teachers

One of the major issues raised in relation to child counseling concerns the involvement of significant persons from the child's life in the counseling process. Although the major focus of this book is on direct counseling with children, working with parents and teachers must also be considered.

The beginning child counselor works with children directly while another member of the mental health team counsels the parents. The child counselor may be involved in some parent and teacher contacts, but it is not until he moves to the next stage of development (see Chapter 2) that he does in-depth counseling with parents and consultation with teachers. This chapter does, however, give the counselor some strategies to use with parents and teachers and discusses the values and issues related to parent involvement.

WORKING WITH PARENTS

The influence of one to two hours of child counseling a week can hardly be expected to produce permanent behavioral change without the support of significant others in the child's environment. An adult or even an older adolescent who is developmentally independent may not need this kind of support in order to benefit from counseling. The child, however, is in a dependent position in his environment, and is not able to control the variables that affect his mental health. The best results in child counseling have occurred when both parents and teachers are involved in either the counseling procedure or a consultation relationship with a counselor.

When the parents are not involved in the counseling process, or when they are quite resistant to the idea of mental health counseling for themselves or their child, there may be a parallel resistance to counseling in the child. Even though the child may ask for and need help, he may not feel free to engage actively in the counseling process. The parents may consent to the child's being counseled, but at the same time be giving unspoken messages to the child not to be actively involved in the process and not to divulge any family secrets. When parents are ready to accept help and begin to trust the counseling process, children will be more free to use it for self-growth.

When parents are absent, or mentally or physically ill, it is impossible for the counselor to involve them in the counseling process. This situation also occurs with parents who reject counseling for themselves but who agree to allow it for their children. Most mental health agencies will not work with children unless there is some form of parent involvement. However, there are usually exceptions made for the child who is desperately in need of counseling and whose parents are absent or not able to engage in the therapeutic process.

There are a number of ways in which parents can be involved in counseling. The choice of a specific method depends on the needs and readiness of the parents to accept a specific type of process. Involvement decisions are made in the initial evaluation period and are based on collected data and parents' approval of a particular approach for treatment.

Whatever method is chosen, the counseling interactions should reflect a nonjudgmental and accepting attitude toward the parents. The tone of the contact with parents should be one of collaboration. The professional person and the family work together as partners for the benefit of the child. Too often professional personnel have neglected to involve parents in the treatment process in a way that enhances their self-esteem and their ability to assume their parental roles more fully. The collaborative relationship is a big step in remedying this gap in delivery of service.

Initiating Parent Involvement

Many referrals for child counseling are initiated by teachers or other persons in the child's environment who notice a child's distress and who want the child to receive help. The parents may also be aware of the child's distress, but for innumerable reasons, such as fear or lack of knowledge, are not able to initiate the process of seeking help for their child. Most parents really love and care for their children, and want to see their children develop to the fullest; however, they may need professional assistance to be able to use the services available to them.

These parents need to work through two issues that are related to their resistance to counseling. First, they must acknowledge that their child does have an emotional problem; second, they need to overcome their own concerns about being involved in counseling. Someone from the counseling team may need to reach out to these parents to help them overcome these two issues before the parents can be involved or involve their child in an evaluation process. This means that a member of the team might make a series of visits to the parents in their home setting prior to their agreement to bring their child to a mental health agency.

The Child Has a Problem

For the parents who are aware that their child is somewhat "different" from others of his own age level, the counselor can validate that this is in fact true and that the child needs professional help to overcome this "differentness." Other parents may be aware of some behavior in their child that is difficult for them and for others, but may feel that the child will "outgrow it." These parents need to be convinced that such a problem is not likely to be outgrown without professional intervention. The counselor can provide information, as with the less resistant parents, but he will need to give much more time and effort to help these parents work through their feelings before they agree to take the first step toward obtaining professional help. These parents may need some type of implicit compulsion, such as withdrawal of a child from school, in order to take their child to a mental health agency for evaluation. Once there, they will again need intensive assistance in order to assure their continued involvement in the treatment process.

Concerns about Using Mental Health Services

Some parents have distorted ideas about what happens at a mental health clinic. The counselor can introduce some reality into their thinking by describing what actually happens when parents apply for help, what the evaluation process is, and what their responsibility will be for involvement in treatment and for financial support of a treatment program. For parents who are culturally different from the counselor, it is helpful to have a mediator or interpreter who is of the same culture as the parents to work with the counselor in helping the parents accept the use of mental health services. It is best, of course, if both parents and counselor have the same cultural background.

Parents Have Problems

Some referrals of children come from families with multiple problems, or from families in crisis. These families may need crisis intervention and casework with some of their other problems before they are able to invest their energy in the individual needs of one of their children. At times the counselor may also need to function as a child's advocate when parents will not or cannot care for their child's needs. For example, in cases of child abuse the counselor may have to seek legal aid in assuring that the child receives the protection and treatment that is his right.

PARENT COUNSELING

In the beginning of the counseling relationship parents may be confused about what they are to do, what their role is, and what the counselor is expected to do. It is helpful if the counselor explores with the parents what their expectations are of the counseling process. When client expectations and treatment realities are quite different, there is a high rate of client dropout. In exploring the clients' expectations of the counseling process, the counselor can gain insight into what type of involvement he might expect of the parents. He can then build counseling interventions around client expectations.

This period of exploration also gives the parents an opportunity to continue to work through their responses to having a child who has been labeled as "different," their feelings about using mental health services, or reality issues involved in starting service.

Many parents also want to know what to tell their child, and also how counseling with children works. The counselor may suggest that parents acknowledge their child's distress, and explain that they genuinely want the child to feel better and that they want to learn how to help. They may explain also that the counselor is a person who helps parents and children to get along better. Sometimes it is very difficult for parents to grasp the idea that, although their counseling may be predominantly verbal, the child's counseling centers around play and a variety of activities. They can be told that play is the medium by which the child relates to the outside world, and it is through play and activity that the therapeutic relationship is established with the counselor. With this kind of information, the parents are in a better position to explain the nature of the counseling process to their child.

Strategies in Parent Counseling

The counselor uses his skills to provide a model of acceptance, respect, concern, and trust for the parents, as well as of healthy communication. He may give information and provide direct alternatives, but he is not directive.

Parents must make choices and decisions themselves as to how they will use the information given. The counselor is supportive of decisions that parents make, and facilitates their being able to make behavioral changes.

In the initial exploration of parent expectations of the counseling process, the parents often express a desire to focus on child management. The counselor accepts this statement, but also encourages the parents to talk about anything they want during the session, including themselves and their background. Parents often seek advice on how to help their child with specific behavior related to normal development, such as fears or aggression, illness or surgery, or family changes such as the addition of a new sibling or death of a family member. The counselor may also provide normal growth and development information so that the parents will have some reality yardstick with which to measure their child's development, and so facilitates an exploration of the parents' responses to the information given. For example, if a couple is having difficulty accepting their child's mild mental retardation, they might perceive the child as grossly different from others and unable ever to have a normal life. When the parents are given factual information about normal intelligence and how people with mild retardation can function very well in society, they are often able to explore together their responses to their child and to begin to have a more accepting attitude.

Some parents need a type of supervision of their parental behavior. The counselor can help parents develop long-term and short-term goals regarding child behavior, and can help them develop strategies related to management of their child. Their counseling sessions may take the form of finding solutions to real-life situations that arise as the parents attempt to implement their strategies.

Some parents may never choose to focus the counseling process on themselves, but often after the initial interviews there is enough trust and acceptance developed in the counseling relationship for the parents to begin to do so. The role of the counselor is then to help them explore their own personal experience by listening and clarifying. When they seem unclear, the counselor helps them to restate their experience more precisely. He empathizes with their distress and, through acceptance and understanding, helps them accept and understand themselves. In later interviews, the counselor may initiate content related to themes that have developed in the child's counseling. He may ask the parents to explore their responses to these themes, and also helps them explore alternative behaviors that deal with these themes.

A specific situation may arise in child counseling that the counselor or the child feels needs to be discussed with the parents. In order to ensure the confidentiality of the child-counselor relationship, it is essential that they both agree on what will be discussed with the parents. They may also decide that a joint session with the parents, the child, and the counselor may be appropriate for the discussion.

The counselor may occasionally also ask for information about family activities as a reality check in working with the child. There are times when the child presents material about which it is extremely important for the counselor to know the environmental reality. There are also times when parents will call the counselor to tell him of significant incidents that occurred in the family or to the child. The child should be kept advised of these contacts with the family.

Length of Counseling Relationship

The length of parent counseling is determined by the type of presenting problems. When the problems arise from difficulties around specific developmental crises, short-term counseling (4—6 sessions) is appropriate. However, when there are more severe or chronic types of family problems, long-term counseling (6—12 months) may be necessary before the parents are able to become more effective in their parental roles. As with child counseling, termination is a mutual decision on the part of both the counselor and the client. There may be times when a parent or both parents will continue in counseling beyond the period of time when the child is in counseling in order to continue to receive support for their behavioral change.

Counseling in the Home Setting

There are times when counseling in the home may be practical and advisable. The needs of the family are the determining factor in the decision for the home as a setting for counseling. The criteria to be considered may include one or more of the following factors.

1. Family situation or problems that make agency or office interviews sporadic or impossible
2. A member of the family needing counseling has medical problems that prevent outside travel
3. When family resistance to counseling might be overcome by tactful assistance with a wide range of needs
4. When the family background and value orientation suggest that parents would respond better to active, reality-oriented counseling

Although the family with multiple problems may frequently be found in the lower socioeconomic group, there are times when families of all socioeconomic classes might fit one or more of these criteria. The home setting also provides for a possible shift in counseling focus from one of talking to one of demonstration and active participation based on observed reality factors. Home counseling ensures continuity of regular appointments and structure that helps to overcome many of the resistances to mental health counseling. Counseling in the home also provides opportunities to include other members of the family who might not normally be included in counseling.

Parent Counseling Groups

Besides counseling with individual parents and families, the counselor may join groups of parents or groups of families together. Besides the usual therapeutic benefits of counseling, both types of groups provide the parents with opportunities to share their experience with others and to gain support from others in the group to change their behavior.

Another type of group work with parents is child-centered group guidance. The goal of guidance groups for parents is to help significant others in their children's lives to be able to foster their children's normal development. The group is planned by and for those parents who want it. The attendance is voluntary and the tone is nonjudgmental.

The counselor should be a skilled group leader who is accepting and who has a background in normal growth and development and child-rearing practices. It is the leader's responsibility to function as a resource person for the group, to facilitate communication, and to keep the group child-centered. It may be a temptation in this setting to deal with marital difficulties, but they should be referred elsewhere or refocused so that the parents look at how a marital difficulty affects the child.

The child-centered group guidance process can offer the parents the following advantages.

1. Support and encouragement to pursue positive trends in child-parent relations
2. An opportunity to have a type of supervised parenthood by trying out behaviors and reporting on them to the group
3. The development of empathy with their children
4. The development of self-acceptance and self-awareness
5. The opportunity to experience mutual give-and-take with other parents who have similar problems

6. The opportunity to identify with the leader as a healthy parent model
7. The opportunity to acquire knowledge of child growth and development
8. A reduction in feelings of guilt and failure
9. Increased control over impulsive behavior

In addition to the free-flowing discussion groups of child-centered guidance, the counselor may develop structured sessions in which he can provide experiential teaching sessions related to communication, application of reinforcement principles, creative family problem solving, management of specific child behavior, and self-awareness.

FAMILY COUNSELING

In addition to parent counseling, there is a growing concern in the mental health field for including the whole family in the treatment process. The rationale for family counseling lies in the fact that the child is affected by his total home environment and in turn affects that environment. The child with symptoms of emotional disturbance is sometimes seen to reflect the distress of all family members.

During the past ten years, the practice of family counseling and family therapy has expanded throughout the mental health field. Those who include family counseling in their practice have developed a variety of styles, modes, and approaches, but there are some basic theoretical positions which they all share.

The goal of family counseling is to improve the quality of life of each family member and of the family as a whole by providing the family with therapeutic experiences in which they have opportunities to grow in self-understanding and self-esteem, and by improving communication and problem-solving skills.

This is a therapeutic process that deals with people in their natural social group and that deals with this group as a system. The process is characterized by action: do-show-tell, confrontation, direct exploration of communication, exploration and trials at alternative modes of behavior, and active modeling by the counselor.

As in parent counseling, the family may be unclear as to what to expect and as to what they are expected to do. Here again the counselor can explore their mutual expectations. He also stresses the importance of having all family members attend sessions, and expresses his valuation of the unique contribution of each member to the total family process. He explains that the major focus in family counseling is on the total family system and how the members relate to one another, rather than on the person who has been identified as having a problem. Besides his recognition of the family members as unique individuals, the counselor is also a model of acceptance of the differences among members. He helps the family members to bring their differences and disagreements into the open and to communicate differences in what they see, think, and feel. This type of process takes the pressure or focus away from the symptom bearer and concentrates on the interactional relationship among family members.

Indications and Contraindications for Family Counseling

Most mental health counselors who practice family counseling believe that any situation for which individual counseling is indicated is also a situation in which family counseling is a highly desirable procedure. There are situations, however, in which family counseling is either contraindicated or impossible. For the adult living alone or at a great distance from any family, family counseling is clearly impossible.

Contraindications for family counseling arise in both the family and the counselor. When the counselor does not believe in, or have the ego strength and maturity to deal effectively with, the power of the family structure, family counseling is not the method of choice. The family itself may not have the motivation or corporate strength to engage in family counseling. Some families appear to be already "dead" and lack sufficient motivation even to contemplate trying to restore or regain life. Other families are so violent or volatile as to be in danger of flying apart with any attempts to interfere in the family system. The decision as to whether to attempt to work with these families is a difficult one, and commands serious considerations and consultation.

Another issue to be considered is whether individual members of the family should be in individual or group counseling in addition to family counseling. There is no definitive research in this area that clearly indicates what is the most effective approach, and there is a great deal of disagreement in the field of family counseling as to the desirability of more than one type of counseling for all members of a family. However, even when families are committed to counseling that includes the whole family, there are some children having greatly delayed development who need the added help that individual or group counseling can provide. Some parents who have severe deficits in ego development can also gain strength through such procedures as individual counseling and sensitivity groups. There are also times when individual family members feel that they cannot talk about certain kinds of problems in the total family group. For example, a father who wants to work through an early traumatic sexual experience may see the counselor alone or with his wife. This material may be used at a subsequent time in the family counseling sessions as it seems to affect the father's relationship with family members, but not in the detail that the father revealed in his individual sessions. It seems altogether reasonable that if conjoint family counseling facilitates healthy communication and problem-solving skills, the child in individual counseling will gain support in his striving toward these healthy behavior patterns by being involved in both processes.

Issues Arising through Inclusion of the Children in Family Counseling

It is usually appropriate for the counselor first to see the parents for several interviews alone. The parents may not be ready to look at their own and family interactions in beginning interviews. They may need a few sessions without the children just to begin to relate to one another as mates without the addition of child interactions. The beginning sessions also give counselor and parents an opportunity to explore their expectations of the family counseling and to decide who will be involved and what the most appropriate setting will be. In these initial sessions the counselor and the parents can also explore how they plan to present the concept of family counseling to all family members so that they will want to be involved. A nonsymptomatic member of the family may resist being involved in family counseling, saying that he is not "sick" like his sibling. Parents will need a great deal of support from the counselor to deal with this type of resistance. The counselor may suggest that the parents and the resistant sibling meet together with the counselor so that each side will have support in seeking a solution and in working through the resistance.

Children of preschool age might not be actively involved in all sessions, but in just a few sessions so that the counselor can see how the whole family relates to one another as a group. For practical reasons, such as short attention span and the need to control behavior, it may not prove fruitful for preschoolers to attend subsequent sessions. For some preschoolers and in home settings, however, the preschool child may be present as a participant observer. He may be playing, drawing, or otherwise occupying himself around the house during counseling sessions so that he can listen and observe. In some situations which directly involve him, he may be an active participant. For example, he may be a part of demonstrations and role-play situations as they arise in the counseling process.

When including children in family counseling, it is also wise to start with certain ground rules that are aimed at controlling and making allowances for the possible behavior of young children. A few rules to use are listed here.

1. No one can destroy furniture or equipment and physically harm another person.
2. No one may speak for others.
3. Everyone must speak so that he can be heard.
4. Everyone must make it possible for others to be heard.
5. Mutual decision is made on how often children may leave for drinks or toileting.
6. The counselor can shorten sessions to conform with the age or behavior of the participating children.

WORKING WITH TEACHERS

Besides parents, teachers are often the most important significant persons in the lives of children. Teachers have numerous opportunities daily to influence personality development in the children they teach. Some are more skilled than others, but few are prepared to deal with the kind of behavior the disturbed child brings to the classroom.

Perhaps one of the first to recognize that teachers need help to deal with the variety of personalities in their classrooms was Alfred Adler. Before there were any school psychologists or school counselors, Adler met with teachers in Vienna. He trained them to be sensitive to individual needs of children and to make observations and interventions. Today there is an ever-increasing focus in teacher education and in classroom experience on the child's emotional growth as well as on his intellectual and social growth.

The mental health counselor can develop a collaborative relationship with the teacher in regard to the child he is counseling, and he can also offer a variety of counseling activities to teachers who need support and direction in helping their children with optimal development.

Teacher Collaboration in Child Counseling

The counselor who establishes a collaborative relationship with his client's teacher is in a position to obtain valuable data about the child's school experience and also to provide consultation related to the management of the child at school to the teacher or school administrator.

In observation visits to the school and to the child's classroom, the counselor gains a realistic view of school philosophy and practice and how this experience affects the child. Prior to making such visits, the counselor discusses his proposed observation with both child and parents. If they agree, the counselor then makes contact with the school authorities to obtain their permission. In this initial contact he states the need to know more about the child's school experience, and he also offers consultation if the school personnel desire this service.

The teacher who might initially be reluctant to approach a mental health counselor for help with a disturbed child may be less resistant if the counselor approaches him in the collaborative role. The counselor emphasizes that he needs to know more about the child, and that the information the teacher can give about the child is vitally important to successful counseling. By means of these classroom observations, the teacher has the opportunity to become acquainted with the counselor and to form a beginning trust on which to build the consultation relationship.

As with parents, these meetings provide the counselor with opportunities to share with the teacher basic themes that have developed in the child's counseling and to explain the dynamics underlying the child's behavior. These meetings may occur on a regular or a sporadic basis. The teacher is also asked to contact the counselor if something arises at school that is significant to the counseling process, or to ask for assistance with specific situations as they arise.

Consultation with Teachers

The mental health counselor in a school setting can express his availability to teachers on both an individual and a group basis. Often a relationship with a teacher is established at the time a child is being evaluated for treatment. The counselor may ask the teacher for information about the child's behavior and ask to observe in the classroom. As previously stated, this process may help the teacher see the counselor as a nonthreatening person and a person who "doesn't know all the answers." Teachers feel encouraged to use mental health counselors if the school administrator supports the counseling activities by being a role model in using the counselor, by providing opportunities for the counselor to have contact with the teachers formally through faculty meetings and informally in the teachers' lounge, and by encouraging teachers who have difficult children to use the services of a counselor.

When the teacher asks for assistance the counselor must keep the focus of the discussion on the child rather than on the teacher and his personal problems. The focus of the teacher consultation is to help the teacher describe the child, to recognize when more data are needed, to suggest what is needed and how to collect it, to help the teacher express his feelings toward the child and describe how he would like the child's behavior to be different, and to develop specific procedures for achieving change.

In the consultation process there are a number of pitfalls that the beginning mental health consultant needs to be aware of and to avoid in order to remain effective. Some of these situations are as follows.

1. The tendency to give advice too quickly and not draw out the teacher's own problem-solving skills
2. Overreaction to the above tendency — that is, remaining silent and offering no verbal direction
3. Choosing to comment on too many areas, and overloading the teacher with too much information
4. Not listening to the central problem being presented, perhaps getting caught up in detail, and not being able to respond with specificity
5. Failing to take into consideration administrative or school policy when suggesting alternatives
6. Assuming the role of supervisor, administrator, or therapist, or allowing the consultee to assume these roles
7. Introducing and forcing his own bias inappropriately
8. Allowing the consultation to be either too wide or too narrow in scope
9. Assuming a position of expertness in the area of the consultee's professional competence (teaching) when it is different from his own (counseling)
10. Not being aware of his own limitations, which fosters the illusion of omnipotence and a "know-it-all" attitude

Group Consultation and Guidance for Teachers

When individual teachers have come to value and trust the mental health counselor, and when administrators are supportive, teachers may ask for guidance and consultation groups.

Guidance groups are organized with the same tone, process, and focus as parent guidance groups. A voluntary activity, it can be very helpful in raising the level of child mental health in the schools. Often the groups will begin discussing general concepts of mental health and child development. They may then turn to discussion of practical skills in handling disturbed behavior. Following these time-limited guidance group experiences, teachers may ask that the groups be extended on a group consultation basis. The teachers have become secure enough with the counselor and with one another to be able to admit that they cannot handle specific behavior, and need help.

Environmental Counseling in the Classroom

In addition to individual and group consultation, the mental health counselor can also be an effective agent for behavioral change by direct intervention within the classroom environment. The counselor in the classroom can help to facilitate the children's normal development and also utilize therapeutic interventions with children who have observable problems. By working therapeutically with children in their normal classroom environment the counselor is able to actualize the following therapeutic dynamics.

1. Maintain the disturbed child in his or her normal classroom setting instead of separating him as "different"
2. Utilize natural situations as they arise in the environment as a basis for interventions
3. Utilize the dynamics of the group to foster behavioral change
4. Function as a role model for both teacher and children through his intervention in disturbed behavior.
5. Develop and implement learning experiences focused on understanding behavioral concepts (such as learning appropriate expression of anger)

The Life Space Interview

The strategies and techniques of Redl's [1] life space interview provide one framework for environmental counseling in a classroom setting. A life space interview is one that takes place between a child and a counselor in the child's natural setting. The content of the interaction between them arises from problems that occur in this natural setting — in this instance, the classroom.

Redl believes that life space interviewing plays an important part in the lives of all children and that adults in any kind of educational role with children — either individually or in groups — can and should take advantage of these strategies for fostering growth. The adult assumes a mediating role between the child and his environment.

The two major goals and tasks of life space interviewing are what Redl terms the clinical exploitation of life events, and emotional first aid on the spot. The difference between these two is not in the nature of the precipitating incident but rather in how that incident is to be dealt with. The decision of which strategy to use is dependent on the nature of the situation and on

the readiness of the child and the adult to use a particular strategy. If the
child and the situation seem to indicate the time and appropriateness of only
emotional first aid, then this strategy is initiated. If, however, there is time
and the child seems open and ready, the adult can use this natural incident
that arises from the environment to explore the relevance of this incident to
the child's problem and to more long-range therapeutic goals.

The clinical exploitation of life events may take different forms at different times with different children. Some children need to be confronted with
their behavior by those who were directly involved in an incident. Others
need to be convinced that they are paying too high a price for their maladaptive behavior — whatever their secondary gain is, it does not outweigh the
negative aspects. For those who have not developed a sense of conscience,
an appeal to a sense of fairness may foster sensitivity to others and the
development of values. And there are some children who seem unaware of
what is going on around them and of what their rights are. They need to be
helped to explore and expand their boundaries of self.

Emotional first aid on the spot helps disturbed children cope with the
demands of daily life that they cannot manage alone. Although there are
usually no long-range gains in this type of intervention, emotional first aid
helps preserve these children's self-concept so that they can be open to more
extensive interventions.

Whether the adult chooses to use a life space interview with a particular
child is based on an appraisal of the total situation as it occurs. The choice
depends on (1) the specific goal the adult has in mind, (2) the setting, (3) the
specific behavior of the child, (4) the state the child is in, and (5) the adult's
emotional ability to intervene therapeutically.

PARENTS AND TEACHERS AS MEDIATORS
OF REINFORCEMENT TECHNIQUES

The skillful use of behavior modification principles can be a successful and
powerful tool for parents and teachers to use for encouraging growth-
producing behavior in children. Behavior modification techniques also provide parents and teachers with a systematic method of observing and analyzing
children's behavior. There are numerous studies that attest to the successful
application of behavior theory in practice both directly and through mediators such as parents and teachers. Appendix G presents case studies with
parents and teachers as mediators.

Learning theory, which underlies behavior modification, identifies a specific relationship between the person and his environment. As the environment changes, so the behavior also changes. With this hypothesis, it is reasonable to expect that the most effective attempts at modifying behavior are in the natural environment of the child. The use of the child's natural relationships in the child's own environment can be an integral aspect of child counseling. The natural environment is a difficult field of operation because the environment is difficult to control, but the rewards can be very fruitful if the task is skillfully pursued.

Mediation of Reinforcement Techniques in the Natural Environment

When behavior modification is implemented in the natural environment by a person who has a normal role relationship to the child — parent or teacher — that person is termed a *mediator*. In this situation, the mental health counselor becomes the consultant to the mediator. The major therapeutic effort is effected with the child through the mediator, although the consultant may on occasion interact with the child directly as a role model for the mediator. The major task of the consultant is to teach the parent or teacher to modify his response to the child's behavior.

One of the problems that arise in the use of parents and teachers as mediators is their resistance, which may stem from a rejection of behavioral approaches generally, a position that rewards should not be given for acceptable behavior, personal disorganization, and severe family disorders. Some of these resistances to the method can be worked through with the counselor. When the resistance arises from the intrapersonal dynamics of the mediator, this method of approach might be contraindicated.

Behavior Modification in the Classroom Setting

In some schools and classes, teachers and administrators have consciously structured curriculum which incorporates reinforcement principles. In these settings, planning and implementing both individualized and group programs can be accomplished with a great deal of success and a minimum of resistance. In schools in which this approach is new, it is often viewed with suspicion and resistance. The best approach in such a situation is to find a teacher who is willing to try, and to aim for a fairly certain success. This type of demonstration often helps other teachers and administrators to overcome their bias against this method.

SUMMARY

It is generally accepted that parent involvement is a crucial part of effective child counseling. Some parents do not understand how important they are in helping their child resolve his problem. Mental health counselors need to take time with these parents to help them become involved in counseling. There are a variety of ways that parents can be involved in the treatment process: individual, couple, family, and parent group counseling.

Teachers are also viewed as important people to be involved in child mental health activity. Counselors can collaborate with teachers regarding a specific child in counseling. Mental health counselors can consult with teachers regarding emotional problems of children, lead teacher guidance groups, and model direct interventions with children in the classroom.

The mental health counselor can also work with parents and teachers as mediators of reinforcement techniques aimed at modifying child behavior.

REFERENCES

1. Redl, F. Strategy and techniques of the life space interview. *Am. J. Orthopsychiatry* 29:1, 1959.

Appendixes

(A) Movement in Counseling–Case Studies

WITHDRAWAL BEHAVIOR – CAROL

Carol, a 14-year-old black girl, was brought to the psychiatric outpatient clinic by her mother. Her primary presenting behavior was withdrawal from social interaction.

Carol could best be described physically as well dressed, neat, overweight, with poor posture (hunching in of shoulders, head down, almost resting on chest, and shuffling of feet when walking). Her movements were extremely slow and very small. The fingers stretched in and out and rubbed the thumbs. Body weight shifted from one side to the other, or the whole body slowly rocked forward and back or sideways. This was the limit to movement when we were alone together. No eye contact was achieved, for Carol wore her hair in bangs which covered her eyes when her head was resting on her chest.

We began our work together by trying to increase her self-awareness by expanding her range of motion of body parts. By having her move the body parts already in motion (fingers, feet, head, whole body unit in rocking), the resistance was not quite so unmanageable. However, any attempt to go further or at a faster pace brought total noncooperation.

The first plan I had in mind was to help increase awareness of body parts and their possible range of motion. Again, only a token attempt was made on Carol's part to become involved in this activity. When she was done

Unpublished data by Georgiann Gielow, 1974.

moving her head once up and down, side to side, and in a circle, she stopped. I would continue for a short time, hoping to discover some technique that would help Carol be more comfortable in moving.

We began to explore shapes as a concrete movement experience. A child who has had limited movement experience can understand this activity and not feel self-conscious doing it. Carol was able to copy the shape I formed, and her interest seemed to increase the number of times she was willing to move. I decreased the amount of face-to-face social contact expected of her by working next to her and projecting our shadow shapes on the wall in front of us.

Slowly I tried to increase her involvement in taking some direction for our activities. Carol initially gave no indication of what she would prefer doing. She indicated negative feelings by total withdrawal, and acceptance by copying my movements. Carol was always given the opportunity to suggest what she wanted to do, but no suggestions were made. Eventually I helped her make small decisions by saying I would make the first shape and she would make the next shape. Again, because of lack of experience with movement, she varied only slightly from my shape. As she became familiar with this activity, she began to become more creative in her thinking.

Because we were still operating on a somewhat mechanical basis, I decided to introduce some social interaction. The next activity was to move the other person's shadow off the wall. We investigated all sorts of ways this could be done (kicking, elbowing, butting with head, pushing with hands, back, shoulders, or side, punching).

We moved from shadow play back to face-to-face contact, but keeping an object as a safe barrier between us. We now investigated how to push, kick, and, in general, move an object around. Then we found we had to change our behavior when the object would not move. These same movements were next tried out on each other. Some movements were done in pantomime form, for it was not allowed for either one of us to get hurt. At this time Carol was beginning to show a preference for controlling my movements, so a game was started which involved an obstacle course. First, I verbally guided her through and lost my turn only when she bumped into something. She became very proficient at guiding me so that I did not bump into objects. This increased her time to control me. However, in order to earn this time, she was learning how to give very explicit instructions instead of the brief movement commands she first gave. Some limited contact was accepted at this time, for we could spin each other around before going through the obstacle course. Carol enjoyed spinning me around. After a while of letting Carol experience total control of me, I began to resist her ease in spinning me to try to match her resistance to my turning her. Again, this was difficult, for she was quite strong.

I tried again for increased interaction by having us move together while touching hands. She resisted, and still resists, this or any other physical contact. We were always stalemated by her overpowering me and forcing me down to the floor. I was no match for her strength, and first felt fear of being overpowered, then of having her experience me as too weak to help her safely vent her pent-up energies. This interaction was most bewildering, because Carol turned all attempts at unison movement into sheer overpowering. When she gained the advantage, she merely held her ground. It was at this time that I shifted the emphasis from pure movement to energy-expending movement. This focus was accomplished by working on expanding the amount of space she used while moving and the tempo of the movements. I began to notice that Carol's reluctance to move had a great deal to do with lack of experience in moving. With the passage of time she seemed to be able to build on the familiar movements and come up with some very exciting ideas.

The follow-the-leader idea was brought closer to a semblance of sharing by both of us moving around the room either next to each other or one in front of the other. Carol initially utilized the kinds of things we had been doing, which indicated that she was retaining something from week to week. The only other indication that Carol was getting involved was her positive comments as reported by her mother. Carol's only spontaneous contribution was to pantomime a burglar.

Carol was slowly changing in appearance. Her posture was improving. She walked instead of shuffled, and she began to have some eye contact, or at least I was aware that she was watching me. At the same time she began to talk more in the counseling group of which she was a member, and which met one hour before we worked alone. I was a coleader in this group, and Carol began to speak softly to me but never to the others.

At this time a friend of Carol's joined the group, and after working with this girl in the group I decided to work with the two together. Carol was ready for this move and showed that she really had progressed. She still does not tolerate any physical contact with me, but she has taken responsibility to have her friend cooperate and move. Verbally, Carol has progressed to expressing her dislike directly or through "smart talk." She still has passive-aggressive behavior, but this is more workable than the withdrawn behavior with which she entered counseling. Carol's mother reports increased social contact with peers instead of the clinging to her exclusively.

In one session we tried a very aggressive activity. Each person held a soft stuffed bat with a hand grip like a sword. We started by fencing and then we tried to knock the bat from the opponent's hand. I had to use two hands to maintain a grip on my bat because Carol really let loose. In the therapy group, comments like "stab in the stomach" are slowly coming to the surface. She can maintain her rights in the face of a very aggressive group and, more important, the group does not see her as fragile and in need of coaxing.

At present the girls are more comfortable working together doing movements they are familiar with: for example, exercises done in gym, cheerleading, and popular dancing. There is a great deal of giggling and smart comments to ease their embarrassment before we settle down to move.

Carol's range of motion has increased along with variety in her use of movements. She tolerates my verbal instructions to use more space and in general to use more energy in moving. This structuring of her movements keeps us in more of a teacher-student relationship, but at this time the social distance seems to be achieving my initial aims. The black-white issue is very strong in both therapy groups, and may account for this keeping of a social distance.

Carol has just begun to scratch the surface of using movement to express feelings, but we both have come a long way already in learning about each other.

AGGRESSIVE BEHAVIOR – JIM

Jim was an 8-year-old boy in a day treatment center. The particular movement behavior reported by his parents involved his hitting them. The first step was to actually see this behavior. Jim's mother came to the center so as to stimulate the child into the behavior. In the second visit to the center, the behavior occurred. Jim became angry at not being able to control his mother. He first tried verbally to get her to interact with another child. His mother did not respond as Jim wanted, so Jim became combative. The counselor watched to see how the mother would handle the behavior, and at a certain point did intervene to assist the mother in stopping the hitting. The counselor's intervention did not affect the child's behavior, and it was only when Jim wanted to calm down that he did so. This same type of interaction occurred two more times. Again the counselor could not control the child while the parent was there. Jim would get hysterical and cause his mother to panic.

Jim's hitting was discussed by the mental health team, and the intervention the team agreed on was that the mother should not allow Jim to hit her. However, the mother did not feel that she had enough strength to work this out herself. The next time Jim vented his anger on his mother, the counselor demonstrated to the mother how to implement "not hitting" by taking Jim's fists in her hands and saying, "You cannot hit your mom; tell her you are angry with her." At the same time the counselor was moving with the child's in-and-out arm pattern. This short, punching movement was finally changed to longer, back-and-forth arm movements, giving the child some resistance to move against and allowing him to expend some of his increased energy. This activity was then turned over to the mother. She was able to copy or role-model the counselor's activity and did not let the child hit her, and she even managed to calm the boy down.

After the initial confrontation with the mother's ability to control him, the outbursts were never as violent, staying on the verbal level, which was much easier for the parents to handle. The hitting had paralyzed the parents from pursuing any effective intervention with the child.

The following are additional examples of Jim's movement behavior and planned interventions. Jim walked with his head down; consequently his eye contact was very limited. This was an area of primary concern because it had been observed in a variety of settings. Intervention was aimed at bringing Jim's head up. The first activity chosen to accomplish this goal was rolling a ball back and forth while he and his counselor sat on the floor. After a short time they moved to a kneeling position and started bouncing the ball. This brought more eye involvement, for Jim now had to locate the ball in space. They next moved to a standing position and alternated between bouncing and catching the ball. Eye contact was now being maintained only briefly. Next the counselor began to move around the room and throw the ball from different directions. Ball bouncing and a variety of other activities further reinforced the desired eye contact.

It was now established that Jim needed a safe way to release his pent-up energies if he was going to feel free to interact with others. Jim maintained a very tight, erect body posture at all times. Activities were now chosen which involved more expenditure of energy, the goal being to increase range and amount of muscle tension necessary to complete an activity, so that Jim would move from his confined body posture to a new and more comfortable position. Jim indicated an interest in musical instruments, but when allowed to play them he showed little results because his energy release was not sufficient to make sounds. A xylophone was chosen to gain the needed energy release, because it requires some effort to obtain sound. This activity also helped focus eye contact, because Jim needed to follow the numbers printed in place of notes in order to create a song. The counselor helped Jim move his arms to achieve the sounds, but when she did not help him, no sounds were produced. Next she used a verbal image of "drop; let go; let your arm drop" as she held his arm above the xylophone. Other activities were also chosen to accomplish the same goal of muscle release in order to gain a desired effect.

Jim was beginning to use his arms instead of holding them rigidly at his side. He was eventually able to generalize and open up his body to stimuli present around him. He began to run, and his peers began to ask him to play. Step by step, slowly, Jim's counselor helped him to develop a more spontaneous type of movement behavior.

This case study not only exemplifies movement intervention but also contains a working description of some of the dance concepts. For example, it was noted that Jim's *range of motion* of body parts was quite limited: the head was held down; the hands moved a bit but only at the side; and the arms did not reach out except when hitting. The *tension level* was quite strong inside, as if Jim were holding himself back. When he came to using a body part, Jim did not have enough force to create a productive movement. His use of *space* was quite limited in that he did not relate to others in space or explore the area around him. His space was located inside himself. When others moved toward him he responded by moving away from them or by drawing his body in closer. His posture reflected an attitude of "leave me alone; don't come near me." All body parts were pulled in toward his center. Locomotion was stilted. He did not move his legs very far apart, so that movement was quite slow.

The counselor understood Jim's background and what had caused these movement patterns, but decided that, because of lack of verbal contact, the initial approach would be best on a nonverbal, physical level. Jim's feelings were being expressed through limited muscle movement. When this muscle movement became more open and he developed a greater repertoire of movements, Jim began to achieve a physical and psychological integration. He began to verbalize more and look more comfortable with himself and his ability to control himself and others in a more acceptable manner.

When Jim began to experience a wider range of movement patterns, he began to move to the aggressive extreme verbally and physically. When this extreme was channeled into acceptable behavior, Jim moved more into the middle or balancing area for the major part of his interactions. During crisis times the old extremes appeared again, but Jim was now open to helping solve the problem so he could again find the new comfort zone on a scale which used to be constantly in a state of unbalance. These changes were accomplished at the child's pace, as evaluated through his movement cues. Jim began to feel safe in exploring different movement experiences. He discovered that it was not merely safe or comfortable to move, but even fun. In moving he was able to expend some of the pent-up energy, and he did not have to work so hard holding it under control.

Jim began to learn who he was and what he could do, thus seeing or feeling himself separate from his parents' feelings. He found that both fast and slow movements were pleasing, and began to choose when to change pace. In moving like his peers (bouncing, swinging, running), he found he could relax his muscle tension. Previously most of his verbalization was on an intellectual level and he could not recognize and give voice to his feelings. As he became freer in his movements his verbalization also became freer. Through expanded movement he released energy to rechannel thinking and feeling. With the developing trust in his counselor and himself, the generalization of trusting spread to his family, peers, and school.

(B) Play in Counseling–Case Studies

PLAY IN INDIVIDUAL COUNSELING – MARK

Mark was referred to counseling because he had withdrawn from interactions with his teachers and peers. He was a 7-year-old boy who had a previous history of hyperactive and aggressive behavior. In kindergarten he was diagnosed as having a severe perceptual disturbance. With special tutoring he was learning to read; however, his withdrawal from interpersonal contacts outside the home was hampering his social and emotional growth. It can be hypothesized that at an earlier age Mark used aggression as a form of expression of anger, but later began to use withdrawal instead of aggression. Children with learning disabilities often have an emotional overlay related to anger and frustration they have experienced in learning situations. Mark's emotional problems were also aggravated by the divorce of his parents when he was entering school.

Mark was referred by his teacher for individual counseling. His mother was being counseled by another mental health professional person regarding her relationship to Mark and her problems of raising a family of four children by herself.

Mark was engaged in play counseling for five months on a one-hour-a-week basis. His counseling terminated at the end of the school year.

Beginning Session

Counselor: Hello, Mark. Come on in. Thank you for bringing him, Mrs. Owen. I will go with him back to your class at 11:30.

(159)

I closed the door gently as Mark moved into the center of the room. He did not look at me but moved quietly and directly to a table that had art supplies on it. He took out a large, bright purple chalk.

Mark: What is this?
Counselor: That is chalk.
Mark: Supposed to be white? (Said in an accusing tone.)
Counselor: You're saying chalk you've seen is white and this one isn't?
Mark: What do you do with it?
Counselor: You can draw.

Although Mark directly conversed with me, he did not really look at me. I recognized his questions as his way of beginning our relationship and finding out what this room was all about. Mark moved to the table, lifted the cover of the large drawing pad, and quickly drew a figure.

Mark: That is a person.

He said this as he looked seriously at the figure. He turned to the chalk box and selected a bright red chalk. He lifted the first sheet and started to draw another. I took the first sheet off and put it near the table, in view. He drew a second figure in less detail and considerably smaller.

Mark: This is another person.

He stepped back and looked at his hands. I took the second sheet off and put it next to the first.

Counselor: One person is bigger and one person is smaller.

Mark rubbed the color from his hands on his pants, but did not acknowledge my comment. I wondered if Mark's drawing symbolized how he saw us two people here: one bigger, one smaller.

Mark returned to the art supplies. He picked up some coiled wire and asked, "What's this?"

Counselor: Wire for making figures and shapes. Those two tools there are for cutting and bending the wire.

Mark took wire and tools to the table. He began to bend and cut the wire. The wire cutting was hard, and he had to use all his energy to cut. Now I could watch him closely, while he was fully engaged in this activity. I was sitting in a chair with castors so I could be just about his height, and I could move freely and comfortably around the room to be with him. Mark's face was impassive even when he was straining to cut the wire. It was almost as if he had a mask on.

He had dark, longish, straight hair, somewhat tousled, very dark eyes, and a bridge of freckles over his nose. He was neither fat nor thin but well proportioned for a 7-year-old boy. He had on a cotton shirt that was wrinkled and stained with what looked like his morning cocoa. He was wearing blue jeans and white tennis shoes. He definitely had a 7-year-old-boy look, with a defensive, aloof tone to his behavior. His body did not look rigid or tight, but it was not free or relaxed either. As mentioned before, he did not maintain eye contact when he talked, but he did ask direct questions to explore our relationship.

After cutting and bending wire for several minutes, Mark put the wire and tools away very quickly. I had been watching him very closely and commenting on what he was doing. Now he moved across the room directly to material that belonged to someone else and that could not be used.

Mark: Can I play with these?
Counselor: No, they belong to someone else. You may play with any of these other materials and toys that are in the room. In this room you can play with these things any way you want; you can do or say anything you want.

Mark did not acknowledge that he had heard me, but moved back across the room nearer to me. For the first time in this session he sat down in a chair, looked at me, and said: "I'm bored."

Counselor: You have played with some of the things in this room, but now you feel bored.

Then Mark returned to the art supplies and said, "What's this?"

Counselor: Clay.
Mark: The box looks like crayons. Should be crayons, not clay.

This was said in an accusing tone. Mark took clay from the box and took the wrapper off. "This clay is new?"

Counselor: Yes.

Mark then turned the drawing tablet over to work on with clay. "I'll make a gingerbread man and put it away in the box." I also started to work with some clay. As soon as I started, he discarded his clay project.

Counselor: Boy, your gingerbread man disappeared in a hurry.

I wondered if my movement to the material caused him to change again so suddenly. Then he reached for the ceramic clay and began to form another figure by taking small pieces at a time and connecting them together.

Mark: This is a snowman.

This figure was less like a man than the first.
I continued to roll and mold my piece as he worked. He suddenly broke the man up quickly and put it away. I followed and put my piece away. He looked at his hands, and I looked at mine.

Counselor: Do you want to wash off the clay?
Mark: Yes.
Counselor: Me too. You go to the boys' bathroom and I'll go to the girls' and we'll meet in the hallway.

After washing I waited in the hallway for him. I could hear the water splashing and I wondered what he was thinking.
Before returning to our room I asked Mark if he would like to stop by the library to get a book to take back with him. As we entered, the librarian approached.

Librarian: Oh Mark, I found that article on leeches you were asking about. Here it is.
Counselor: Would you like to take it into our room?

Mark nodded ever so slightly and we went on to our room. He looked at the pictures of the leech and the article accompanying them. Then he went to the crayons and got a whole box and started to draw a leech.

Mark: There is a movie about giant leeches.
Counselor: That must have been scary.
Mark: No, just science fiction. Where do leeches live — in the ground?
Counselor: Let's see. Yes, it says they do live in moist ground. And they do have rings just like you drew. I wonder which is the head.

Mark: This part that is round. How long do they live?
Counselor: Well, this article doesn't say.
Mark: Must be longer than us.

Mark then added a black rock, red ground, orange flowers, and a mailbox to his picture. He did not make any move to take the sheet off the tablet, but went down farther in the tablet and started another picture. This time I did not tear off the sheet, for I sensed that I had intruded or interfered before by taking them off. As he started another picture I asked him if his teacher had explained why he was coming to this room to play instead of to her room to work. He shook his head very slightly to indicate no.

Counselor: I think I saw you shake your head no — like she didn't say anything to you. I guess you're wondering who I am and what this playroom is all about. (No acknowledgment of my statement.) Have you any ideas why you are here instead of your work room? (No acknowledgment.)
Mark: How come I play here when this is a learning school? (Said in an accusing tone of voice.)
Counselor: Well, Mark, your mother and teacher are really concerned about you. They know you are doing your schoolwork okay now, but they notice you don't talk to or play with the other kids any more. Sometimes kids have problems that are bothering them that keep them from doing things they want to do. This is a place where you can talk about or do anything you want. My name is Mrs. Pothier, and I'll be seeing you here on Thursdays at this time each week.

Mark continued to draw. He drew dinosaurs and a volcano. He started another picture.

Mark: Can I leave the room any time I want?
Counselor: No, our time together will go until 11:30 like your class.

Mark went back to art supplies for more crayons and noticed a red can that he had not explored before. He opened it and found candy.

Mark: Can I have one?
Counselor: Yes, you can.

He took a piece of candy and replaced the lid to the can and returned to drawing, chewing his hard candy vigorously. He started another picture which included cavemen, a fire, and a volcano.

Mark: What did cavemen eat?
Counselor: I don't know, but I guess some animals or birds.
Mark: What were their names?
Counselor: I don't know.
Mark: This is a pterodactyl.

In the middle of the picture he drew a bird with large teeth. Then he left the drawing and put his arms out to the side like wings; he moved quickly across the room saying, "Pterodactyl goes like this." In this movement he was more spontaneous than he had been during the whole session. Then he returned to the picture and, while filling in detail like sky and sun, he spoke again.

Mark: What did the cave children learn? No schools.
Counselor: Maybe different things than kids learn today.

I was about to explore this with him a little more when he closed the drawing pad, put away the crayons, sat on the chair, and asked: "Can I go now?"

Counselor: Yes, it is almost time to go. Would you like another piece of candy first?
Mark: Yes. (He got the candy and replaced the lid.)
Counselor: Okay, let's go find Mrs. Owen. I'll look forward to seeing you again next week at the same time, Mark.

Mark's behavior in this first session was typical of many children. He used the play and art materials; he asked questions about them and the room to begin to define for himself what this new experience would be about. In attempting to explore the reasons for these play sessions he was typically not able to respond; therefore I offered an explanation. I was pleased that Mark could ask his question about play in a learning school, and also that he could begin to open up the subject of schools and learning through the caveman drawings.

Play Activity

In the second session Mark began a routine of play activity that was to be repeated with variations for the rest of his counseling sessions.

Session 2

Mark: What's this? (Moved toward Bozo; punched him.)
Counselor: That's a Bozo. Okay to puch or hit him.

Mark pushed a couple of times, then moved over to the tape recorder.

Mark: A tape recorder.
Counselor: That's right. And you can listen to it any time you want during our time together.

Mark picked up the mike and moved the button on and off. I checked to make sure it was still on.

Mark: What shall I say? Can't think of anything.
Counselor: Anything you want. (Pause.) You could tell a story if you wanted.

Mark put the mike down and went over to the toys. He looked in the basket and began to take out toy soldiers, tanks, and guns.
I slipped off my shoes and sat on a pillow next to him.

Mark: Why you take shoes off? (His tone sounded like: You shouldn't take your shoes off.)
Counselor: You noticed that I took my shoes off. I like to take my shoes off when I sit on the floor.

Mark took all of the soldiers out of the basket and lined up two teams opposite one another. He looked at each soldier and then assigned it a position. Two leading opponents and the rest of the soldiers and equipment were divided facing one another. Then in *Scene 1* he had each soldier kill another; he made a gun sound and the opponent fell over dead. When all were down he raised up some to continue the battle. Except for gun sounds he made no other sound; he kept his head down and his face impassive. Finally all the soldiers were down again. *Scene 2:* All soldiers arranged similar to Scene 1. I commented that there were two groups of soldiers facing one another — reflecting what I saw.

Mark: How can I tell the two groups apart if their uniforms all same color? Two groups should have different colors. (Accusing tone in Mark's voice.)

I was aware of a defensive feeling when he made this statement, and remembered that we had had a similar interaction in the previous session. I wondered if this was a pattern of behavior for Mark.

In this second scene he knocked all the soldiers and equipment down again. This time without sound or specific shooting action he just pushed everything over quickly with a sweep of his hand.

Counselor: You knocked everyone down again.

Then Mark started putting the soldiers up again. I had the feeling that when I commented on anything he viewed it as a criticism. I would have to note more closely his patterns of action after my reflections.

Scene 3. Mark situated the soldiers in the same positions again. He worked methodically and without sign of enjoyment but with the same impassive face. Occasionally he looked up at me. During this scene he moved quite close to me in his play, but it was as if I were not really close. While setting up the battle he tried to put standing soldiers inside a truck but found that he could not put the top on tightly, and removed the soldiers. Later he put lying-down soldiers in the truck and found that the top fitted. Still later, in setting them up he tried again to put a standing soldier in the truck with the top on. He tried hard to make the top fit. His face and body were still impassive even with this frustration. He finally took all the soldiers out of the truck.

Mark: Where do you get all these toys?
Counselor: I brought some — some I had.
Mark: You have kids?
Counselor: Yes, but they're grown now.
Mark: Why you keep the toys?
Counselor: I keep them for boys and girls like you that come to play here.

When he finished setting up the battle, he counted the number on each side; one had 22 soldiers; the other had 14.

Counselor: One side has lots more than the other. I wonder which will win.
Mark: This one (pointing to the group with 14 soldiers).
Counselor: That group has less soldiers and less equipment. Why do you think they will win?
Mark: Because of the trucks.
Counselor: Oh. The truck is bigger? What about the trucks?
Mark: The water. (He pointed to a water can on a truck.)

Counselor: How does that help them win?
Mark: They can't fight without water.
Counselor: Oh.

Mark swept his hand over the soldiers and trucks until they were all down again. He did this almost casually, as if the important part was getting set up, not the battle that ensued. Mark looked at other toys in the basket. He was having difficulty finding what he wanted.

Counselor: It's okay to dump the toys out if you want.

Immediately he did so. Did he see my comment as an order or command to be obeyed? He set up Indians.

Mark: Where are the cowboys? (Again, his tone was "there should be cowboys; you should provide cowboys.")

He found a cowboy and put him on a horse. He then moved to a plastic boat.

Mark: What's this? (Before I could say anything) It's a boat. What kind? A ferry?
Counselor: It could be a ferry.

Then he filled the boat with small cars.

Mark: This is a ferry going to England. (He moves a few feet away with the "ferry boat.")
Counselor: There goes the ferry boat to England. Now it is coming back.

Mark returned, dumped the cars out, and then dropped the boat. He looked around. He hit Bozo a few times, looking at me as he punched. I nodded and smiled.

Counselor: You punch well.

He punched a couple of more times, then sat down near me again. Again I noted a change in activity after my comment. He fingered the dart gun which I had placed outside of the basket on the floor. Then he picked up a dart.

Mark: This fits in the gun.

With no comment from me he put the dart in; it seemed hard for him. He shot it at the floor and hit another dart that jumped up. He looked at me quickly and then away. I observed interestedly and smiled. He retrieved the first dart and then shot at Bobo at short range so that it gave a loud thump. Mark again looked at me. I nodded and smiled. He put the gun down quickly and looked at the toy Indians again. He seemed to change activity with positive statements.

Mark: How long do I have to stay here?
Counselor: About five more minutes.

Mark looked at the candy can.

Counselor: Would you like a candy?

Mark looked, still impassive, and reached out for a piece; I took one too. Mark looked in a basket, as if looking for something else to do. He brought out an alligator puppet and opened and closed its mouth. I brought out a girl puppet on my hand. He brought the alligator over and snapped at the girl's head.

Counselor: Ouch! You're hitting my head. Oh!

He bit a few more times; then reached for another puppet, female; he had the alligator bite her.

Counselor: The alligator is biting the lady.

Then Mark got a car out; he put the puppet in the car, with the alligator on the other hand.

Mark: Teenager.
Counselor: Teenager going for a ride in the car.

For the first time Mark moved to another part of the room. He pushed the car all the way down, with the alligator biting an arm of the puppet. Then he put three more puppets in the car and repeated the scene with the alligator biting at the people.

Counselor: Mark, the time is gone for today. I'll see you next week here in the same room.

Mark left very quickly without looking at me.

Sessions 3—9

During these sessions Mark continued to construct battle scenes with soldiers, guns, and trucks; cowboys and Indians; and dinosaurs. He constructed between three and five scenes in each session, making very little comment about the battles or anything else, and few battle sounds. At one point I tried to encourage him to make battle sounds. His response was: "No, I don't want to make too much noise. It bothers others." His facial expression was unchanged in his play.

He came in and left the room without looking at me. During the sessions he often sat near me on the floor, sometimes with his body touching mine; but in spite of the physical closeness I sensed his emotional distance. I commented from time to time that I felt he shut me out and that I felt frustrated in not being able to communicate with him.

Sessions 10—12

In session 10 Mark set up four different battle scenes that had a different structure. Previously there had been a classic battle with both sides advancing in the session. These scenes were more like an ambush. I commented on the difference in his play. He did not acknowledge this, but when he left that day he looked at me and waved as he went out the door.

In session 11 he noticed that there were some soldiers missing. He said that someone must have taken them, and asked me to get him some more. Mark seemed to be saying that these soldiers were important for his work in the playroom. His play in this session was less formal or structured than at any other time. Instead of a big battle scene, a few soldiers engaged in hand-to-hand battle. Mark was even able to make sounds of battle as he played.

I felt encouraged that he was getting freer in his play and in his expression of aggression; however, the next session (12) found him more rigid than ever and very anxious about the time. I commented to him on the difference between his play last week and this, and wondered if there were any connection. He was not able to respond, but spent the last ten minutes of the session anxiously staring at the clock.

During this week I had reports from Mark's mother and teacher that he was beginning to talk and play with his siblings and peers. The change in his behavior started at the time his play structure changed.

Sessions 13—15

In session 13 Mark incorporated block towers in his play with the soldiers. He put the soldiers on top of the towers and shot them off with darts. Glancing sideways, he looked at me but made no sounds or comments.

In session 14 he made his towers very close together with soldiers on the top. He knocked them all over and said, "They didn't get killed; they're not dead." He then put a man doll in between the blocks and smashed him and also had an airplane dive-bomb the man. He spoke angrily and made angry sounds. In the next session Mark went back to his towers and soldiers. He surprised me by asking if he could tape the battle and listen back to it. He had ignored the tape recorder after the first session.

Session 16

In this session Mark had tower battles, shot soldiers with darts, and blew up balloons and shot at them. In all this activity he was animated and smiling, enjoying and talking about what he was doing. I commented on this change in him and said that his mother and his teacher said he seemed happier with them and other people too. Toward the end of the session he walked around me in circles asking and answering questions. We were actually carrying on a conversation, and the social distance had disappeared.

Ending Counseling

We had four concluding sessions before the school year ended. During this time Mark continued to maintain his openness with me, and his play became even more expansive and varied. My reflections did not cause him to stop or change activity, and there were no more critical statements such as were common in early sessions. He continued to progress in his social relations with his teachers and peers.

DIRECTED PLAY ACTIVITY IN GROUP COUNSELING*

The group was composed of six racially mixed boys aged 10 to 12 years. The reasons for referral to counseling included social withdrawal, aggression, poor peer relationships, and inability to express feelings.

*Unpublished data by Marcia McLain-Douville and Mary Lambert, 1973.

The following goals were formulated with a consideration of the developmental tasks of preadolescence and the particular needs of each boy: (1) to provide an accepting and safe atmosphere in which each boy could identify and express feelings, attitudes, and ideas about himself and his environment; (2) to facilitate a greater sensitivity to the feelings of others in the group; (3) to provide an opportunity for peers to learn from one another's experiences and behavior, e.g., more appropriate ways of communicating and expressing feelings; (4) to allow the members the opportunity to participate in deciding individual and group goals; and (5) to enhance ego-strengthening, positive self-concept, and acquisition of insight.

After the beginning stage of group development was well established, the series of play activities were planned which were aimed at achieving group goals.

The Grab Bag

This experience was chosen first because it was the least threatening of the activities to be used.

In this activity, a paper bag filled with slips of paper was passed around the group. Two basic kinds of words were put into the bag. The first kind were words which tended to be emotionally laden, such as *father, mother, brother, sister, fight, sad,* and *death.* These words were chosen because the leaders felt that they would help the boys to express feelings about some of their conflict areas. The words *black* and *white* were not added because it was felt that these words were too "loaded" with meaning for either boys or leaders to handle. The other words chosen had particular significance to the preadolescent, such as *girls, friends, bully,* and *sports.*

Each group member picked one slip of paper, read the word on it, and described his feelings about the word to the rest of the group. Other group members' responses were encouraged. After everyone had had a chance to talk or respond to a word, each boy was allowed to write down two words he wanted to add to the bag. Words added by the members included *faith, war, happiness, sorrow, hate, pollution, robbers, love,* and the leaders' first names.

The goals for this technique were the following: (1) to encourage equal group member participation, (2) to increase group cohesiveness, (3) to encourage members to express feelings and concerns, (4) to increase flow of interaction among members, and (5) to act as a warm-up exercise for eventual role-playing by enabling the group to work together.

This activity proved to be effective in engaging even the most nonverbal member to participate and stimulated group decision-making and cooperation.

It seemed to meet all of the therapeutic possibilities, and was so successful that the members requested that it be repeated the following week.

I've Got a Worry

The boys had started to share some feelings in the previous activity, and group trust appeared to be heightened. This second technique was chosen to facilitate expression of more personally relevant material.

Each member wrote a worry on a blank card, and the leaders read aloud the worries. A short period of time was spent talking about the worry. The concerns of the members consisted of "being worried when parents were late getting home," "life and living every day," and "winning a baseball game."

The goals were (1) to encourage freer expression of feelings by writing anonymously, thus protecting members from overexposure; (2) to facilitate group decision-making by deciding what worry would be discussed first; (3) to provide the opportunity to check out the reality of worries; (4) to provide each member of the group the opportunity to validate and react to his own concerns; (5) to provide the opportunity for support from the peer group; and (6) to provide the opportunity for peers to learn from one another's concerns.

The discussion was primarily superficial, and the members requested that the grab bag technique from the previous week be repeated. The possible reason for this could have been that the boys shared as much about themselves as they were ready, and were not able to go into more depth at that time.

Strength Bombardment

The use of this technique depends upon a high level of trust and group interaction. The leaders felt that the boys were working on this level.

The technique was presented to the group in the following way: "Today we are going to do something different. Each person — if he wants to — will take his turn sitting in the middle of the circle. The person in the middle will begin by saying something good about himself. You are not to say anything bad about yourself. You may say as many or as few good things as you want to about yourself, but you have to say at least one good thing. After you are finished, the group members will say good things about you. During the time the group members are talking, you are not to say anything. The group members cannot say anything bad about you. This may be hard for all of you to do. Sometimes it is much easier to say bad things about yourself or about others. A lot of times we don't hear good things about ourselves which are good for us to know. If you don't feel like you can say anything good about another person, you don't have to say anything."

Each time a member made a positive statement he received a jelly bean.

The goals of this technique were (1) to increase recognition of positive feelings about self; (2) to provide opportunity to receive positive feedback from others; and (3) to enhance self-esteem and positive self-concept, and to reduce self-criticism.

The main features the boys admired in themselves and in each other were being "good" in sports and school subjects, with girls, in playing musical instruments, in fighting, in being a "nice guy," in "conning," and in being "sneaky." A comment about the activity from one group member was: "It was fun 'cause everybody said what they liked about somebody."

Negative Feelings

This activity was a takeoff from the previous one. Each member sat in the center of the circle and expressed negative feelings about school, teachers, family, and society. The members were not allowed to express negative feelings about other members or themselves. Each boy received credit for a negative statement by receiving a jelly bean. The jelly bean reward showed acceptance for negative feeling expression.

The goals for this activity were (1) to provide structure for ventilation of negative feelings, and (2) to show that expression of negative feelings is acceptable.

Specific dislikes centered on parents, siblings, teachers, restrictions, chores, and behavior of other peers. All the boys participated enthusiastically, and the jelly beans seemed to add a game-like quality which fostered expressing personally relevant feelings.

Role Playing

This was the most comprehensive and productive activity. The other techniques were in ways preparing the boys for role playing. Because the readiness of the group for this type of technique is important, an initial assessment was made prior to presentation of the activity. An alternate activity was planned if the members seemed to be in a high mood level and unable to "settle down and work." One alternate activity, called "Future Enactment," involved asking one member to get up and act out what he thought he would like to be doing in twenty years. The other group members were to guess the occupation the boy acted out. This activity was much more charade-like, but still tapped their fantasy life and self-concept. In one meeting this activity was used solely. It was also used for a "warm-up" for subsequent role-playing sessions. Examples of some of the occupations acted out were archeologist, FBI man, sports players, "John Wayne," executive, playboy, gangster, scientist, artist, and fireman.

The goals for the role playing were (1) to facilitate expression of feelings and problems by a way other than direct verbal communication, and (2) to aid each member to gain insight into his own behavior and the behavior of others, i.e., teachers, parents, and peers, by experiencing and viewing cause-and-effect relationships.

Preparation for Role Playing

The technique of role playing was presented to the group members in the following manner. The leaders stated that one thing they had noticed was that the boys had many feelings about getting "detentions" (school restrictions), and that an activity had been planned around this problem.

The warm-up involved asking the boys to get comfortable in their chairs and to remember a time when they got a detention. They were asked to recall all of the details they could about the event: for example, where it was given, who was involved, and what kind of feelings they had at the time. Even as brief as this warm-up exercise was, it was almost too long, for moments after the introduction the question was raised: "Who's going first?"

The boys were told that the leaders thought that many of them could probably talk about their detentions, but one way of helping the group to really understand what the situation was like was to act it out. They were told that they could pick one other person to help out with the scene, for the leaders felt that this would make the experience less threatening and more enjoyable. Alternatives to participation were stressed, by stating that no one was required to participate, and that anyone could observe instead. A volunteer was asked to begin the sessions.

Role Play Experience

The leader started the scene by asking the volunteer to tell the audience what he was thinking just before getting the detention. This maneuver aided him in getting into his part, and allowed the audience to see his thinking. Then the leader warmed up the other actor to his part by asking: "What are you doing? What do you think about him?" Then the leader turned to the group and said: "This should be good; let's watch what happens." This statement helped the group feel more a part of what was happening. It was planned that the leader would immediately cut the scene after the teacher gave the boy the detention and focus immediately on how the boy was feeling, and then get the reactions and comments from the audience. At this point the leaders decided to enact further scenes in order to ventilate feelings or to suggest other ways of handling his behavior.

There were scenes of ventilation involving yelling at teachers and bullies. Even the quietest member did a scene in which he described the scene, assigned roles, and directed other members in the action. Other role-playing involved suggesting better ways for the teachers to handle the scenes, and ways the boys could have changed their own behavior. For both group members and leaders, this activity was enjoyable and productive.

Tell-Your-Feeling Road

In an attempt to enhance integration of the group experiences and facilitate separation and termination, the leaders planned a termination activity. For a couple of sessions prior to the end of the group, the boys had requested that the leaders do "something special." An easily constructed model car was given to each boy. The cars were brought as gifts, as an act of caring, and as a remembrance of the group experience. An activity was needed to help mobilize the anxiety of the termination process. By being able to build the cars, the boys "had something to do," and were able to use the structure to share, talk back and forth, and focus their high energy level.

The leaders planned an experience for integration. Twenty feet of butcher paper together with felt-tip pens were brought to the group to draw a "road map." The boys were told this map was to be of the group. For example, they were told that the cars represented them, and the road represented the group experience. Suggestions were made to the boys like: "What were you like at the start? Where were the hard spots in the road? What is it like at the end?" At the beginning of the experience the boys wrote down words like "muddy spots, sand pits, clay, big truck coming, quicksand, boulders, and lake." As momentum in the group built, and one group member wrote down the "first day of talk class," leaders enthusiastically commented on this phrase and from this point the boys began to write down many significant events that had happened throughout the group experiences. Examples of their integration statements were: "talking about movies is no fun," "movies are over," "stop-and-pick-word-bag road," "talking road," "talking about mother and people in family," "jelly bean road," "worry road," "act, acting-out, and action road," "chocolate-chip-cookie road," "punch [beverage] road," "Wednesday [day of group] road," "Mary-and-Marcia [leaders' names] road," and "tell-your-feeling road." Specific termination statements were: "the end of talk class" and "The sad part was when they left; will you come back?" It seemed from their statements that they considered it normal to have feelings and concerns, and that it was okay to talk about them.

Conclusion

The termination demonstrated that a strong group identity and cohesiveness had been achieved. For example, all of the comments on the paper were group-oriented except for those of two boys, who wrote their own names. This fact reflects the importance of the peer group and games to the preadolescent. The boys' reluctance to talk about the group outside of the meeting, and strong refusal to allow anyone else to join the group, were further evidence of their cohesiveness.

As a whole, the directed play activities aided expression of feelings and discussion of common problems. In addition, group cohesiveness, decision-making, and cooperation were enhanced. It was significant that everyone participated in each activity. A comment from a group member expressed this well. "It [the activity] was fun, 'cause everybody had a feeling for the game, and everybody liked doing it."

(C) Art in Counseling-Case Studies

ART IN INDIVIDUAL COUNSELING – LEE ANN

Lee Ann, a 12-year-old girl, was referred for mental health counseling by a court judge following a hearing in which she was placed under the guardianship of her father and stepmother. Lee Ann had previously been living with her very disturbed mother. At the time of the hearing her mother was judged unfit to care for her daughter, although the mother did have visiting rights.

Lee Ann attended a regular public school in which she participated in some special classes for emotionally disturbed children. She was observed to function at a grade level below that of her chronological age. Regression was the major behavior pattern that Lee Ann used to defend against the anxiety which arose because of previous interpersonal interactions. The most apparent regressed behavior was her immature speech and unkempt appearance. At home and at school she also had difficulty carrying out responsibilities that are usually expected of a 12-year-old girl.

Because Lee Ann had been exposed to a detrimental environment for most of her life, long-term, individual counseling was prescribed. Lee Ann was too old for play materials, and her verbal ability was very poor. Thus art became a medium that was important for her to use for communication and for working through emotional problems. In this case presentation I will describe a few of the most significant experiences that occurred over a two-year period.

Spontaneous Art Activity

House and Family Themes
During the first month of counseling Lee Ann used crayons on manila-colored, 9 X 12-inch construction paper. Although she varied her themes somewhat,

her pictures usually included a house, a tree, flowers, a grass line, a skyline, and a smiling yellow sun — drawings that are usually done by a child 5 to 7 years old. Sometimes she said nothing about these pictures, but at other times she would tell me who lived in the house and how happy they were. Her ideal family included her father, her stepmother, her brother (who was in the Navy), and her cat, Softy. Cats, and Softy in particular, appeared in her drawings on and off throughout counseling. In one house picture she drew Softy on the front step.

Lee Ann: Softy loves me and I love him.
Counselor: How do you know?
Lee Ann: He sleeps with me and curls up in my lap. I feed him.
Counselor: How can you tell if people love you?
Lee Ann: They feed me; give me clothes — sometimes. I don't want to talk about that any more.

Then Lee Ann marked out her drawing of the house and cat. The cat seemed to symbolize a dependable, secure kind of love; but to love human beings was difficult and not predictable.

Sexual Themes

Through counseling sessions with Lee Ann's father and stepmother, I learned that Lee Ann constantly sought affection from her father by following him around, sitting in his lap, and generally intruding herself between her parents. This behavior was also reflected in Lee Ann's house drawings. She would draw pictures of the house with father and stepmother in a bed. Then she would cross them out and draw a picture of a baby in bed with the father. Another time she would draw the father hugging and kissing a young girl. When she did these drawings, she would become so anxious that her speech was hardly intelligible. In her art she seemed to alternate between viewing herself as an adolescent and as a baby, and in both situations her sexual feelings were causing her to exhibit anxious behavior.

Lee Ann also used clay to work through some of her sexual feelings. In one session she modeled a figure with prominent breasts. Her anxiety level was high, as evidenced by her regressed speech and her increased laughter. Following the modeling, I asked her if she was concerned about her own breast development. She could not speak, but nodded. I commented that she was beginning to mature physically and that she might have strong sexual feelings developing too. I explained normal adolescent growth and development, physical and emotional, including menstruation and some of the normal feelings of girls about menstruation.

The sexual theme also recurred in relation to boys. At one session she drew a long, penis-shaped figure. I noticed that her speech was especially unclear, and suspected anxiety related to sexual content. I asked: "Can you tell me about what you drew, or draw another picture?"

She became very red in the face, giggled, and nodded. Then she drew a primitive picture of a male putting his penis in a female. She hid her face and laughed almost hysterically.

Counselor: Can you tell me what's happening?
Lee Ann: Hangman.

This meant that she wanted me to guess the word she wanted to use by playing the "hangman" game. She made spaces for a four-letter word which I eventually guessed to be "fuck." She was calmer now, and was able to tell me about a friend of hers who fucked boys and how frightened she was that it would happen to her. At this point I talked with her about the ambivalence I saw in her wanting to be loved but being afraid. She nodded agreement and said, "It's hard to grow up." I stated: "That's true. And I'm here to help you."

At a later session she was able to use clay again to express her feelings about sexual material. She again modeled a girl with breasts but this time with a vagina. Then she modeled a boy with an erect penis. She had them engage in sexual intercourse. Again, she was very anxious, but was able to express her feelings of wanting this experience but of being afraid.

Love-Hate

The strongest ambivalence that Lee Ann had was toward her mother. She was always upset by her mother's visits because of her mother's inappropriate behavior. In fact, the visits were so disruptive that they were eventually held under supervision of juvenile authorities. One time Lee Ann came to a counseling session after a supervised visit. She was quite visibly upset and unable to express herself verbally. She grabbed a black crayon and a large piece of newsprint. She drew a small, witch-looking person on one side of the page and a larger, strong-looking female on the other. Then she was able to say, "My mother is a witch. She's emotionally disturbed. I am stronger than she is. I don't have to be sick like her. I hate her."

I said that she did not have to be sick, that she was different from her mother, and it was all right to have negative feelings toward her mother.

At other times she was able to express her ambivalent feeling toward me through drawing. After a very difficult session at which I had pushed her hard to accept some of her own negative behavior, she drew a picture of a rat with the title "Pat the Rat." Another time near Valentine's Day she was very anxious throughout the whole session. I could hardly understand her speech, and was puzzled about what was going on. At the end of the session she quickly drew a large heart with red crayon and printed I LOVE YOU. She handed it to me and left hurriedly.

Aggressive Behavior

At times Lee Ann needed help in learning ways to express her angry feelings that surfaced on the slightest provocation. We developed one method through art to "let off steam." When she came to a session with pent-up anger, I encouraged her to use large pieces of colored chalk on rough 24 X 48-inch construction paper. The medium encouraged large motions; sometimes she started with short, accentuated dots and slashes, and at other times vicious circles. As her anger began to dissipate I encouraged large, smooth, gentle strokes. By the time this exercise was over, she was drained of her angry feelings, and often curled up in a chair or relaxed on the floor. I encouraged her to use this method of relieving her angry, tense feelings at home, and talked with her parents about art supplies and encouragement for this activity.

Free Form Drawing

Another art activity that seemed to allow Lee Ann to express herself more freely verbally was free form drawing. Lee Ann would often take out large colored paper and large colored chalk at the beginning of a session. Sometimes she would fill the paper with different colors, and at other times she would draw intricate designs. Occasionally she would invite me to add colors or designs to her drawing. While she drew she talked about something of importance that was going on in her life.

Telling a Story

At times Lee Ann used her pictures to tell me a story. In a session after she had attended a summer camp for the first time, she drew pictures of all the activities that were meaningful to her. When she was finished and we had talked about the different activities, I asked her if she had any words for her camp experience. She said, "Pleased, proud, and surprised." I agreed that I was pleased and proud of how well she had behaved at camp.

Bridge for Discussing Problems

Prior to one session, I received a telephone call from Lee Ann's stepmother, who stated that Lee Ann had stolen candy from a neighborhood store. In the session I asked Lee Ann what her stepmother might have phoned about. She shrugged and said, "I don't know." Then she proceeded to trace the outline of her hands with crayon on paper, over and over. I asked if her hands could be involved in what her stepmother phoned about. Then she was able to say, "Stealing." Using the focus of the hand drawings, we discussed how she could exert control over what her hands did.

Directed Art

There were times when I felt that Lee Ann could benefit from a directed art activity. These activities were especially helpful at times of crisis in Lee Ann's life.

Self Portrait

When Lee Ann's home environment became disruptive or uncertain, she usually responded by increased anxiety and uncertainty about who she was. At these times she seemed to gain in awareness of a reality-based self by means of drawing portraits. In these portraits she used large, colored chalk, either the end or the flat side, and large pieces (24 × 48 inch) of construction paper.

In order to minimize her own criticism of her pictures and to decrease the effects of censoring, I asked her to draw with her eyes closed and with her left hand. Then I would ask her to choose a color of chalk and paper for a drawing of a happy face, then sad and mad. After each drawing she would open her eyes, look at the picture, talk about it, and then select colors for the next portrait. To further help her with checking out the reality of her behavior, I would ask her to state what percent of the time she was happy, mad, or sad. If I felt that her estimates were unrealistic, I used this as a base for correcting her perception of herself.

An alternative activity was to ask her to draw the same portraits with eyes open, eyes closed, and right and left hands. Then with this large selection I had her rate the ones she liked from best to least. This process also provided a springboard for discussion of differences and similarities. One time we mounted the pictures she selected as most likeable. I hung them in the counseling room during her visits to further help her value herself and her art product.

Circles, Squares, and Triangles

Another technique that I used when Lee Ann was quite anxious involved making circles, squares, and triangles on large newsprint with crayons. As with the self portrait, I asked her to draw with both her accustomed and unaccustomed hand and with her eyes open and closed. After she had done a whole series she would rank-order them from best to worst and give them a percent grade. In this process Lee Ann, although very anxious, could engage in a nonthreatening art activity that was reality-based, for which she could take credit, and for which she could make decisions.

Family Portraits

As mentioned earlier, Lee Ann's drawings often portrayed her real family life and her ideal family. Periodically I asked her to draw how she saw her family. These drawings usually gave accurate cues as to what was going on in Lee Ann's family life.

At one point during counseling a crisis occurred when her father died and her stepmother was not able to care for her alone. Lee Ann was placed in a children's shelter until appropriate care for her could be arranged. She was naturally very upset by all the changes, grief for her father, and fear about what would happen to her. Initially I asked her to draw story pictures about the experiences of her father's dying and her coming to the shelter. She drew many pictures of her father's dying, of angels, and of her hatred of the shelter.

In sessions at the shelter we dealt with what her alternative living situations might be and which ones would be best for her. I asked her to draw each situation and to assign each a rating. She drew a picture of the shelter with a rating of 50 percent, a picture of her mother with a rating of zero percent, and then wrote "foster home" with a 100 percent rating. I asked her if she could picture what a foster family would look like. As I suspected she might, she drew her ideal family from left to right: father, mother, Lee Ann, and two younger brothers. Also included were four cats. In addition she described the type of house and relationships in the home. I was able to help her to be open to the idea of a family that would be less than her ideal by means of discussion of the realities of what might be available to her, and of the fact that few families were like her ideal.

Postscript

Lee Ann was eventually placed in foster care. Her first two foster homes turned out to be as disastrous as her natural family life had been, but in her eighteenth year she was adopted into a family that turned out to be as close to her dreams as her drawings had portrayed throughout counseling.

DIRECTED ART ACTIVITY IN GROUP COUNSELING

The group was composed of six girls aged 11 to 12 years who were referred to counseling because they had difficulty getting along with peers, because they had a poor self-image, and because they were all having some academic difficulty. The goals were improvement of communication and interaction skills, resensitization to their own feelings and those of others, and increase in self-image. After a period of learning to know and to gain some trust of one another, I initiated with their agreement a series of 10 directed art activities aimed at achieving these goals.

In each session the girls were presented with a specific art activity that had a focus related to the group goals. Some of the activities were done by the girls as individual projects. In other activities, the girls worked in dyads or as a group. After each art experience the girls had ample opportunity to discuss what they had done, compare their product to one another, and share their feelings. In addition I took color Polaroid photographs of their art products. These photos were used by the girls for further identification with their art experience and for evaluation of their own emotional changes.

Self Portrait — Chalk Drawing

The girls were told that they were going to have an opportunity to explore parts of themselves through drawing. Large pieces of colored construction paper and colored chalk were available to them.

The following instructions were given.

1. Select a piece of paper and chalk and find a place in the room where you can work comfortably without touching someone else.
2. When you are settled, close your eyes and begin to get in touch with how the paper feels: What is the texture? How long is it? How wide is it?
3. Now explore the chalk. How does its texture differ from the paper? How long is it? Can you communicate with your chalk?
4. Now begin to think about yourself right now. What do you look like? How do you feel?
5. Now draw a portrait of yourself from the shoulders up.
6. When you are done, open your eyes, look at your portrait, and then share with someone else what you drew and how you felt.

Some of the girls giggled during the warm-up time, indicating some nervousness, but when they started drawing, each girl became very serious. There was more giggling and laughter when they opened their eyes and began to share. The last part of the session was spent in sharing the similarities and differences in their pictures as a total group. Even the quietest of the girls participated in drawing and sharing.

Safe Place – Clay

The group was told that they were going to have an opportunity to use clay to describe for themselves a safe place. Ceramic clay was available in previously formed balls, and the following instructions were given.

1. Take a ball of clay and find a comfortable place in the room to work.
2. Close your eyes and begin to explore the clay, being aware of its texture. Is it hot or cold? How hard do you have to push it?
3. Now begin to think about what is a safe place for you. When you have decided on the safest place, begin to make a sculpture of that place with your clay.
4. When you are ready, open your eyes and look at your sculpture; then share with someone whose safe place looks most like yours.

The girls were very quiet as they began to manipulate the clay. One girl, however, did express disgust at the feel of the clay. I suggested that she stop for a few minutes and, if she felt like it, to continue modeling the clay. She was still not able to touch the clay after her time out, so I asked her to find some paper and crayon and to write her feelings about the clay and to draw a safe place. With this direction she was able to continue. In the sharing time as a group, this girl was able to tell how the cold clay reminded her of touching her dead grandmother when she went to the funeral.

The girls made prideful statements about their safe places, and also expressed surprise that others might have similar structures and similar safe places.

Self Appreciation – Collage

The girls were told that in this session they would have a variety of materials to use in making a collage picture of themselves that "maximizes how they feel about themselves." Each girl was provided with a large poster board base for her picture, glue, and access to colored paper, string, yarn, cotton, wrapping paper, and magazines with pictures. The instructions were as follows.

1. Take a large poster board and find a place in the room where you can work without bothering someone else.
2. Get in a comfortable position, close your eyes, and begin to think about your "best self" – what are your best points; how do you look when you are feeling at your best?

3. When you are ready, open your eyes, take material to make your collage, and make a picture that describes your best self.
4. When you are done, share your picture with someone whose picture is different from yours.

In the group sharing, the girls talked about how difficult it was for them to pick out things they liked about themselves. Being preadolescent, they were beginning to become very self-conscious of their appearance. They asked if they could do the same thing the next week, but focus on the things they did not like.

In the next session I used the same instructions, except that I asked them to focus on the parts of themselves that they did not like. The girls found this task easier to do, and most of their comments about themselves were exaggerations of their appearance: hair too long, too short, too straight or curly; body too fat or too thin; face too pimply.

After they had ample opportunity to express their negative feelings, I asked them to compare the two collages they had made and to pick out their strongest and weakest parts. This time they could take more credit for their positive parts, and the negative ones lost their overpowering strength.

Dyad Cooperation — Constructs

In this session the girls were told that they would have an opportunity to work together with a partner. They were to take notice of how they were able to work together. The material available for use was cuisinaire rods, which are smooth wooden rods of different lengths and colors, used to teach mathematical concepts. The instructions were as follows.

1. Choose a person to whom you are most similar in the group to work with.
2. Gather a pile of rods and make a construct that represents an object you both like.
3. When you are done, walk around and see what the others have made.

At first the girls seemed hesitant about selecting the girls they wanted to work with. They held back until I suggested that two girls who were obviously close work together. Then the others were able to choose. Some of the dyads talked about what they would build first, whereas others went right to work on their constructs. There was some initial competition about the distribution of the rods because the groups that started to work right away took more than their share of rods. They agreed to give up enough to make a fair share all around. While they were working, the girls talked with each other a great deal, and there was a steady hum of people working together harmoniously.

In the large group sharing, each dyad presented their construct and related that they worked well together. One dyad said they had had a dispute over what to make but, once they started, they cooperated in their work.

In the next session I asked them to make the same kind of construct, but to make it with the person they were most different from. It seemed easier for them to pick someone who was different than it had been the week before to select someone similar. Again, there was bickering over how many rods each dyad was to have. The group was very careful to count out the exact number of each size for each dyad.

There was much discussion in the dyads about what they would make. Some of the discussions became arguments. One dyad spent the whole time trying to decide; one made separate constructs; and the last dyad made a construct but neither girl seemed very pleased with it.

In our group discussion I asked the girls to focus on the differences between their experiences with someone who was like them and with someone they saw as different from themselves. They were able to go beyond their immediate group situation and talk about how they acted in similar ways outside the group, especially in the school setting.

Group Cooperation – Construct

In this session I told the girls that they would have an opportunity to work through some of their difficulties related to working with someone unlike themselves by making a group construct. The material available to them was a large piece (6 × 6 feet) of newsprint, collage materials, glue, and crayons, and the instruction was:

1. With the material available to you, construct a "world" together.

Without much discussion, each girl staked out a spot for herself and proceeded to make objects and people in that small area. As they finished their own area, they began to look around and see that they really had not worked together. It was then that they began to talk together about what they needed – houses, a school, a hospital, roads, cars, and trees. Gradually they began to move out of their own self-centered area to develop a cooperative community. Before someone put something new in, she asked for the group's permission.

In the following discussion, the girls stated that they were able to work better with people they did not like when they were all working together than when they were in the dyads. They felt that their "friends" were there to support them when they were all together.

Group Cooperation — Clay Structure

In this session the group continued to work on their group interactions through group clay sculpturing. The instructions and process were similar to the group construct. They were told that they as a group could make any kind of sculpture from a 20-pound bag of ceramic clay.

The girls worked on the sculpture as they had initially in the group construct. Each one took some clay for herself and began to shape and mold it. Even the girl who previously had not been able to use clay was able to participate with the encouragement of group members. After they had molded individual pieces of clay for a while, they began to put their pieces together in the middle of the circle. They spent most of the rest of the session putting pieces on the sculpture and admiring one another's contributions. At the end of the session they asked me to save the sculpture and if they could have pictures of it.

Evaluation — Graphic

During the last two sessions the girls were involved in evaluating their self-growth. In the ninth session I returned Polaroid prints of all their art products to them. I asked them to spend a period of time looking at their pictures and thinking about ways they had changed since the beginning of the group session.

I then told them that they would be involved in their last art activity and that the focus was on evaluating themselves. They had available large poster board, strips of colored paper, and glue, and they were instructed:

1. Make a graph that shows if you have changed — how you have changed — and that also indicates what parts of the group experience contributed to changes or distracted from changes.
2. When you are finished, write a description of your graph.

Because the girls spent most of their session looking at their pictures and making their graphs, it was decided to spend the last session sharing their graphs with one another.

Each of the girls expressed herself uniquely in her graph. Some made fairly traditional types of graphs; others were more innovative — making objects or human figures to express their growth. Each of the girls in some way or another expressed that she felt better about herself and her relationship with others. They did identify different parts of the group experience that contributed to their growth, but all expressed an appreciation for the group clay sculpture. They made comments such as: "We really were together." "It was a different feeling than I've ever had before." They were not able to make many negative statements. The girl who had a strong response to the clay mentioned it, but also said it had helped her with the feelings she had about death. This experience also impressed others, who said they felt uncomfortable when the girl was talking about her dead grandmother. Several girls said they did not want the group to end.

As they left with their graphs and pictures they decided to take the clay sculpture and pass it around among the group members.

(D) Clinical Assessment and Treatment Plan—A Case Study

CLINICAL ASSESSMENT — MARIO

Mario was a 6-year-old boy in the first grade at the time of assessment. He was 47 inches tall and weighed 59 pounds. Findings on his physical examination at Children's Hospital Clinic had been negative.

General Appearance and Behavior

Mario was an attractive little black boy with an afro hair style. Very frequently he sucked the last two fingers of his right hand while his left hand was manipulating objects or toys. If his left hand was otherwise unoccupied, Mario held his left ear, oftentimes tucking it into itself.

Mario often seemed totally involved in his own thoughts, oblivious to instructions being given by the teacher to the whole class, involved perhaps in playing with a tiny toy on his desk and in sucking. When he saw an activity across the room he often went to interfere or become involved. Sometimes he attempted to appeal in a friendly way by putting his arm around another boy's shoulder or showing a toy as if offering to share it.

On the playground Mario was all over the place. During free play his class was supposed to stay in one area of the yard, but he was everywhere. All the teachers knew him. He did not play cooperatively without adult supervision. If he was confronted or resisted he became offensive, and hit out at others.

Mario's behavior can be summarized by saying that he was amiable if

Unpublished data by Elizabeth Jordan, 1973.

satisfied; but sullen, uncommunicative, and stubbornly resistant if reprimanded by an adult, assaultive with children who threatened his will, a ringleader among his fellow aggressors, and fearful and obedient in the presence of his mother. He sucked a great deal, indicating unsatisfied oral needs. He was not involved in creative play or exploration.

Symptoms

Mario was referred for consultation because he acted out and was aggressive. His mother had been called to school regarding his behavior. His teacher described him as lovable but defiant. His responses to discipline or scolding were anger, resistance, defiance, unwillingness to cooperate, and withdrawal. When scolded for hitting another child, Mario would refuse to participate in any activity, academic or otherwise, and would go under a table and suck and hold his ear. At the beginning of the year he had not wanted to come to school. His older sister had come and sat with him a couple of days, which helped him to get started.

Mario's adjustment at the time of assessment was better than it had been in September, but to quote his teacher: "Everything will be fine; then all of a sudden there will be three children crying, 'Mario hit me!' "

Mario ranked in the 25th percentile on the Metropolitan Readiness Test. His IQ had been tested, but the scores had not been returned to the school at the time of assessment.

Family Environment

Mario was the youngest of seven children. He lived with four of them, his mother, and his stepfather in a clean, comfortable, attractively furnished flat in a primarily white and Oriental neighborhood. His mother had remarried during the past year, and the family moved to their current address just before school started. The eldest two children, a boy and a girl, were grown and out of the home. The son is married and has a 3-year-old son. One of the children at home, the oldest, is a daughter who graduated from high school in June. She is not working or attending school. The remaining children are a 16-year-old brother, a 13-year-old sister, and a 10-year-old brother. Mario and this brother share a bedroom.

Mario's mother described a very rigidly run household where the children performed their duties as she told them — no arguing, no questions asked. She had "no trouble with them at home; they know I mean what I say." She initially described Mario as never having had trouble at school previously, and he had had a year of nursery school before attending kindergarten. Later she recalled his kindergarten teacher's having said that there was trouble with sharing, and also related that there had been some problems with her other children along the way.

Mario was very orderly at home, knew exactly where to put his clothes after school, and did it faithfully. His 10-year-old brother was then responsible for hanging up Mario's clothes because Mario could not reach yet. Mario could prepare his own sandwiches, clean his own part of his room, and perform other such tasks expected of him.

In response to my descriptions of some of Mario's behavior at school, his mother said that she was sure that he did not intend to hurt anybody. Eventually she related some of his behavior to "frustration." She discussed his sucking, and was willing to see Mario's need for some counseling.

School Environment

There were 21 children in Mario's class. His teacher was a kind, considerate, understanding person who cared about all the children, including Mario. Willing to ignore much of his maladaptive behavior and to reward his good behavior with praise, she told him that she would not let the other children hit him and that he could not hit them. Her approach was one of caring, and she was consistent in her responses. She felt that Mario had settled down quite a bit since September. The children reinforced Mario's behavior by tattling on him even when he was virtually innocent. Mrs. Jones was aware of this, and reproached them for petty tattling.

Mario was academically behind in school. His teacher worked with him individually and in small groups. Whether he had a neurological learning problem needed to be determined; that he had emotional problems seemed quite apparent.

Reality Adaptation

Mario's sex-role identification seemed appropriate and crystallized, as was manifested by his clothing, his behavior, his affect, and his association primarily with boys at his age. It seemed that he saw himself as masculine.

Mario's conscience and moral standards development seemed erratic. He pretty much did what he wanted with peers, short of hitting them every time he would have liked. He manifested some conscience, as illustrated in his taking another child's ball, being confronted, and replying, "I was getting it for you." His internal prohibiting mechanisms were immature. He responded to external forces against his specific behavior, as noted by his glancing toward an adult when getting ready to throw a bean bag at somebody. His thoughts about what he should do socially were immature.

Mario distorted reality in terms of his offensive behavior. He was active and well coordinated. He was often uninvolved, and isolated himself. Sometimes he and another child would play alone in "the clubhouse," which was a throw rug under a table near the teacher's desk.

Interpersonal Relations

Mario's attitudes toward others varied. Many times peers seemed to be a threat to his ego; his parents were regarded by him as frightening, and other adults as interfering. When he was angry over an encounter with an adult he isolated himself. Otherwise he usually avoided adults, and sometimes appealed to them in his own behalf. A few of the children appeared to be afraid of Mario; others returned his verbal abuses; others ignored him; and still others participated with him. The little girl who sat next to him tried to help him with his schoolwork, and he seemed to accept this. Sometimes he looked to her for direction. I never saw him be unkind to her.

Attitude toward Self

Mario seemed to see himself partly as an ill-behaved, combative, abusive "bad guy," and partly as an appealing person. I felt that the bases for these attitudes were learned and were in response to what he had been taught about himself. He compensated for his feelings of inferiority by rebelling, striking out at those weaker than he, and resisting those stronger. Discharges of anger relieved his frustration. In striving to preserve himself, he tended to destroy himself by turning others from him.

Quality of Affect

When Mario was angry it was obvious by his facial expression and his "body language." His smile, which I did not see often, was appropriate. He made attempts to participate with the other children; sometimes he was imitating and not responding spontaneously. An example of this was his joining the other children's laughter in response to a story the teacher was reading. Mario had been sucking and looking into space when the amusing sentence had been read.

Anxiety

It seemed that Mario's anxiety was moderate to severe. He manifested anxiety by acting out when he felt threatened or frustrated, and by withdrawing and sucking when he felt defeated or down or was not being externally stimulated. In the face of his mother's threat he probably showed fear.

Patterns of Control

Generally Mario had little capacity for controlling his emotions when he was among peers. He was impulsive and acted on his impulses. His capacity for self-expression was limited, for it seemed that his opportunities for exploration, creativity, and warm, loving relationships had been thwarted in his infant, toddler, and preschool years. He did derive pleasure from play experiences and from the control of others that his aggressive expression gave him. His capacity for displeasure was great if he was not satisfied.

Defense Patterns

Mario used verbal defense of his actions, and physical aggression, regression, withdrawal, and resistance when defeated.

Central Conflict

Mario's central conflict seemed to be between behaving as his self-concept dictated and behaving as others said he should. He did sometimes ask for permission before doing something; however, if it involved an emotional conflict, he acted on impulse. Following his act he sometimes was conscious of the discrepancies of his behavior.

CLINICAL TREATMENT PLAN

Working Goals

1. Make contract regarding reason for counseling, meeting time, length of contract
2. Provide a setting and environment for counseling by providing toys suitable for expressing anger and frustration and for dealing with feelings of deprivation. Such toys as a punching bag, gun, knife, pegboard, paints, play dough, water, puppets, dollhouse, soldiers, airplanes, cars, trucks, boats,

and blocks seem appropriate for expressing aggression. A soft doll, bottle, blanket, pillow, puppets, and dollhouse seem appropriate for expressing feelings of deprivation.
3. Establish trust
4. Encourage self-expression by accepting Mario on his own ground — accepting his behavior along with him by means of a nondirective approach
5. Set limits as they are needed during the process
6. Counsel with Mario's mother, helping her to look at some of her own feelings
7. Consult and confer with school personnel

Long-Term Goals

1. Effect change in Mario's feelings about himself — elevate his self-concept
2. Reduce Mario's anxiety
3. Effect change in Mario's behavior outside the playroom

(E) Stages in Counseling–Case Studies

STAGES IN INDIVIDUAL COUNSELING – JERRY

Jerry was an attractive 8-year-old boy referred to a mental health clinic because of his behavior, which disturbed his family and his school. He was described at that time by his mother as not being able to get along with either his siblings or the children at school. At home and at school he was consistently involved in fights, his behavior was totally unpredictable, and there were several incidents of cruelty toward animals and younger children. At school he was withdrawn; except for his fighting, his activities were solitary for the most part, and his ability to function in the classroom was greatly impaired.

Jerry had been examined previously at the clinic, at the age of 3 years. At that time his mother was concerned about his aggressive behavior and his lack of speech, and because she thought he might be retarded. At that time a development history revealed that he was growing within normal limits, and psychological testing indicated low average intelligence with the possibility of higher results when he could verbalize more adequately. The family history indicated that there was marital discord between the parents, little positive attention to the boy by his father, and a household which was disorganized and in which there was little consistency in handling any of the children. The family unit consisted of the mother and father, who were both well educated and with artistic interests; an older sister; and twin brothers two years younger. The clinic's recommendation to the family at this time was to give the boy more personal, affectionate attention.

When he entered kindergarten Jerry was again seen at the clinic because the family was still concerned about the possibility that he was retarded. At this time he tested in the high average range, but his emotional disturbance seemed quite obvious. The parents were reassured about his intelligence, and the recommendation to the parents was again to give Jerry as much attention and affection as possible to avoid serious maladjustment.

When he was examined at 8 years, his psychological testing indicated emotional disturbance and a higher degree of intelligence than previously determined in the testing process. It was recommended at this time that Jerry should be started in counseling and that he should be enrolled in a small private school which the family had been considering for him. Therapeutic goals were set for Jerry, with consideration of his behavior and of the possible dynamics behind this behavior which could be intimated from the family history. The goals of counseling were to provide a concerned, consistent relationship with an adult in which his unmet needs would be fulfilled. His mother was involved in a parents' counseling group.

Beginning Counseling

It was expected, because of the history of Jerry's aggressive and destructive behavior, that he would use play material to act out the behavior that had given him difficulties both at home and at school. The first 10 sessions found Jerry a very rigidly controlled boy who played carefully, and who at all times kept social distance from me. Attempts by me to introduce activities which could lead to some type of aggressive play, so that there might be some behavior to begin to talk about, were to no avail. Jerry did not allow himself to act out his aggressive feelings in the playroom. During this time his tone of voice and facial expression were quite flat and without much affect of any kind. Another characteristic that exemplified his behavior at this stage was his conscious awareness of time. Jerry would ask me several times during the hour how much time there was left, and would sometimes ask if there were enough time for a certain activity. As he was able to move into real fantasy play, the preoccupation with time disappeared.

Working Stage

It was around the tenth counseling session that Jerry began to act out a series of scenes with the use of the dolls and playhouse in which much aggression and destructiveness were demonstrated. Jerry approached this play material readily at the beginning of each session, much as a worker does who is engrossed in working through a problem-solving task. At first I watched this fantasy play as the giant doll proceeded to kill and destroy and then become the good giant who heals and restores. After a few sessions of watching or observing this play, I began to take part in it. At first I interjected myself with a doll as a playmate and admirer of the giant doll. Jerry seemed to welcome this intervention by incorporating my doll into the fantasy and by eventually assigning a role to me, which usually turned out to be that of the son, while Jerry acted out the strong, good, and protecting father.

Interventions through Play

By actually entering into the fantasy, I was able to ask questions and enter into Jerry's real thoughts and feelings. Entering into the action also gave me the opportunity to act as a role model to Jerry. An example of this type of intervention into fantasy play occurred when Jerry as the father took his son on a trip to the mountains. They traveled the long trip by "camper," which was previously filled with all types of camping equipment and food. In the mountains the two spent a glorious day skiing and sledding on the slopes. However, when it came time to eat, the father did not want to eat any of the supplies from the camper, but insisted on roasting the leg of a dear friend who had died in an accident. Although I did participate in the building of a fire and the preparing of the roast, when the invitation to eat of the human flesh was offered to me I refused. The refusal was accepted by Jerry, and he as the father subsequently fulfilled the request of his son for hamburgers by taking him to a drive-in for dinner, after eating and enjoying the roasted leg himself.

Jerry acted out many sequences with the giant doll in counseling, and seemed to be working through some type of conflict in the process. There was never a time when he was able to give to me a clear picture of what the giant doll meant to him. He was, however, able to work through the conflict-laden material by means of fantasy play and with his counselor entering into the fantasy play as a participant-observer.

Terminating Stage

Evaluation

There were changes in Jerry's behavior. In the playroom Jerry became less rigid in his movements. His voice and body assumed a more relaxed tone, with more affect involved in all of his verbal and nonverbal communication. Whereas he had previously maintained social distance with me, he was now able to relate not only to the fantasy character being played by me but also to me as a person. Outside of the counseling situation he was observed at home by his mother to be able to play better with his siblings and to tolerate the frustrations and teasing offered by his older sister, and to show concern, care, and affection for a pet rat which often became his bedmate. At his new school his aggressive, sadistic behavior disappeared, and he was able to experience the feeling of success in readily mastering new learning skills, in which his teacher reported excellent progress.

Ending

I discussed with Jerry his observed changes in behavior in counseling, at home, and at school. I suggested that he might begin to think about ending counseling in about a month. He said he did not want to stop — that he needed to come to the playroom more than ever. Because his family situation was still unstable and because Jerry was able to make such a clear statement of his need, counseling was continued until the end of his school year.

In the final stage of counseling, Jerry's play had much less conflict material. He used play materials more for age-appropriate task mastery. His verbal communication was more direct and usually related to what he was doing in counseling or to something that had happened at school or at home.

When the time came to end Jerry was ready to leave, and seemed to have worked through the feelings of ambivalence which he had expressed previously. In the last session, when it was time to leave he said, "I'm finished now. Good-bye."

STAGES IN GROUP COUNSELING

The setting for our group meetings was in a classroom of the school which the boys attended. The room was used for exercise and dance. It was quite bare except for a round table and six chairs, a tumbling mat, and six large, stuffed pillows. There were windows on one side, a basketball standard on one wall at the end, and a blackboard on the wall at the other end. The equipment available to the boys included a kickball, a basketball, a nerfball, a Frisbee, two sets of popguns which shot Ping-Pong balls, and games of Monopoly, checkers, chess, and cards. Art supplies were also available: paints, chalk, crayons, and plain and colored paper and clay. The group was to meet one and one-half hours weekly for 16 weeks. I had no coleader.

The group membership consisted of five boys aged 10 and 11 years. They were referred for counseling for the following reasons: Michael, frequent crying; Mario, immaturity; John, rigid behavior; Jerry, aggression; and George, daydreaming.

Beginning Stage

Session 1

As the boys came into the room they seemed awkward and somewhat embar-
rassed. I greeted each one as he entered, and then I sat down on one of the
large pillows to watch. They did not speak to one another, but they did begin
to look around the room and to engage in some type of activity. John found
the cards and sat at the table playing solitaire and looking at the others. After
walking all the way around the room, Mario sat next to me on the floor and,
without speaking, also watched. George found the basketball and began
shooting baskets. Mike played catch with the nerfball by himself, but fairly
near to George. And Jerry strutted around the room pouting and intruding
his physical presence on each boy except Mario. He stayed at a distance from
Mario and me.

About ten minutes after they had all arrived I asked them each to get a
pillow and sit on the floor in the corner where I was. While they were dis-
engaging from their activity I got out crayons, pencils, chalk, newsprint sheets,
and a long piece of newsprint. George and Jerry were the last members to
settle themselves, and each positioned himself somewhat out of the group
circle.

I stretched the long newsprint paper out on the floor and wrote my name
across the paper, using a large space. I asked the boys each to get a piece of
chalk and write his name on the paper. Each boy selected a chalk and wrote
his name. Mario used very little space; John printed his legibly; Jerry scrawled
his largely and sloppily; Mike and George wrote neatly, using more space than
would be used in normal writing. I asked each boy to identify his name and
make one statement about himself. I started off by identifying my name,
saying it, and saying that I was the group leader. I called on Mike, who identified his name and said that he was a good wrestler. I asked Mike to choose
another boy. Mike chose Jerry, who said he thought this was a dumb class.
He pouted and refused to choose another boy. I chose Mario, who said he
liked to play kickball. Mario chose George, who said he liked to play basketball.

The boys were beginning to become restless at this point, so I brought out
the snacks (juice and cookies) to the table area. John and Mario came over
to help; the others took turns shooting baskets. Finally all the boys sat down
at the table and started to eat. Jerry took more than half the cookies, but
no one said anything to him. While they were eating I reviewed some of the
rules I had described with them individually: regular and punctual attendance;
confidentiality; the rule that they could not hurt themselves or one another

or destroy property willfully; and the rule that decisions would be made by consensus. I asked them if there were any more rules they wanted. George looked at Jerry and said, "Yeah. How many cookies a guy gets." Nobody was willing to take this statement any further, but I recognized that this was a first step in confronting Jerry with his behavior. I told them that the group would meet weekly for one and one-half hours, and that in each session there would be time for free play; some structured activity; snacks; and talking. I also said that I would plan activities from time to time like crafts, art, or outings, and that I wanted them to think about things they wanted to do. The group ended with George, Jerry, and Mike shooting baskets. While I cleaned up, John helped me and Mario watched both groups.

Session 2
This session went much like the first one except that the structured activity dealt with what they wanted for themselves out of the group. I asked them to either write or draw what they wanted from the group for themselves.

John wrote, but the rest of the boys drew pictures, which they then shared with one another. John wrote that he wanted to learn to play kickball better. Mike drew himself as Mr. Atlas and said he wanted to be strong all the time. Mario drew himself shooting baskets with another boy. He said he wanted to be able to play with George. Jerry drew a picture of himself with boxing gloves on, and although he showed the picture he would not say anything about it. George drew himself drawing a picture of himself. He laughed when he showed it, but made no further comment.

Session 3
In this session, I had planned to engage the group in a "follow-the-leader" obstacle course activity that used most of the equipment in the room. I was aware that the group seemed different when they arrived. I sensed that they were tense and more active. At the end of the free play time they did not come to sit down when I said it was time, but continued their free play. I went ahead and set up the obstacle course and, because no one seemed to listen to me, I wrote the activity I had planned on the board. John and Mario looked at it and did engage in following the course for a short time while George shot baskets and Jerry and Mike used the Frisbee like a boomerang meant to kill one another. I recognized that this was probably the beginning of a transitional stage before the group could move into the next stage. I sighed, knowing that it would be hard, wishing I had a male coleader for support, and realizing that we had to live through this stage before we could progress into the working stage.

Sessions 4–7

The sessions proved to be a continuance of the same type of activity. They threw balls at the wall clock, breaking its hands; they threatened to break the windows; they threw balls and pillows at one another. The contagion was so great that even John and Mario were caught up in it. The throwing became so fierce that they set a limit of how far away a person had to be when throwing or shooting guns, but they had trouble enforcing it. They also set a limit on not throwing the basketball at one another after several boys had cried when they were hit. To break up the threatened group disorganization, we went outside for a walk in a nearby park, but this also became a source of anxiety for me, for they played a game of tag on the tops of the picnic tables. Another strategy I implemented, with more success, was the removal of paints, crayons, and clay to prevent possible misuse of these materials.

This period was anxiety producing for me, and it was difficult to keep from intervening except when someone asked for support or protection and to prevent total group disorganization. I watched carefully to make sure that no one was seriously hurt, and I was ready to intervene if necessary.

Besides being active physically, they also tested me with the use of "power words": fucker, motherfucker, shit, piss, etc. When one of the boys would say one of these words, someone would usually look at my response — either the boy who said it or one of the others.

During this period there was little serious talk except at snack time, and that usually consisted of: "What class are you in?" "Do you get detention?" These exchanges usually lasted about five minutes. There seemed to be a constant shifting of alliances from week to week and within individual sessions.

In the seventh session an unusual incident occurred that seemed to help them move into the working stage. They had been shooting the popguns at one another as teams. Suddenly both the teams ganged up on Jerry, whom they cornered behind the table. Instead of fighting, as they expected him to do, Jerry cringed in the corner and cried. The others looked anxious and frightened at the collapse of their strong, cocky adversary. At this point I intervened by having each boy sit down on a pillow near to where Jerry was. I sat near Jerry, offering him verbal support for his position and at the same time acknowledging the fear I saw in the others. They talked a little about not knowing what had happened, and gradually the tension was reduced. I had planned popcorn for the snack time, so moved them on to making and serving popcorn. Each of the boys was either actively involved or a participant observer in this process. My thought was, "At last a productive group activity!"

During snacks, George suggested that we talk about some of the activities we could do together, and asked if we could go to the playfield for kickball next week. I asked the others if this was okay. They all assented; even Jerry mumbled an assent.

Although there were times of stress in future sessions when the group regressed, this session seemed to bring an end to the hectic behavior of the beginning stage.

Working Stage

Session 8

When the boys had assembled for this session, I was pleased to see them take the responsibility for getting the material together to go to the playing field. Although there was not a place to play basketball, George brought the basketball, which he dribbled down and back. Mike carried the kickball and tossed it back and forth to Mario as we walked. John offered to carry the cookies and juice. Jerry said he wanted to bring the Frisbee. As we walked to the field Jerry walked beside me, except for short forays to retrieve the Frisbee.

At the field they organized a game of "One-O-Cat" kickball with Mike and George taking leadership roles in planning where bases should be and what positions people would start in. I became their participant-observer and supporter from the sidelines. The three most physically able boys, Mike, Jerry, and George, were very competitive with one another but considerate and helpful toward the immature Mario and the rigid, awkward John. Mike, Jerry, and George seemed almost as pleased as Mario when the latter made a home run with their assistance through a dropped fly ball.

Because I was the keeper of the time, I suggested that we had about 20 minutes left: 10 minutes for snacks and 10 minutes to walk back. Without any discussion, Jerry evenly distributed the cookies and poured juice for everyone. They talked about the ball game and shared experiences that had happened to them at school. The favorite theme was "that awful teacher" who always picked on them and their fantasies of what they would like to do to "her."

Sessions 9–13

In these sessions the boys continued to take increased responsibility for their behavior and for planning what they wanted to do. Generally they seemed to be more comfortable with their planned outings to the playing field, and when they did stay in the activity room their behavior tended to be more tense and regressed.

One session was particularly illustrative of their ability to work together and be responsible for one another. This session involved making and flying kites. The activity was planned by the boys the week before at their usual snack-talk time. It was kite season with good winds, and the playfield was ideal for such an activity.

I brought manufactured kites that needed to be put together, thinking that this was within the skill of all the boys. They divided the kites by choosing favorite colors and designs, and each boy took a ball of string. They decided to make the kites at the field rather than inside. When they started to assemble the kites it was apparent that some boys had greater skills than others. Mike, George, and Jerry had theirs ready in a couple of minutes while John and Mario were still fumbling with the sticks and string. George moved over to help Mario, and Jerry helped John. Mario and John watched closely and asked questions about how to do certain parts of the construction. Meanwhile, Mike was putting a big tail on his kite. Jerry looked up and told him it was too big and he didn't need one at all, but Mike told him to go "fuck off." Mike then ran across the field with his kite behind him, only to have it crash to the ground and break. Jerry shouted, "I told you so," to which Mike retorted, "Fucker." I could see the tears begin to start in Mike's eyes, and asked him to come over to the group. Mike came reluctantly and with his head down. I commented on what had happened, on his response, and how hard it was for him. The other boys offered supportive statements and told him matter-of-factly that he just shouldn't have put a big tail on. Mike shrugged and said, "Yeah, I guess not." They drifted away from the group then to fly their kites with Mike sitting near me, watching wistfully. George was most successful in getting his kite to stay up, and called over to Mike to fly it for him so he could take a break. Mike refused at first, and then went over to fly George's kite for him.

I felt that the boys had come a long way in being sensitive to one another's needs and in taking responsibility for one another and the group process. I continued my role as gatekeeper with interventions at a minimum.

In session 12 I asked the boys if I could plan an activity for the next session using art media. They all agreed that I could present it and they would participate. What I wanted to help them begin to look at was their growth as a group and how they functioned individually in the group. The plan I had in mind consisted of having the boys construct "their world" using a variety of material which included an 8 × 10 foot paper base, crayons, paint, chalk, paper, rope, and yarn. The instructions to the boys for the experience were "to make their world" by using the large paper base and any material available in the room, and to "identify themselves in 'their world.'"

In planning this activity I was acutely aware of the timing in relation to both the group process and where the individuals were. They had passed through the tumultuous beginning stage and had indicated that they could take responsibility for planning and implementing group activities. When I talked with them about the planned activity they indicated their willingness and even eagerness to be involved.

My therapeutic goal, as previously stated, was to help them look at and take credit for their growth as a group and where they were individually in relation to the group. I felt that the members were able to experience and look at group growth, but I was not equally certain that individual members could look with ease at their own part in group growth and participation. For example, I was not sure how much John could be in touch with his participation in the tumultuous beginning stage, or whether George and Jerry could take credit for how they were able to help Mario and John. I thought that, if these boys became in touch with this material during the experience, they might need extra support to deal with their feelings, and perhaps would need help in refocusing. I discussed my plan with a colleague, who agreed that it had therapeutic merit and that the timing was right.

When the boys arrived for the session they were excited and curious about the large paper and the different kinds of material. I gave the instructions for the focus of the experience, along with a statement of permission not to be involved if they did not want to. They all agreed to participate, and no one expressed the need to withdraw.

They did not talk to each other as they started, but began collecting material for their work. As they found what they thought they needed, they went to the paper and began to work. Each one made some kind of a structure fairly near the perimeter of the paper, and then began to look around at the others. George said he was going to make a road over to Jerry. With this action by Jerry, the others began to add parts to the middle of the world. Mario drew a big green playing field, a ball, and players. Mike added a boy flying a kit with four people around him. John drew a series of picnic tables with figures on top of them. George had been watching as each new part was put in; when the others seemed to be finished George took some yarn and started weaving it in and out of each structure until all the parts were connected. Then he sat back and just smiled at the rest of us. George seemed to be saying: "See, all these things are connected." He also seemed to be taking pride in his part in bringing the group together.

The boys walked around, looking from different angles at what they had done. After a few minutes I asked them to sit down by their original structure. I asked them to make a short statement of their response to the world they made and what they liked best. John started by saying that he didn't know that his world was so big, and what he liked best were the roads to the different people. He called on Jerry, who stated he liked George's road. Next Mike was called; and he stated that he liked the kites and the kite flyers. He also said that he didn't realize how many roads their world had and how they were all connected. Mario then said that he liked the playing field and kickball game best and that he was glad it was part of his world. Finally, George made his statement of pride in his roads and the way he connected all the parts.

I was aware of the symbolism involved in the roads and structures, but I felt that the boys did not need to discuss the symbolic nature of what they had each experienced because they had integrated, through action, the feeling of group togetherness and their unique part in it.

Because our group was time-limited to 16 sessions, I reminded them in the thirteenth session that there were only three sessions left. I asked them to think about what they wanted to do for the ending sessions. Several boys expressed surprise that we were ending; another said he didn't believe it.

Terminating Stage

Session 14

After my reminder of the fact of termination in the previous session, the boys did not volunteer any discussion about termination. In this session, however, they began to act very much as they had in the beginning stage. There was running, throwing, and shouting of obscenities. At snack time I commented that their behavior was much like it had been during our earlier sessions together, and wondered if it had anything to do with my talking about termination. At first they ignored my comments, then they began to plan what they wanted to do the last two sessions. They decided they wanted a kickball game for the next session and a picnic for the last time together.

Session 15

After kickball, the boys decided to return to the activity room for snacks and to plan the picnic. While they were eating, George started talking about his first impression of Jerry and how he didn't like him then but did now. This freed the boys to check out perceptions with one another. Finally, George asked me how I could have stood them when they were all acting so awful. I said it had been hard sometimes, but that I did care for each of them and that I did understand their need to act the way they did. They almost forgot to talk about the picnic, but they planned what each person would bring as they went out the door.

Session 16

Because the food they had decided on included cooking (hot dogs and marsh-mallows), I volunteered to bring the fire supplies. I also brought such things as plates and napkins that they probably would not think of.

The major activity of this session revolved around the fire and fire building. This activity was similar to the kite building in terms of different skills and cooperation. It took a while to get a good fire going, and they must have each used a book of matches; however, each person had the experience of building and controlling fire. They ate enormous quantities of food and played kick-ball; and, when we returned to the school after the activity, the boys split up very quickly, mostly with comments like, "See ya."

Evaluation of Group Experience

During the 16 weeks of group life, some of the behaviors that were problems to individual children were modified. Mike was able to experience criticism and failure in the kite-flying episode without falling apart, and could accept support and direction from the group. Mario was able to engage in active play with the other group members and to respond with more age- and sex-appro-priate behavior. John was able to allow himself to engage in "acting-out" behavior with the group during the transition stage; later, he actually learned to play kickball. Jerry learned that he could be accepted just for himself and did not have to resort to aggressive acts to gain attention. He also related to the other boys in a more friendly manner. And George was able to take credit for his strength and what he was able to give to others. Each boy showed evidence of developing several more normal, age-appropriate coping behaviors.

As a group the boys were able to move beyond the tumultuous beginning stage to a working relationship in which they were more cooperative and had more self-discipline and acceptance and tolerance of one another. The boys were also able to take increasing responsibility for group behavior and for group activities.

(F) Setting Limits in Counseling–A Case Study

A CASE STUDY – KARL

Most child counselors consider limits to be an essential aspect of counseling with children. Although there are certain basic limits that are considered conducive to effective treatment, these limits are allowed to evolve from the relationship between counselor and child as a unique product of their interactions. The child's thoughts and feelings are accepted and respected, but he encounters limits on his actions. The setting and breaking of limits constituted the major part of my counseling experience with Karl.

In school Karl disrupted his class and broke rules on the playground. At home he was manipulative, disobedient, and difficult to manage. Everyone saw Karl as a bad, unacceptable child, and every day Karl lived up to this negative image. It followed then that he brought with him to our relationship his characteristic way of relating to people. He, too, believed in his "badness," and every limit that I set and he broke was supposed to convince me of this too.

Although the broken limits created turmoil and uncertainty in our relationship, each resolution brought renewed trust, increased self-exploration, and the possibility for self-growth.

Time Limit

In the first few sessions Karl used the five-minute warning to begin to finish his play and prepare to leave. A couple of times he stalled slightly but, with reassurance that he could come back, he was able to leave.

Unpublished data by Page Kelly Brenner, 1971.

(207)

During the ninth session he was very involved in playing with the animals and soldiers.

Counselor: Karl, there are about five more minutes.
Karl: Oh jeez.

And he started the soldiers firing at the animals, which were charging at the entrance that the soldiers were guarding.

Karl: Three more minutes?
Counselor: No, about one more minute now.
Karl: Brrm, brrm, make room for the cars.
Counselor: The cars are coming out now. It's just about time to go, Karl.
Karl: About?
Counselor: Just about. (Pause.) Now our time is up.
Karl: Wait. I want a . . .

We discussed where he was to go now — back to his classroom or out on the playground for lunch.

Counselor: Time's up for today, Karl.
Karl: First of all, these guys have to get on the truck or they'll get killed.
Counselor: You'd like to stay longer and finish your story, but it's time to go. You can come back on Wednesday.

Karl's testing of the time limit continued to be a recurrent theme throughout the sessions with him. He tested it by changing the subject, using stalling tactics, or using the "wait, just this" routine.

Toys Remain in Playroom

In the fourth session Karl was playing with the toy soldiers and cars, and he ask if he could keep the car.

"Karl, you may play with the car here, but it has to stay in the playroom so it will be here when you come." He accepted this.

At the end of the sixth session, as we were leaving he pulled the baby of the family out of his pocket and asked if he could keep it, looking at me sheepishly with pleading eyes.

"You like the baby and you'd like to have it. You can play with it again the next time you come, but it has to stay in the playroom."

Child Remains in Playroom

During the second session Karl was looking out the window, and asked if he could go out.

"You may go out if you like, but if you do you won't be able to come back today."

In the fourth session he announced that he was going out to get a drink. I sensed that he might have needed to get away at that point, and said that if he felt like that he could go across the room for a while and come back when he was ready.

From that point on I kept a jug of water in the room for drinks.

In the ninth session he kicked Bozo over to the door, opened it, and went out, trying to get me to chase him. When I did not, he came back in.

"Karl, remember a long time ago we talked about if you wanted to leave before the time was up it was okay, but you couldn't come back into the playroom." He went back to the dollhouse, where he had been playing earlier.

Health and Safety

In the process of exploring the room during the first session, Karl found a perfume bottle with a tiny bit of perfume in it. First he brought it to me to smell. Then he went over to the radiator and spilled a few drops on it and looked at me. I accepted this, but said nothing. He then went to the window and dropped the bottle out onto the playground.

"Karl, there are many things that you can do in the playroom, but I cannot allow you to do anything that might hurt somebody. On the way back to your classroom we can stop on the playground and you can put the bottle in the trash can."

He did this later with no hesitation.

Destruction of Property

Karl walked in the door for the second session, went right to the toy shelf, and loaded the guns with the suction darts. He began looking around the room, especially at the window and the clock.

"Karl, I think you know what can be shot at and what can't."

I nodded my head in agreement, and he drew a bull's-eye on paper to use for a target.

Physical Attacks on the Counselor

The first time this issue arose was during the seventh session, when Karl had spent most of the time boxing and wrestling with Bozo. He picked up Bozo by the neck and swung him over his head.

Karl: I'm gonna hit you with it.
Counselor: You'd like to hit me with it, but I don't want to be hit. (He put Bozo down and hit him away from me.) Karl, if you'd like to hit me some; time, you can tell me.
Karl: Who?
Counselor: You.
Karl: Like who?
Counselor: If you'd like to hit me sometime, it's okay, but *tell* me; don't hit me.
Karl: Oh ... who wants to hit a girl?

Then he went to the blackboard and wrote: BOZO IS A CLOWN, A HIT-TING CLOWN.

In the sixteenth session, Karl became angry because I repeated something that he said.

Karl: Don't repeat what I say, or else I'll give you a slap. (Pause.) Can you beat me up? Are you tougher than me?
Counselor: You're wondering if I'm gonna beat you up if you tell me you'd like to give me a slap.
Karl: But you can't beat me up, right?
Counselor: No, I won't beat you up; but your thinking that you might like to beat me up doesn't hurt me. Not unless you were to beat me up would it hurt. You can wish or you can think without it being real. (Pause.) Sometimes people think when they have had thoughts about other people, Karl, that they should get punished, that they've been bad just for having the thoughts. It's okay to have bad thoughts — just not bad actions, right?
Karl: Right!

Karl had indicated that he feared retaliation for the verbalized wish to attack. I tried to reassure him that the thought alone could not hurt, and that it is permissible to have those thoughts.

Broken Limits

The entire four months of counseling with Karl were characterized by limit setting and limit breaking. It would follow, then, that the issue of limits was the most important ongoing one in his life at school and at home. The most recent conference with his parents supported this assumption. His aggressive behavior and lack of self-control in school were a constant source of difficulty for his teacher and, of course, for him too. The management of limit breaking and the understanding of the motivation for the act when it occurred was a continual challenge.

During the counseling experience with Karl, it seemed that the broken limit plunged our relationship into confusion and uncertainty many times. Each time we struggled and suffered until we found a new limit that we could share. And each time the resolution brought renewed trust and an increased willingness for him to share more of his troubled feelings with me.

I will describe some incidents of broken limits and the growth experiences which occurred with their resolution.

As Karl explored and tested the relationship with me during the first six weeks, all of the basic limits that I mentioned earlier had been set. The process of structuring was well under way.

During the seventh week it became apparent that Karl's trips into the storeroom were intended to break the limit, and had a purpose. Karl walked into the storeroom, and appeared to be interested in the things that were on the shelves.

Counselor: Karl, that's the storeroom, and I'd rather you stay out here. Please come out.
Karl: I'm stuck!
Counselor: You want me to come after you?
Karl: Yeah! Come on, come on after me.
Counselor: You like to be chased.
Karl: Yeah! Come on.
Counselor: I'm on to you. I know you like to be chased.
Karl: Okay, come here. Try to find me.

When I did not chase him and told him there were only a few minutes left, he came running out.

In the next session, however, we explored it further. The scene began just like the previous one.

Counselor: You like me to chase you outa there.
Karl: Yeah!
Counselor: Well, what do you want me to do if I chase you? Do you want me to catch you?
Karl: Yeah, come on!
Counselor: If I catch you, what do you want me to do?
Karl: Just bring me on the other side. Come on! (getting exasperated).
Counselor: Bring you on the other side? You want me to grab you with my arms and take you on the other side?
Karl: Yeah! Try to catch me.
Counselor: If there's something you'd like me to do, you can ask me about it.
Karl: I'm dying (tauntingly), just come and catch me 'cause I'm on top of something.
Counselor: You think if you tell me you're on top of something I'll come quicker?
Karl: Yeah. Come on. Please! (now more pleading than demanding).
Counselor: Karl, you're in the storeroom and this is our playroom. If you want me to catch you, come out here, and perhaps we can figure out what you want.
Karl: Okay, come up here. I'm gonna fall.

Again he tried every trick he knew to manipulate. And then after a pause:

Counselor: Do you want me to hold you? To catch you and hold you?
Karl: Uh-huh.
Counselor: I guess that's a little hard to ask for.

I went into the storeroom and carried him out and sat him on my lap. He sat there rather stiffly without saying a word for a few seconds, and then ran to the middle of the room.

Counselor: Is that what you wanted?
Karl: Yeah (with an anxious laugh).

This was the first time that physical contact had been introduced into our relationship. In the session that followed, I very clearly and firmly restated the storeroom limit, and Karl spent the entire session seeking more physical contact. He wanted me to put him into and lift him out of some empty boxes. He wanted to sit on my lap and be carried around the room. His ambivalence showed in his vacillation between wanting affectionate contact and wanting to hit me. This was the beginning of the physical aggression directed at me that also needed a limit to be set.

Even though the storeroom limit had been clearly defined and one of Karl's reasons for breaking the limit explored, it was necessary to come up with a method of enforcing it.

In the beginning of the sixteenth session I explained that the contents of the storeroom did not belong to us and that he was not allowed to go in there. The first time he broke this limit, he would get a time-out period. This would involve sitting on a chair for a minute to get control. If he broke the limit a second time, the candy would be put away, and if it happened a third time I would have to take him back to his classroom.

Karl's response was to go to the door of the storeroom and look in. He stood on one foot and put the other into the storeroom.

"You're trying to see if I mean what I say, huh, Karl?"

Then he stopped testing and began to play.

He accepted my limit, and once again our relationship had the necessary structure for exploration and growth. During his play following this experience, he explored a new area of conflict. There were several interruptions when his anxiety rose because an important but frightening idea was seeking expression. It was a measure of his ego strength, my supportive interventions, and the new trust between us that he was able to finish this play sequence.

During the next four weeks, Karl's anger became more focused, and both verbal and physical expressions of it became directed toward me. Once I recognized the "dirty" words he muttered. He wrote and said them more often when he was angry. He continued to test the storage area limit.

During the twentieth session he fleetingly mentioned "tittyballs" (breasts) and reacted as though he'd said something "dirty." I let him know that I was sure that was something of interest to him and that it was something we could discuss. He spent the rest of the session mixing a concoction of paint with his hands. I let him know that the mess he was making was fine, but that he must confine it to the paint table and not pour it onto the floor. It seemed that he was testing with the paints how "dirty" he could be in our relationship — what kinds of questions about sex he could ask.

Also during this four-week period, the time-outs began to fail as a means of helping him gain control over limit breaking. New limits had to be set if we were to continue, and I explained the following to him:

that I would hold his hand all the way to the playroom because I could not allow him to run away ahead of me;

that if he did break away our session would be five minutes shorter;

that if he pointed the guns at me or broke limits with other play materials, they would be put away for that day;

that we would continue to use the one-minute time-outs to help him get control

that if he wouldn't stay in the time-out chair I would have to take him back to his classroom.

I really had very mixed feelings about setting the ultimate limit of taking him back to his classroom. Somehow it seemed punishing and rejecting to me, and yet, in trying to think of alternatives, I could think of none. For the time being, however, I could hope and believe that the limit breaking would not come to that.

I had to use the leaving as an ultimate limit because I had nothing else, but I was not completely comfortable with it. The rules were reviewed and explained in the beginning of the twenty-first session, and Karl proceeded to test them. He went straight to a pile of boxes and climbed up.

Counselor: You're not to be on that pile of boxes, Karl. I see you're going to try to see if I mean what I say. I think you are ready for your first time-out.

Karl: No! (shouted, and he ran across the room).

Counselor: Here is the time-out chair. I'll give you a chance to get in it for one minute. If that doesn't work, then you're going back to your room.

He stalled and resisted, but I gave him a chance to make up his mind which way he was going to have it. He sat on the chair and then sent two darts in my direction.

Counselor: Karl, you know what things are allowed to be shot at and what aren't.

Karl: Yeah.

Counselor: The guns are going away and you're gonna finish your time-out.

Karl: No, no. Not the guns!

And he ran across the room, but I grabbed him and took the guns and put them away.

Karl sat on the chair for the time-out and then went looking for the guns.

Karl: Let me see. Where are those guns?

Counselor: The guns have been put away for the day and the storeroom is off limits.

Karl: Where are they? WHERE? WHERE?
Counselor: You're wondering where they are and you'd like to have them back.
Karl: Yeah! I promise I won't shoot them at you (said pleadingly).
Counselor: The guns will be back next time but not today.
Karl: Okay, if you don't give them to me I'll break this dart. It's up to you.
Counselor: The dart is to be shot out of the gun, Karl, and if it's broken it can't be shot. So that's up to you. The guns are away for today, but they'll be back next time. There are many other things to play with.

The testing ended and the new limit held. Karl got out the soldiers and cars and began playing on the floor in front of the dollhouse. I sat nearby, watching and listening. As in previous sessions, the broken limit and its resolution enabled him to explore more of his feelings — this time his hostile feelings toward rivals.

The manifest and latent content of this play sequence was amazing to me. On one level he was talking to me, asking me what other children came to the playroom, what toys they used, and whether I played with these children. On another level he was talking for the soldiers as he moved them around.

Counselor: Karl, do you kinda wish you were the only child that came to use this playroom?
Karl: Yeah.
Counselor: And you wish other people didn't use the toys, too.
Karl: Yeah. (For the soldiers) Okay, stand by. Don't let anybody else spot it. Now *guard* it!

The play and conversation went on and then I said:

Counselor: Sometimes you wish that this room was only used as a playroom and that we were the only people who came here.
Karl: Yeah! That would be good.
Counselor: It's okay to wish that, Karl. It's okay to wish that you were the only one who came here. I bet that sometimes you wish that when you're at home, too.
Karl: Yea-a-ah!
Counselor: Sometimes you wish that little sister hadn't come along.
Karl: (For the soldiers) He's shooting at the elephant. Boom, boom! Okay, one down; strike out.

Although he really did not get into the angry feelings toward his sister, it seemed that the soldiers very subtly got rid of her. The positive relatedness of this session continued throughout, and it ended with Karl wanting me to hold him and carry him.

During the next three weeks, however, Karl's testing and limit breaking reached unexcelled heights, and our relationship plunged to the depths of confusion and uncertainty.

He tested splashing and messing with the paint to see at what point it would be taken away. He shot the guns at me, and they were removed. He climbed on the boxes and turned off the tape recorder and got a time-out. He refused to hold my hand and ran ahead of me to the playroom, and received several five-minute penalties. He became furious when I followed through with an alternative for the limit he broke. He bribed and manipulated like a pro. He hit and kicked me, and found it very hard to confine his anger to verbal expressions, even with assistance. When the time-outs failed to work, the ultimate limit of having to terminate the session had to be invoked — twice about five minutes early; and the next two sessions lasted only 20 and 10 minutes, respectively. It was true that he left with a sense of relief.

At this point I did not know what to do next. I fluctuated between trying to realize that limits were an important issue for Karl and that there was a reason for his exaggerated response, and feeling that I was failing if I could not handle these issues in the playroom. I was disappointed and felt manipulated, frustrated, and rejected.

I decided that I would give him more help in adhering to the limits. I would hold his hand and keep him from climbing on the boxes. I would continue to remove objects. And the only thing I would take him back to the classroom for would be attacks on me.

And then came the twenty-seventh session. I went to pick Karl up and he came willingly, holding my hand the whole way. I sensed the calm — the difference — and was relieved. When we got to the playroom he got right to the point.

Karl: Hey, do you have the book ... how to make ... how to ... the book of seals?
Counselor: You'd like a seal book — about seals?
Karl: Yeah. How ... how seals are made (quickly, and with an anxious laugh).

I got out the book *How Babies Are Made,* and although we did not learn much about seals we looked at a great many pictures about flowers, chickens,

dogs, and human beings, and how males and females differ anatomically and
how they reproduce.

Because of the turmoil of the past three weeks and the trust that had been
added to our relationship, he knew what he could do to evoke a limit-setting
response from me. When his anxiety got high, he used this for relief. He ran
to the boxes and I enforced the limit. Then he could resent the limit, be
angry with me, and try to hit me. He went through the whole repertoire:
shooting guns, turning off the tape recorder, throwing clay at me.

Counselor: You know, Karl, I think that sometimes things go on in here that
scare you. And when you feel a little scared you start throwing things. I
understand that; I won't let you throw things, but I understand that sometimes you get scared.
Karl: Okay, I'll — (and dashed to turn off the tape recorder).
Counselor: It's okay if you can't, I'll stop you. (He did it again.) The answer
is no; you cannot turn off the tape recorder. You're testing me to see if I can
stop you.

Later he scribbled on the table with a crayon, and I gave him some paper.

Counselor: Paper is for drawing — not tables. (He took chalk and wrote on
the radiator, and I removed the chalk and the crayons.) You're wondering if
I can stop you every time you do something you're not supposed to. The
answer is I will stop you —
Karl: Okay.
Counselor: — every time.

The last three weeks we worked through termination, and it was as turbu-
lent, or perhaps more so, than I expected. Perhaps the ultimate limit of time
illuminated all the other limits. I let him know that I understood how angry
he was.

Counselor: You're angry with me today, and you'd like to hurt me. But no,
Karl, I won't let you kick me.

He called me names and shouted at me, and I tried to show him I accepted
this and understood.

Karl: You know you're stubborn. I'll hit you. You know, you are a *real
pest,* I mean it. I really mean it.

Counselor: I know, Karl. You think I'm a real pest today. Sometimes I won't do what you want.

He expressed his increased dependency in numerous demands on me to help him in his play. I accepted this and tried not to make an issue out of it.

Karl: Make that clay into a ball or else I'll kill you. You make that ball or else I'll throw that chair at you! (shouted).

He not only climbed on the boxes, but started kicking them and knocking them over. He tried to break the dollhouse with his foot. These activities I had to limit as well as the physical attacks on me.

In the thirtieth session I reinforced the boundaries of our play area by painting a line on the floor, and reiterated the limit about hitting me and, if he broke this, I would have to return him to his classroom. He responded well. He let me know that he had broken the limit regarding toys leaving the playroom, and I had to enforce the limit.

Karl: I took the baby tiger home, and I'm never bringing it back.
Counselor: It must be very important to you.
Karl: Uuh-huh-h —
Counselor: I understand that you might like to keep it, but I need to have it back because it belongs to the playroom.

Several days went by, and then he brought it back on the next day to the session. By the last two sessions it seemed that the uncontrolled aggression and destructiveness were spent.

The final session gave me my first glimpse, in concrete terms, of the positive results of our working relationship, with all its uncertainties, turmoil, limit setting, and limit breaking. Karl and I were discussing the baby tiger he had taken and brought back.

Karl: Do you ever give out detention notes?
Counselor: Do I ever give out detention notes? What do you think? What's your idea?
Karl: I say you don't.
Counselor: You say I don't. That's right.
Karl: WHAT? YOU DON'T GIVE OUT DETENTION NOTICES! Woo-ooooo ooooo!
Counselor: Other people give out punishments, but I don't, huh?

Karl: How come? How come you don't? 'Cause you're not a teacher?
Counselor: Yeah, I guess so (not being able to think of a better answer).
Karl: Do you *wish* you were a teacher?
Counselor: No, I like what I'm doing.
Karl: How come?
Counselor: I enjoy it.
Karl: You *enjoy* it? (in disbelief).
Counselor: I enjoy playing with you.
Karl: When I do all those *bad* things — turning off the tape recorder, going in the storeroom — you enjoy *that?*
Counselor: Yes, I still enjoy playing with you!
Karl: All the time?
Counselor: Yes. I know that there's a reason why you do those things, Karl.
Karl: Yeah, why?
Counselor: I don't know exactly why.

While this conversation was going on, Karl was busy running string across the room from the radiator to a chair, exactly where the line was indicating the boundary of our play area. There was something quite positive about his taking an active role in clarifying this boundary.

My response during this interaction was a very emotional one. I was able to continue speaking, but had to blink hard to keep the tears back. I was happy, relieved, and excited all in one.

Even though it was hard for him to imagine, Karl had been unable to defeat one adult thus far in his life. I did not respond to his manipulative, "acting-out" behavior with punishments and "bad child" labels. Because this was an unaccustomed response, I imagine that it made him anxious many times. But there was a part of him — the part that believed in his own inherent worth and wanted to be realized — that seemed to reach out to grasp the opportunity for growth that I had offered.

(G) Parents and Teachers as Mediators of Reinforcement Techniques – Case Studies

PARENTS AND TEACHERS AS MEDIATORS IN BEHAVIOR CHANGE

Behavior modification through mediators was used in conjunction with individual counseling with an 8-year-old boy with a learning disability. Both his parents and his remedial reading teacher were concerned about Michael's inability to concentrate and his obvious lack of motivation to pursue academic tasks which were remedial in nature. Mike saw these activities as babyish and not interesting because of their repetitive nature. Mike wanted to be able to read as others do, but he lacked the motivation to work through all the remedial steps. In his counseling sessions with me he readily admitted to his frustration and hopeless feelings about himself. I asked him if he thought it would help to talk with his parents and teacher about some of his feelings and to see if we might look at some ways of helping him become more motivated to pursue his remedial work. He was feeling so helpless and hopeless about himself that he could scarcely give an answer, but he did agree that I could talk with them.

In talking with Mike's parents I found that they too had begun to feel quite hopeless about him. They expressed doubts about his intelligence and his future, and could not see anything positive about him. His father said he was lazy, and his mother said he just couldn't do anything well around the house. I suggested that Mike needed motivation at home as well as at school, and asked them if they would care to be involved in a program that would concentrate on improving Mike's total motivation. I explained the principles of behavior change through changing the environmental reward system. They agreed to try because anything was better than the way they were currently feeling about Mike. I asked them to talk with Mike about what we discussed and to begin to identify behaviors that they could give positive reinforcement for and those they could ignore.

When I talked with the parents one week later, they had already identified some behaviors that they would feel quite comfortable in reinforcing, such as wiping dishes, picking up his room, and feeding his dog. Behaviors that they felt they could ignore were whining when he was reminded of tasks he was to do, and slowness in doing them. They had decided, with Mike, to make a chart of the tasks to be done, with stars for each task completed. At the end of a week, if he had earned a certain number of stars in each category, he could buy a phonograph record for his collection, which was very important to him. In the beginning the number of stars needed to earn a record was relatively small, based on the observed number of tasks that he usually completed in a week. The target number of stars for earning a record was set just above this baseline. As Mike's motivation improved, gradually more stars were needed to earn the record.

In addition, both parents planned to make an extra effort to give social reinforcement through verbal praise and pats on the back when he did his tasks without being asked, without whining, and at a fairly steady pace. When he whined or dawdled over his work, the parents planned to ignore this behavior.

The parents reported back to me weekly by phone, and Mike brought his charts in to show me during counseling sessions. The parents had some difficulty in ignoring the negative behavior, and the father seemed particularly sensitive to the whining and slow or erratic behavior. They did, however, have more success in reinforcing the positive behaviors, and in our telephone conversations I began to pick up tones of pride in how well Mike was responding to the program.

At the same time I was also talking with Mike's remedial teacher, who had also experienced a great deal of frustration in working with Mike. She too agreed to work on a behavior modification plan aimed at improving his motivation. We started with a meeting between Mike, his teacher, and myself. I facilitated communication between Mike and his teacher in which each could openly and directly express frustration. Then we began to look at how they could work together so that Mike could use his teacher's skills more productively. One thing that became apparent was that there were days when Mike really felt like working and other days when he just felt as though he could not do anything. His teacher recognized and accepted these feelings, but insisted that Mike needed to do some work each session. I suggested that at the beginning of each session they negotiate how much Mike would do on a particular day. If he was able to be involved in and complete this much work, he would earn a star. Using the same type of reward structure as that being used at home, he could earn phonograph records. This suggestion was agreeable to both of them.

The teacher had also become accustomed to paying attention to and scolding Mike for dawdling and whining. In subsequent discussions with her I suggested that she try to ignore these behaviors and give extra social praise for his accomplishments.

There were difficult days for both Mike and his mediators in implementing these programs of behavior modification, but after a few months of consciously focusing on changing the environmental reward system, the vicious circle of hopelessness began to be broken. Mike still had difficulty accepting his disability and his need to be involved in a remedial education program, but he was motivated to keep at it with the end goal of learning to read.

BEHAVIOR MODIFICATION IN THE CLASSROOM SETTING

In some schools and classes, teachers and administrators have consciously structured curriculum which incorporates reinforcement principles. In these settings, planning and implementing both individualized and group programs can be accomplished with a great deal of success and a minimum of resistance. In schools where this approach is new, it is often viewed with suspicion and resistance. The best approach in such a situation is to find a teacher who is willing to try, and to aim for a fairly certain success. This type of demonstration often helps other teachers and administrators to overcome their bias against this method.

Teacher Asks for Help

An opportunity to provide just such a demonstration occurred in an elementary school. Miss J., a new fourth-grade teacher in the school, asked for a consultation in the second month of school. Her complaint was that she could not get many of the children to work up to the capacity she knew they had. She also complained of the sullen attitudes toward her that they expressed. I suggested that I spend a period of time making observations in her room and that we meet again after this time to discuss what I had seen and heard in her classroom. In my first observation I was aware of a vague feeling of discomfort in myself. It was not until I reviewed my notes that I realized that my response had been to the amount of negative reinforcement that Miss J. was giving. I decided that I would need more definitive and concrete data for my conference with Miss J., so I made a series of observations with the focus on the number of negative and positive reinforcing behaviors in stated periods of time. I also recorded the antecedent and consequent behavior of the teacher and children. The collected data clearly validated my first observation that Miss J. gave very little positive reinforcement and had an exceedingly high rate of negative reinforcing behaviors. The recorded antecedent and consequent behaviors indicated that Miss J. gave attention to restlessness, incorrect answers, talking out of turn, and moving out of one's seat. She ignored, or barely acknowledged, correct answers, remaining in seats, and quiet, attentive behavior.

In my meeting with Miss J. I was tempted to present her with the observed data, but felt that she would only become defensive. I started with telling her about another teacher with a similar type of class that I was able to help through behavior analysis and the systematic use of reinforcement principles. I asked her to read *Living with Children* [1] and then to talk with me again. In our next session she said she thought that she knew what was wrong with her class: she "had been rewarding the wrong behaviors." It was then that I could show her the baseline data related to her classroom behavior, and begin to explore with her how she could change. She was able to say that she had some guilt feelings about ignoring negative-type behavior, which she thought might have come from the way she was raised. She did state, however, that she saw value in trying another method since she was so miserable with the class as it was. We did not use a chart with stars, but Miss J. did attempt to keep account of her negative and positive reinforcing behaviors each day. We met once a week to talk about how the week had gone. These meetings provided me with the opportunity to give Miss J. positive reinforcement for her efforts. At the end of a two-month period, she said she noticed that the children seemed less sullen, and were engaged in more productive behaviors. She asked me to observe her class again so that we could compare these data with the baseline. The comparative data per se were reinforcing in terms of her continued behavioral change, but the change in her relationship with the students and their increased productivity were even more reinforcing.

Behavioral Management

This success gave me an opening to work with another teacher. Mrs. R., a first-grade teacher, asked Miss J. over coffee in the teachers' lounge why she did not complain about her class any more. Miss J. explained what had happened in her class and how she did not complain any more.

Subsequently Mrs. R. asked for a consultation regarding two children in her classroom with widely divergent behavior: one very withdrawn and one exceedingly hyperactive. She felt that their behavior was interfering with their ability to learn. I asked Mrs. R. to read *Living with Children* [1], and also planned a series of observations of the two children about whom she was concerned.

Withdrawn Behavior

In the initial observation, Tina, the withdrawn girl, showed little initiative in starting any activity. For example, when the children had a period of time for drawing, Tina would sit in front of her paper and do nothing if she had to initiate a trip to where the crayons were kept. She spoke very little, and when she did her speech was quite indistinct. I did notice, however, that she was attentive to all that went on in the classroom and that she did complete assigned work. In subsequent sessions I observed the following behaviors for baseline data.

1. Initiates communication with peers
2. Responds to peers verbally when approached
3. Volunteers to give response to teacher's questions or activities
4. Speaks clearly

Observation data revealed that Tina never volunteered to respond, that she did respond when other children talked to her, that she never initiated conversation with her peers, and that her speech was consistently unclear.

I suggested that, because Tina did seem to be an active observer and listener, she might need some special assistance to be able to respond with what she did know and to take a more active role in the learning process. I asked Mrs. R. to try to think of ways she could provide a bridge for Tina to begin to respond. Mrs. R. thought that she might start with their storytelling time, during which she would tell or read a story and then ask the children questions. Mrs. R. decided that she would ask Tina to answer at least one question at each story period, and that she would give Tina social praise for her ability to participate and for speaking in a voice that others could understand. At first Tina seemed surprised and reticent when called on, but with Mrs. R.'s encouragement she was able to respond. Mrs. R. also engaged Tina in active participation as leader of nonthreatening games such as "Simon Says." In these activities Tina could use skills within her ability and begin to relate to her peers through play activities. At the end of a one-and-a-half-month period

I observed Tina's behavior again. She had significantly increased her verbal communication with peers; she seldom volunteered for leadership roles or to give answers; but when asked to participate she would become actively involved with a voice that could be clearly understood.

Hyperactivity

The management of Mrs. R.'s hyperactive child proved to be a much more difficult problem because of the disturbance he caused in the class, and because of the fact that Mrs. R. could not provide positive reinforcement at appropriate times because of her other classroom duties. Richie was one of 25 children in his first-grade class. He spent a great deal of time running around, talking to other children, sharpening his pencil, and playing with the toys. In baseline observations he was observed to spend three five-minute periods at his seat working and 30 minutes in other activities around the classroom. Obviously Richie was not able to be effectively involved in the learning process. I asked Mrs. R. if she would feel comfortable talking to Richie about his behavior and in exploring ways to help him use school more for himself. When we met together, my role was to facilitate communication and to help them explore alternatives. After they had each had an opportunity to express frustration about the other, they began to explore different ways of behaving in the classroom. Mrs. R. agreed that Richie could not spend long periods of time at seat work, that he needed to be able to move about, and that he could not complete total work assignments. Richie agreed that he would complete a certain amount of seat work, then move about, but only to play quietly without disturbing others. He would then return to complete the amount of work agreed upon. Richie's reward for fulfilling this contract was social praise and stars on a chart. The chart was used to receive further praise from both the school principal and Richie's parents. The other children were asked to ignore other activities that Richie did, and not to speak to him when he was out of his seat.

Mrs. R. needed a great deal of encouragement and support to ignore Richie's out-of-seat activity and to allow him to use his play time. Richie tested and teased for almost a week before he began to decrease the "out-of-bounds" classroom activities. He did not earn many stars during this time, but because he was not getting reinforcement for his acting-out behavior, he gradually began to engage more in his seat work as agreed upon, and was eventually able to gain more positive reinforcement for his increased adaptive behavior.

REFERENCE

1. Patterson, G. *Living with Children.* Champaign, Ill.: Research Press, 1968.

Supplementary Reading List

JOURNALS RELATED TO CHILD MENTAL HEALTH COUNSELING

1. *American Journal of Orthopsychiatry*
2. *American Journal of Psychiatry*
3. *Behavior Therapy*
4. *Bulletin of Art Therapy*
5. *Child Psychiatry and Human Development*
6. *Child Welfare*
7. *Children Today*
8. *Community Mental Health Journal*
9. *Dance Magazine*
10. *Journal of Abnormal Psychology*
11. *Journal of the American Academy of Child Psychiatry*
12. *Journal of Child Psychology and Psychiatry*
13. *Journal of Psychiatric Nursing*
14. *Journal of School Psychology*
15. *Perspectives in Psychiatric Care*

CHILD COUNSELING AND PSYCHOTHERAPY (Chapter 6)

1. Adler, A. *The Practice and Theory of Individual Psychology.* New York: Harcourt, Brace, 1924.
2. Allen, F. *Psychotherapy with Children.* New York: Norton, 1942.
3. Axline, V. *Play Therapy.* Boston: Houghton Mifflin, 1947.
4. Bandura, A. *Aggression: A Social Learning Analysis.* Englewood Cliffs, N.J.: Prentice-Hall, 1973.
5. Bandura, A., and Walters, R. H. *Social Learning and Personality Development.* New York: Holt, Rinehart & Winston, 1963.

6. Bender, L. *Child Psychiatric Techniques.* Springfield, Ill.: Thomas, 1952.

7. Bijou, S. W., and Baer, D. M. *Child Development.* New York: Appleton-Century-Crofts, 1961.

8. Carek, N. J. *Principles of Child Psychotherapy.* Springfield, Ill.: Thomas, 1972.

9. Dollard, J., and Miller, N. E. *Personality and Psychotherapy.* New York: McGraw-Hill, 1950.

10. Fagan, J., and Shepherd, I. (Eds.). *Gestalt Therapy Now.* New York: Harper & Row, 1970.

11. Fagin, C. M. *Nursing in Child Psychiatry.* St. Louis: Mosby, 1972.

12. ____. *Readings in Child and Adolescent Psychiatric Nursing.* St. Louis: Mosby, 1974.

13. Finch, S. *Fundamentals of Child Psychiatry.* New York: Norton, 1960.

14. Freud, A. *The Psychoanalytic Treatment of the Child.* London: Image, 1956.

15. Howells, J. C. *Modern Perspectives in Child Psychiatry.* Springfield, Ill.: Thomas, 1965.

16. Haworth, M. R. *Child Psychotherapy.* New York: Basic Books, 1964.

17. James, M. *Born To Win: Transactional Analysis with Gestalt Experiments.* Reading, Mass.: Addison-Wesley, 1971.

18. Kanner, L. *Child Psychiatry.* Springfield, Ill.: Thomas, 1962.

19. Lippman, H. *Treatment of the Child in Emotional Conflict.* New York: McGraw-Hill, 1962.

20. Loomis, M. E., and Horsley, J. A. *Interpersonal Change: A Behavioral Approach to Nursing Practice.* New York: McGraw-Hill, 1974.

21. LeBow, M. *Behavior Modification – A Significant Method in Nursing Practices.* Englewood Cliffs, N.J.: Prentice-Hall, 1973.

22. Moustakas, C. *Psychotherapy with Children.* New York: Ballantine, 1970.

23. Patterson, G. *Living with Children – New Methods for Parents and Teachers.* Champaign, Ill.: Research Press, 1968.

24. Perls, F. *Gestalt Therapy Verbatim.* Lafayette, Calif.: Real People Press, 1969.

25. Perls, F. *In and Out of the Garbage Pail.* Lafayette, Calif.: Real People Press, 1969.

26. Perls, F. S. *The Gestalt Approach.* Ben Lomond, Calif.: Science and Behavior Books, 1973.

27. Perls, F., Hefferline, R. F., and Goodman, P. *Gestalt Therapy.* New York: Delta, 1965.

28. Rachlin, H. *Introduction to Modern Behaviorism.* San Francisco: Freeman, 1970.

29. Rank, O. *Will Therapy.* New York: Knopf, 1936.

30. Reisman, J. *Principles of Psychotherapy with Children.* New York: Wiley, 1973.

31. Reese, E. *Analysis of Human Operant Behavior.* Dubuque, Iowa: Brown, 196

32. Schiffman, M. *Gestalt Self Therapy.* Menlo Park, Calif.: Self Therapy Press, 1971.
33. Simmons, J. E. *Psychiatric Examination of Children.* Philadelphia: Lea & Febiger, 1969.
34. Skinner, B. F. *The Analysis of Behavior.* New York: McGraw-Hill, 1961.
35. Smith, B. K. *No Language But a Cry.* Boston: Beacon Press, 1968.
36. Taft, J. *The Dynamics of Therapy in a Controlled Relationship.* New York: Macmillan, 1933.
37. Tharp, R. C., and Wetzel, R. J. *Behavior Modification in the Natural Environment.* New York: Academic, 1969.
38. Winnicott, D. W. *Therapeutic Consultations in Child Psychiatry.* New York: Basic Books, 1971.

GROUP COUNSELING WITH CHILDREN

1. Barcai, A., Umbarger, C., Pierce, T., and Chamberlain, P. A comparison of three group approaches to underachieving children. *Am. J. Orthopsychiatry* 43:1, January 1973, p. 133.
2. Gazda, G. M., and Peters, R. W. Analysis of research in group procedures. *Educational Technology* 13:1, January 1973, p. 68.
3. Gazda, G. M. *Group Counseling: A Developmental Approach.* Boston: Allyn & Bacon, 1972.
4. Ginott, H. *Group Psychotherapy with Children.* New York: McGraw-Hill, 1965.
5. Howard, W., and Zimpfer, D. G. The findings of research on group approaches in elementary guidance and counseling. *Elementary School Guidance and Counseling* 6:3, March 1972, p. 163.
6. Jefferies, D., and Schiaffini, K. Group counseling with children: An annotated bibliography. *Educational Technology* 13:1, January 1973, p. 48.
7. Konopka, G. *Therapeutic Group Work with Children.* Minneapolis: University of Minnesota Press, 1949.
8. Mahler, C. *Group Counseling in School.* Boston: Houghton Mifflin, 1969.
9. McBrien, R. J., and Nelson, R. J. Experimental group strategies with primary grade children. *Elementary School Guidance and Counseling* 6:5, March 1972, p. 170.
10. Ohlsen, M. M. *Group Counseling.* New York: Holt, Rinehart & Winston, 1970.
11. Ohlsen, M. M. (Ed.). *Counseling Children in Groups: A Forum.* New York: Holt, Rinehart & Winston, 1973.
12. _____. Readiness for membership in a counseling group. *Educational Technology* 13:1, January 1973, p. 58.
13. Scheidler, T. Use of fantasy as a therapeutic agent in latency-age groups. *Psychotherapy: Theory, Research and Practice* 9:4, Winter 1972, p. 299.
14. Slavson, S. R. Group psychotherapy with children. In Slavson, S. R., *Child Psychotherapy.* New York: Columbia University Press, 1952.

15. _____. Group therapy for young children. *Nervous Child,* April 1945, p. 196.

MOVEMENT AND DANCE IN COUNSELING *(Chapter 8)*

1. American Dance Therapy Association. *Second Annual Conference Proceedings,* 1967 (included in *Monograph No. 1,* 1971); *Fourth Annual Conference Proceedings,* 1969; *Fifth Annual Conference Proceedings,* 1970; *Sixth Annual Conference Proceedings,* 1971; *Seventh Annual Conference Proceedings,* 1972; *Monograph No. 1,* 1971; and *Monograph No. 2,* 1972. Available from A.D.T.A., Suite 216-E, 1000 Century Plaza, Columbia, Md. 21044.
2. Bernstein, P. L. *Theory and Methods in Dance-Movement Therapy.* Dubuque, Iowa: Kendall/Hunt, 1972.
3. Birdwhistell, R. L. *Kinesics and Context.* New York: Ballantine, 1970.
4. Canner, N., and Klebanoff, H. *...and a Time to Dance.* Boston: Beacon, Press, 1968.
5. Chace, M. The power of movement with others. *Dance Magazine,* June 1964.
6. Cole, N. R. *Children's Arts from Deep Down Inside.* New York: John Day, 1966.
7. Davis, M. *Understanding Body Movement.* New York: Arno, 1972. (An annotated bibliography.)
8. Dell, C. *A Primer for Movement Description: Using Effort-Shape and Supplementary Concepts.* New York: Dance Notation Bureau, 1970.
9. H'Doubler, M. *Dance: A Creative Art Experience.* Madison: University of Wisconsin Press, 1970.
10. Hackett, L. C., and Jensen, R. G. *A Guide to Movement Exploration.* Palo Alto, Calif.: Peek, 1966.
11. North, M. *Body Movement for Children.* Boston: Plays, 1971.
12. _____. *Movement Education.* New York: Dutton, 1973.
13. _____. *Personality Assessment through Movement.* London: MacDonald & Evans, 1972.
14. Pesso, A. *Movement in Psychotherapy.* New York: New York University Press, 1969.
15. _____. *Experience in Action.* New York: New York University Press, 1969.
16. Schoop, T. *Won't You Join the Dance?* Palo Alto, Calif.: National Press, 1973.

PLAY ACTIVITY AND CHILD COUNSELING *(Chapter 9)*

1. Biblow, E. Imaginative play and the control of aggressive behavior. In Singer, J. L., *Child's World of Make Believe.* New York: Academic, 1973.

2. Boston Children's Hospital Medical Center. *What to Do When There's Nothing to Do.* New York: Delacorte, 1968.

3. Cassell, S. The suitcase playroom. *Psychotherapy: Theory, Research and Practice* 9:4, Winter 1972, p. 346.

4. Corsini, R. J. *Role Playing in Psychotherapy.* Chicago: Aldine, 1966.

5. de la Torre, J. The therapist tells a story: A technique in brief psychotherapy. *Bull. Menninger Clin.* 36:6, November 1972, p. 609.

6. Fineman, J. Observations on the development of imaginative play in early childhood. *J. Am. Acad. Child Psychiatry* 1:167, 1962.

7. Gardner, R. A. *Therapeutic Communication with Children — The Mutual Story Telling Technique.* New York: Science House, 1971.

8. Gardner, R. A. The mutual story-telling technique in the treatment of anger inhibition problems. *Int. J. Child Psychotherapy* 1:1, January 1972, p. 34.

9. Gilmore, J. B. Play: A special behavior. In Haber, R. N. (Ed.), *Current Research in Motivation.* New York: Holt, Rinehart & Winston, 1966.

10. Groos, K. *The Play of Man.* New York: Appleton-Century-Crofts, 1901.

11. Hartley, R., Frank, L. K., and Goldenson, R. M. *Understanding Children's Play.* New York: Columbia University Press, 1969.

12. Hartley, R. E. *The Complete Book of Children's Play.* New York: Crowell, 1963.

13. Kalff, D. M. *Sandplay: A Mirror of the Child's Psyche.* San Francisco: Browser, 1971.

14. Klinger, E. Development of imaginative behavior: Implication of play for a theory of fantasy. *Psychol. Bull.* 72:277, 1969.

15. Kritzberg, N. I. TASKIT (tell-a-story kit), the therapeutic storytelling word game. *Acta Paedopsychiatr.* 38:9, 1972, p. 231.

16. Moreno, J. L. Psychodrama. In Arieti, S. (Ed.), *American Handbook of Psychiatry,* Volume II. New York: Basic Books, 1959.

17. Opie, I., and Opie, P. *Children's Games in Street and Playground.* Oxford, England: Oxford University Press, 1969.

18. ____. Games (young) people play. *Horizon* XIII, 1971, p. 16.

19. Otto, H. *Group Methods to Actualize Human Potential — A Handbook.* Beverly Hills, Calif.: Holistic, 1970.

20. Peller, L. Libidinal phases, ego development and play. *Psychoanalytic Study of the Child,* Volume 9, 1959.

21. Piaget, J. *Play, Dreams, and Imitation in Childhood.* New York: Norton, 1962.

22. Piers, M. W. (Ed.). *Play and Development.* New York: Norton, 1972. (A symposium with contributions by Jean Piaget and others.)

23. Ruevini, U. Using sensitivity training with junior high school students. *Children* 18:69, 1971.

24. Schiffer, M. *The Therapeutic Play Group.* New York: Grune & Stratton, 1969.

25. Schutz, W. C. *Joy: Expanding Human Awareness.* New York: Grove, 1967.

26. Singer, J. L. *The Child's World of Make Believe.* New York: Academic, 1973.

ART ACTIVITY AND CHILD COUNSELING (Chapter 10)

1. Barron, F. *Creativity and Psychological Health.* Princeton, N.J.: Van Nostrand, 1963.
2. Bender, L. *Child Psychiatric Techniques.* Springfield, Ill.: Thomas, 1952.
3. Betensky, M. *Self-Discovery through Self-Expression.* Springfield, Ill.: Thomas, 1973.
4. Cole, N. R. *Children's Arts from Deep Down Inside.* New York: John Day, 1966.
5. D'Amico, V., Wilson, F., and Maser, M. *Arts for the Family.* New York: Doubleday, 1966.
6. Demis, W. *Group Values through Children's Drawings.* New York: Wiley, 1966.
7. DiLeo, J. H. *Children's Drawings as Diagnostic Aids.* New York: Brunner/Mazel, 1973.
8. _____. *Young Children and Their Drawings.* New York: Brunner/Mazel, 1970.
9. Freeman, N. N., and Janikown, R. Intellectual realism in children's drawings of a familiar object with distinctive features. *Child Dev.* 43:3, September 1972, p. 1116.
10. Gantt, L. *Art Therapy: A Bibliography,* January 1940–June 1973. Rockville, Md.: U.S. Department of Health, Education, and Welfare, 1974.
11. Ireton, H., Quast, W., and Gantcher, P. The draw-a-man test as an index of developmental disorders in a pediatric outpatient population. *Child Psychiatry and Human Development* 2:1, Fall 1971, p. 42.
12. Joesting, J., and Joesting, R. Children's quick test, picture interpretation, and Goodenough draw-a-person scores. *Psychol. Rep.* 30:3, June 1972, p. 941.
13. Kellogg, R. *The Psychology of Children's Art.* New York: C.R.M., 1967.
14. Kramer, E. *Art as Therapy with Children.* New York: Schocken, 1971.
15. Laosa, L. M., Swartz, D., Jr., and Holtzman, H. Human figure drawings by normal children: A longitudinal study of perceptual-cognitive and personality development. *Developmental Psychology* 8:3, March 1975, p. 350.
16. Lewis, H. P. (Ed.). *Child Art — The Beginnings of Self Affirmation.* Berkeley, Calif.: Diablo, 1966.
17. Miel, A. (Ed.). *Creativity in Teaching.* Belmont, Calif.: Wadsworth, 1961.
18. Naumberg, M. *An Introduction to Art Therapy.* New York: Teachers College Press, 1973.

FAMILY DYNAMICS AND COUNSELING (Chapter 14)

1. Ackerman, N. W. *Treating the Troubled Family.* New York: Basic Books, 1966.

2. Anthony, E., and Koupernik, C. (Eds.). *The Child in His Family, Volume I.* New York: Wiley-Interscience, 1970.

3. ———. *The Child in His Family, Volume II, The Impact of Disease and Death.* New York: Wiley, 1973.

4. ———. *The Child in His Family, Volume III, Children at Psychiatric Risk.* New York: Wiley, 1974.

5. Anthony, E. J., and Benedek, T. *Parenthood: Its Psychology and Psychopathology.* Boston: Little, Brown, 1970.

6. Block, D. A., and La Perriere, K. Techniques in family therapy: A conceptual framework. In Block, D. A. (Ed.), *Techniques in Family Psychotherapy.* New York: Grune & Stratton, 1973.

7. Cacciatore, E. W. Conjoint therapy as an adjunct to individual therapy. *Journal of Psychiatric Nursing* 11:19, 1973.

8. Fagin, C. *Family Centered Nursing in Community Psychiatry.* Philadelphia: Davis, 1970.

9. Franklin, P., and Prosky, P. A standard initial interview. In Block, D. A. (Ed.), *Techniques in Family Psychotherapy.* New York: Grune & Stratton, 1973.

10. Goren, S. The family as a unit in treatment. In Fagin, C. M. (Ed.), *Nursing in Child Psychiatry.* St. Louis: Mosby, 1972.

11. Gorman, J. Delivery of mental health services to children of resistive parents. *Journal of Psychiatric Nursing* 11:3, 1973.

12. Howells, J. G. *Theory and Practice of Family Psychiatry.* Edinburgh and London: Oliver & Boyd, 1968.

13. Jackson, D. The study of the family. In Ackerman, N. W. (Ed.), *Family Process.* New York: Basic Books, 1970.

14. Levine, R. Treatment in the home: An experiment with low income, multi-problems families. In Riessman, F., et al. (Eds.), *Mental Health of the Poor.* New York: Free Press of Glencoe, 1964.

15. Minuchin, S. *Families and Family Therapy.* Cambridge, Mass.: Harvard University Press, 1974.

16. Napier, A. Y., and Whitaker, C. Problems of beginning family therapists. In Block, D. A. (Ed.), *Techniques in Family Psychotherapy.* New York: Grune & Stratton, 1973.

17. Papp, P., Silverstein, O., and Carter, E. Family sculpture in preventive work with well families. *Family Process* 12:197, 1973.

18. Satir, V. *Conjoint Family Therapy.* Palo Alto, Calif.: Science and Behavior Books, 1964.

19. ———. *Peoplemaking.* Palo Alto, Calif.: Science and Behavior Books, 1972.

20. Slavson, S. R. *Child-Centered Group Guidance of Parents.* New York: International Universities Press, 1958.

21. Solomon, M. A. A developmental, conceptual premise for family therapy. *Family Process* 12:179, 1973.

22. Sussman, M. B. Family symptoms in the 1970's — analysis — policies and programs. In Hymovick, D. P., and Barnard, M. U. (Eds.), *Family Health Care.* New York: McGraw-Hill, 1973.

LITERATURE AND CHILD COUNSELING

1. Almy, M., Chittenden, E., and Miller, P. *Young Children's Thinking*. New York: Teachers College Press, 1966.
2. Ashton-Warner, S. *Teacher*. New York: Bantam Books, 1963.
3. Axline, V. *Dibs in Search of Self*. New York: Ballantine, 1964.
4. Baruch, D. W. *One Little Boy*. New York: Delta, 1964.
5. Bettelheim, B. *Truants from Life*. Glencoe, Ill.: Free Press, 1955.
6. Erikson, E. Jeannie. In Erikson, E., *Childhood and Society*. New York: Norton, 1960.
7. Fisher, D. C. *Understood Betsy*. New York: Grosset & Dunlap, 1941.
8. Frank, A. *The Diary of Anne Frank*. New York: Cardinal Pocket Books, 1967.
9. Gibson, W. *The Miracle Worker*. New York: Knopf, 1969.
10. Green, H. *I Never Promised You a Rose Garden*. New York: Signet, 1965.
11. Itard, J. M. G. *The Wild Boy of Aveyron*. New York: Appleton-Century-Crofts, 1962.
12. Killilea, M. *Karen*. New York: Dell, 1970.
13. Long, N. J., Morse, W. C., and Newman, R. G. *Conflict in the Classroom*. Belmont, Calif.: Wadsworth, 1965.
14. Riese, H. *Heal the Hurt Child*. Chicago: University of Chicago Press, 1962.
15. Rubin, T. *Jordi*. New York: Ballantine, 1963.
16. ____. *David and Lisa*. New York: Ballantine, 1963.
17. Stone, I. *Passion of the Mind*. New York: Signet, 1972.
18. Widerberg, S. *I'm Like Me*. New York: Feminist Press, 1973.
19. Williams, M. *The Velveteen Rabbit*. Garden City, N.Y.: Doubleday, 1958.
20. Wright, R. *Black Boy*. New York: Harper & Row, 1966.

Index